REFLECTIONS
FOR
DAILY PRAYER

ADVENT **2026** TO
EVE OF ADVENT **2027**

ROBERT ATWELL
ALLY BARRETT
TOM CLAMMER
DAVID FORD
JONATHAN FROST
PETER GRAYSTONE
MARY GREGORY
TIM HEATON
COLIN HEBER-PERCY
RACHEL MANN
JULIA MOURANT
NICHOLAS PAPADOPULOS
EMMA PARKER
JITESH PATEL
ESTHER PRIOR
ANDREW RUDD
BROTHER SAMUEL SSF
ANGELA SHEARD
ANGELA TILBY
JANE WILLIAMS

Including Holy Week Reflections by
ISABELLE HAMLEY

Church House Publishing
Church House
27 Great Smith Street
London SW1P 3AZ

ISBN 978 1 78140 524 6

Published 2026 by Church House Publishing
Copyright © The Archbishops' Council 2026

All rights reserved. No part of this publication may be reproduced or stored or transmitted by any means or in any form, electronic or mechanical, including photocopying, recording, or any information storage and retrieval system without written permission, which should be sought from: copyright@churchofengland.org

The opinions expressed in this book are those of the authors and do not necessarily reflect the official policy of the General Synod or The Archbishops' Council of the Church of England.

Series editor: Catherine Williams
Liturgical editor: Peter Moger
Designed and typeset by Hugh Hillyard-Parker
Printed by CPI Bookmarque, Croydon, Surrey

EU GPSR Authorised Representative
LOGOS EUROPE, 9 rue Nicolas Poussin,
17000, LA ROCHELLE, France
E-mail: Contact@logoseurope.eu

What do you think of *Reflections for Daily Prayer*?

We'd love to hear from you – simply email us at

publishing@churchofengland.org

or write to us at

Church House Publishing, Church House,
Great Smith Street, London SW1P 3AZ.

Visit **www.dailyprayer.org.uk** for more information on the *Reflections* series, ordering and subscriptions.

Contents

Table of Contributors	2
About the Authors	3
About *Reflections for Daily Prayer*	7
The Nourishment of Daily Prayer	8
ADVENT Monday 30 November to Thursday 24 December	10
CHRISTMAS Friday 26 December to Tuesday 5 January	32
EPIPHANY Wednesday 6 January to Monday 1 February	42
PRESENTATION Tuesday 2 February	65
ORDINARY TIME BEFORE LENT Wednesday 3 February to Tuesday 9 February	66
LENT Wednesday 10 February to Saturday 27 March	72
EASTER Monday 29 March to Saturday 15 May	112
ORDINARY TIME AFTER PENTECOST Monday 17 May to Saturday 22 May	154
ORDINARY TIME AFTER TRINITY Monday 24 May to Saturday 30 October	160
ORDINARY TIME: ALL SAINTS TO ADVENT Monday 2 November to Saturday 27 November	298
Seasonal Prayers of Thanksgiving	322
The Lord's Prayer and The Grace	325
An Order for Night Prayer (Compline)	326
Index of readings	330

Table of Contributors

Page	Author
10–21	Esther Prior
22–33	Andrew Rudd
34–45	Angela Tilby
46–57	Emma Parker
58–69	Jonathan Frost
70–81	Brother Samuel SSF
82–93	Mary Gregory
94–105	Brother Samuel SSF
106–117	Isabelle Hamley
118–135	David Ford
136–147	Colin Heber-Percy
148–153	Isabelle Hamley
154–165	Tom Clammer
166–177	Emma Parker
178–189	Rachel Mann
190–201	Angela Sheard
202–213	Julia Mourant
214–225	Nicholas Papadopulos
226–237	Peter Graystone
238–249	Jitesh Patel
250–261	Jane Williams
262–273	Tim Heaton
274–285	Robert Atwell
286–297	Julia Mourant
298–309	Ally Barrett
310–321	Peter Graystone

About the Authors

Arun Arora is the Bishop of Kirkstall in the Diocese of Leeds. Prior to this he served in churches in Durham, Wolverhampton and Harrogate. He has worked in Church Communications in lay and ordained capacities in Birmingham, York and eventually London as Director of Communications for the Church of England.

Robert Atwell is the former Bishop of Exeter and Chair of the Liturgical Commission. He is the compiler of two anthologies of readings to accompany the lectionary, *Celebrating the Saints* and *Celebrating the Seasons,* and most recently has published a book on the prophet Jonah, *Bewilderment: a spiritual guide.*

Ally Barrett is Associate Vicar of Great St Mary's, the University Church, in Cambridge. She is a published writer, hymn writer and painter.

Tom Clammer OC is a freelance spiritual director, writer and theological educator. He retired from stipendiary ministry in the Church of England in 2019 following the onset of Multiple Sclerosis. He is a professed brother and novice master of the Anglican Order of Cistercians. He lives in Salisbury.

Jonathan Frost is Bishop of Portsmouth, Chair of the National Society for Education, and the Church of England's lead bishop for education. He is a lifelong supporter of Fulham Football Club.

David F. Ford OBE is Regius Professor of Divinity Emeritus in Cambridge University, a Fellow of Selwyn College and a Reader in the Church of England. His publications include *Meeting God in John: A Companion for Lent, Holy Week, Easter and Beyond*, and *The Gospel of John: A Theological Commentary.*

Peter Graystone is a Reader at the Church of the Good Shepherd, Carshalton Beeches, in Southwark Diocese. He is the author of many books, the latest of which is *All's Well That Ends Well: Forty Days with William Shakespeare.*

Mary Gregory is the Bishop of Reading. She has also served as Canon for Arts and Reconciliation at Coventry Cathedral and as a parish priest. Before ordination, Mary worked in the Prison Service as an officer and as a governor. She loves creativity – her own and others – and sweeping horizons.

Isabelle Hamley is an Anglican priest, speaker and writer. She is currently Principal of Ridley Hall, Cambridge. She has written widely on issues of justice, violence and mental health.

Tim Heaton is a parish priest and rural dean in Dorset and an honorary canon of Salisbury Cathedral. He is the author of the best-selling Lent course *The Long Road To Heaven*. He loves walking in the Lake District and spends a lot of time in the vegetable garden.

Colin Heber-Percy was an award-winning screenwriter and academic prior to ordination. He writes regularly for various magazines and newspapers. His book *Tales of a Country Parish* (published in 2022) was a bestseller. His most recent book, *Lost in the Forest*, was one of *The Spectator*'s books of the year 2025.

Rachel Mann is a priest, award-winning poet and writer, and broadcaster. She is has written 16 books and is due to retire as Archdeacon of Salford and Bolton in July 2026.

Julia Mourant, now semi-retired, has been engaged in spiritual direction for many years, most recently as Programme Leader for the Course in Spiritual Direction at Sarum College, Salisbury. She has also held diocesan posts in vocations and training. Her most recent book, *The Spiritual Director,* was published in 2025.

Nicholas Papadopulos has served as Dean of Salisbury since 2018. He was formerly Canon Treasurer of Canterbury Cathedral, and Vicar of St Peter's Eaton Square, London. Before ordination he worked as a barrister specializing in criminal law.

Emma Parker leads a church in Durham Diocese and previously trained people for lay and ordained ministry at Cranmer Hall. She has authored *The Importance of Outsiders to Pauline Communities: Opinion, Reputation and Mission,* and co-authored *Growing Together in Faith: Thinking Theologically about Ministry with Children and Teenagers.*

Jitesh Patel is Assistant Director and Lecturer in Theology at St Mellitus College East Midlands and Associate Vicar at Holy Trinity Leicester. Jitesh has been in parish ministry for 16 years and has recently authored the Practical Theology work *Charismatics and Postmodernity*. He is married with two daughters.

Esther Prior is the Bishop of Aston in the Diocese of Birmingham. Formerly Vicar of St John's Egham, she brings a deep passion for mission, discipleship and leadership development. With roots in Malawi and Zimbabwe, and theological formation at Trinity College, Bristol, she is committed to fostering diverse gospel-shaped communities.

Andrew Rudd is the author of *The Quiet Path: Contemplative practices for everyday life* (2024) and *The Listening Path: Living attentively* (2026). A poet and teacher, he preaches, leads retreats and offers spiritual accompaniment. He is a Licensed Lay Minister in Frodsham, Cheshire.

Br Samuel SSF is an Anglican Franciscan friar, part of a community of brothers living, praying and working in East London. Assisting in local parishes and seeing individuals for spiritual accompaniment, he is also involved with teaching a Franciscan view of creation.

Angela Sheard is a priest in the Church of England. She trained for ordination at The Queen's Foundation, Birmingham, and served her curacy at St Martin-in-the-Fields, London. She currently works at The Queen's Foundation as Anglican Tutor and is also undertaking doctoral research.

Angela Tilby is a broadcaster, writer, theological educator and priest of the Church of England. Formerly a BBC producer, she taught early church history and spirituality at Westcott House, Cambridge, before ministering in Christ Church, Oxford. Now retired, she is Canon Emeritus and Chaplain at Portsmouth Cathedral. Angela is author of *Science and the Soul* and *The Seven Deadly Sins*.

Jane Williams is the McDonald Professor in Christian Theology at St Mellitus College. She is the author of a number of books, most recently, *Giver of Life: The Holy Spirit in the Creed and the Christian Life Today* (SPCK, 2025) and *The Sacraments: Responding to God's Loving Invitation* (SPCK, 2024).

About *Reflections for Daily Prayer*

Based on the *Common Worship Lectionary* readings for Morning Prayer, these daily reflections are designed to refresh and inspire times of personal prayer. The aim is to provide rich, contemporary and engaging insights into Scripture.

Each page lists the Lectionary readings for the day, with the main psalms for that day highlighted in **bold**. The collect of the day – either the *Common Worship* collect or the shorter additional collect – is also included.

For those using this book in conjunction with a service of Morning Prayer, the following conventions apply: a psalm printed in parentheses is omitted if it has been used as the opening canticle at that office; a psalm marked with an asterisk may be shortened if desired.

A short reflection is provided on either the Old or New Testament reading. Popular writers, experienced ministers, biblical scholars and theologians all contribute to this series, bringing with them their own emphases, enthusiasms and approaches to biblical interpretation.

Regular users of Morning Prayer and *Time to Pray* (from *Common Worship: Daily Prayer*) and anyone who follows the Lectionary for their regular Bible reading will benefit from the rich variety of traditions represented in these stimulating and accessible pieces.

This volume also includes both a simple form of *Common Worship* Morning Prayer (see inside front and back covers) and a short form of Night Prayer, also known as Compline (see pp. 326–9), particularly for the benefit of those readers who are new to the habit of the Daily Office or for any reader while travelling.

The Nourishment of Daily Prayer

In the introduction to her book *Just as I am,* the theologian and spiritual director Ruth Etchells writes honestly about her occasional struggles with daily personal prayer. The desire to embrace distraction or to focus on the inconvenience of time or place takes on a sudden urgency when prayer is viewed as a task. But the joys and benefits of regular disciplined prayer lie waiting to be discovered. 'This personal dialogue with God is the very oxygen of our spiritual bloodstream,' she writes 'and without it we grow faint on the pilgrimage ... it is vital for our soul's health that we know God here in our dailiness.'

There is much to be said for understanding daily prayer not so much as a task but as nourishment.

Paying attention to the health of our souls requires developing habits and disciplines that will lead us to a deeper relationship with the lover of our souls. A focus on our spiritual wellbeing includes understanding a pattern of daily prayer as life-giving and sustaining, providing much needed balance to daily demands. Such an understanding holds prayer as a liberating and creative reshaping of life that provides the room for us to sit and luxuriate in the presence of God, enabled by liturgy that opens our lips and forthtells our praise.

We live in a time when the focus on personal physical health and wellbeing is increasingly enabled through technology on smart devices. This is also true for our soul's health, with the *Reflections for Daily Prayer* app providing an opportunity – in the words of the Apostle Paul to the Thessalonians – to 'rejoice always, pray continually and give thanks in all circumstances'. The app also serves as a reminder that, while we may be alone when we pray, we never pray alone. The millions of downloads since the app was launched reflect the reality of our own prayers joining together with the chorus of voices through time and across the globe, joined together in prayer.

The everyday opportunity to join our voices with those of the saints and angels whose praise ever flows towards the throne of God is too good to miss. For myself, I know that there are times when that opportunity will be the best thing that I will do all day. That in the midst of work, tasks and to-do lists, this precious time spent with God will have provided me with the spiritual oxygen I need, enabling me to breathe and to receive breath.

By understanding daily prayer in this way, the opportunity arises to see it not as a ritualistic burden but rather a platform for liberation, freeing ourselves from our daily realities to spend time in the presence of God; where eternal perspectives enter in and the possibilities of daily renewal by the Holy Spirit can set us free – in the words of Henri Nouwen – to choose joy. The choice to pray recognizes that there is no better conversation to start or end our day than a personal dialogue with the one who accompanies us throughout.

While there are undoubted benefits to be had for us as individuals in holding to and developing the liberating discipline of daily prayer, this should never be mistaken for a narrow individual focus. Prayer remains the starting point for action when reflecting on our own place in God's actions in the world, which he created and loves. As the German theologian Karl Barth wrote: 'to clasp the hands in prayer is the beginning of an uprising against the disorder of the world.'

When the disorder of the world causes us to fear or tempts us to despair, daily prayer can reorient us to the knowledge of God's faithfulness and presence. To not be afraid. To be reminded of the encouragement of the psalmist to take heart and be of good courage. To trust in a Divine order in the midst of worldly disorder and, through daily prayer, to declare that trust once more. This is not to remove ourselves from engaging in solutions. A world made right comes not only through the picket line or the protest march or the policy decision, but through the hands clasped in prayer. Amid a life where all things are intimately connected with one another, the gift of daily prayer allows us to cooperate with God in summoning a new future into being.

+ Arun Arora

Advent

Monday 30 November
Andrew the Apostle

Psalms 47, 147.1-12
Ezekiel 47.1-12
or Ecclesiasticus 14.20-end
John 12.20-32

Ezekiel 47.1-12

'... there will grow all kinds of trees for food' (v.12)

Three times in my life, I have had visions of a river. Here are two of them.

The first was in the late 1990s at St Luke's Church in Harare. I saw a river, rather like Ezekiel's river – one that grew deeper and deeper as it flowed out from the sanctuary. Soon after, we experienced a mini revival. Looking back now, I wonder if God was quietly equipping the church for the trials ahead, for in the early 2000s, when St Luke's, alongside other Anglican churches resisting government control, was forced out of its building, they found themselves in a season of unexpected persecution.

The second was in 2001 at a chapel service at the theological college in Bristol, where I trained. I saw a river, like the one Jesus speaks of in John 7, flowing from the innermost being of a believer. What followed was a season of prayerfulness so remarkable it was noted in the college's annual report.

Ezekiel's vision points us to a river that brings life wherever it flows, transforming deserts into gardens and making trees bear fruit in every season. Advent calls us to long for that life-giving river, Christ himself, who comes to make all things new. We wait for his coming with expectancy, not passivity: stepping into the river, allowing it to carry us deeper, letting it flow through us for the healing of the world. Advent hope is not dry or stagnant – it is a river, moving, widening, deepening, until all creation is renewed.

COLLECT

Almighty God,
who gave such grace to your apostle Saint Andrew
that he readily obeyed the call of your Son Jesus Christ
    and brought his brother with him:
call us by your holy word,
and give us grace to follow you without delay
    and to tell the good news of your kingdom;
through Jesus Christ our Lord.

Reflection by **Esther Prior**

Advent

Psalms **80**, 82 *or* **5**, 6 (8)
Isaiah 43.1-13
Revelation 20

Tuesday 1 December

Isaiah 43.1-13

'When you pass through the waters, I will be with you' (v.2)

There are seasons when challenges rise higher than we think we can bear. But God's promise is steady and sure: you will not be overwhelmed.

But how do we trust these words? First, the one who makes the promise matters. It is the Lord, the God with a track record of rescue – parting seas, feeding in the wilderness, defeating giants, securing futures. This God says, 'Do not fear'.

Still unsure? Remember, he is your Creator. The one who formed you can surely sustain you. Still unsure? He has called you by name, inscribed you on the palm of his hand. You are his. Still unsure? He has redeemed you, paid the price to bring you back, to save you from drowning in sin and sorrow. To be sure, look at the cross of Christ and see there his love for you and for me displayed for all eternity.

In Advent, we remember how this redeeming God came near in Christ. The child of Bethlehem is the Lord who walks with us through the flood, the Saviour whose cross secures our rescue, the King who is coming again. And so we wait in hope, trusting his word: 'Do not fear … you are mine.'

COLLECT

Almighty God,
give us grace to cast away the works of darkness
and to put on the armour of light,
now in the time of this mortal life,
in which your Son Jesus Christ came to us in great humility;
that on the last day,
when he shall come again in his glorious majesty
to judge the living and the dead,
we may rise to the life immortal;
through him who is alive and reigns with you,
in the unity of the Holy Spirit,
one God, now and for ever.

Reflection by **Esther Prior**

Advent

Wednesday 2 December

Psalms 5, **7** *or* **119.1-32**
Isaiah 43.14-end
Revelation 21.1-8

Isaiah 43.14-end

'I am about to do a new thing!' (v.19)

There is a challenge that echoes down to us from Isaiah: not to cling to the past in a way that prevents us seeing what God is doing now, or keeps us from joining in his work of redemption and recreation. Of course we must celebrate our story, because in it we recognize God's faithfulness. But we should not be so wrapped up in the past that we miss God's presence today and his work among us now. Isaiah puts it this way: 'Do not remember the former things, or consider the things of old.'

This is a word of Advent hope. Advent reminds us that God is always breaking in with something new. Long ago, Israel's story was full of memories of rescue – Exodus, Sinai, return from exile. But Advent points us to the greater rescue: the coming of Christ, God-with-us, who makes all things new. And it calls us to look ahead still further to the day when he will come again to complete the work of renewal.

So, here is the invitation: keep pressing forward in God's unfolding plans. Embrace the multi-dimensional change he brings. The past gives us courage, but the future gives us hope. Advent is God's reminder that the best is yet to come, and he calls us not to miss it.

COLLECT

Almighty God,
give us grace to cast away the works of darkness
and to put on the armour of light,
now in the time of this mortal life,
in which your Son Jesus Christ came to us in great humility;
that on the last day,
when he shall come again in his glorious majesty
　to judge the living and the dead,
we may rise to the life immortal;
through him who is alive and reigns with you,
in the unity of the Holy Spirit,
one God, now and for ever.

Reflection by **Esther Prior**

Advent

Psalms **42**, 43 *or* 14, **15**, 16
Isaiah 44.1-8
Revelation 21.9-21

Thursday 3 December

Isaiah 44.1-8

'I will pour my spirit upon your descendants' (v.3)

I never met my paternal grandfather, Sekuru Isaac, but I was raised on stories of a spiritual giant who planted his first church at the age of 95. My grandmother, Gogo Estere, whose name I bear, was a prayer warrior. One of my sisters says she lives with a strong sense of our grandfather's protection, while I have always felt that I fly on the wings of my grandmother's prayers. As we shared these insights, we realized we didn't need to choose one or the other.

Scripture teaches that blessings flow through generations. We can rejoice in the prayers and faith of our grandparents, while also claiming the greater blessing that flows through Abraham, fulfilled in Christ, the Lion of Judah.

Isaiah 44 speaks directly into this: 'Do not fear, O Jacob my servant ... whom I have chosen ... I will pour my spirit upon your descendants ...' God's promise is not simply to individuals, but to families, to generations, to communities yet unborn.

This is the heart of Advent hope. Just as Israel waited for the Messiah, so we stand in that same flow of promise, rooted in the faith of those before us, yet looking ahead to the fulfilment of God's kingdom. Advent reminds us that the Spirit who has been poured out is also the Spirit who is making all things new. Thus blessed, we wait with hope.

COLLECT

Almighty God,
as your kingdom dawns,
turn us from the darkness of sin to the
light of holiness,
that we may be ready to meet you
in our Lord and Saviour, Jesus Christ.

Reflection by **Esther Prior**

Advent

Friday 4 December

Psalms **25**, 26 *or* 17, **19**
Isaiah 44.9-23
Revelation 21.22 – 22.5

Isaiah 44.9-23

'I have swept away your transgressions like a cloud' (v.22)

I always knew my grandmother as a passionate Christian, but she would sometimes give us glimpses into her life in Zimbabwe before Christ. She was a witch, fully immersed in practices of darkness and idolatry. She knew first-hand the counterfeit power of such things, and I often wonder if her strong sense of God's power came from having seen the other side so clearly. She understood its lure and was always admonishing us to pray, so that our eyes would remain open and our understanding true.

What she treasured most was the greatness of God's forgiveness. She had done many bad things in those years of darkness, but when Jesus brought her into the light, the shadow of her sin was pushed back, never to be cast over her again. She lived in the freedom of Isaiah's words: sin swept away like mist before the rising sun.

This is the message of Advent. Into a world captivated by idols and shadows, God comes with redeeming power. The child born in Bethlehem is the light no darkness can overcome, the one who sweeps away our sin and restores us to himself. Advent calls us to live like my grandmother – eyes open, hearts awake, confident that forgiveness is real and the future is secure. We wait for the day when Christ will come again, and every shadow will be gone forever.

COLLECT

Almighty God,
give us grace to cast away the works of darkness
and to put on the armour of light,
now in the time of this mortal life,
in which your Son Jesus Christ came to us in great humility;
that on the last day,
when he shall come again in his glorious majesty
    to judge the living and the dead,
we may rise to the life immortal;
through him who is alive and reigns with you,
in the unity of the Holy Spirit,
one God, now and for ever.

Reflection by **Esther Prior**

Advent

Psalms **9** (10) *or* 20, 21, **23**
Isaiah 44.24 – 45.13
Revelation 22.6-end

Saturday 5 December

Isaiah 44.24 – 45.13

'I will give you the treasures of darkness ... hidden in secret places'
(45.3)

Do you remember during the pandemic when nature seemed to renew itself under the reprieve of our absence, and communities drew closer as neighbours supported each other? Do you remember the applause, the gratitude expressed to frontline workers? My mother, ever the pragmatist, declared it would not last because 'human beings never learn'. In the main, she was right.

Yet as I observed those changes alongside her cautionary words, I sensed God magnifying Isaiah's promise: 'I will give you the treasures of darkness ...'

The pandemic disrupted our ordinary rhythms. In that time some of us discovered treasures we might otherwise have missed – new patterns of prayer and worship, rediscovered family bonds, deeper awareness of creation, an awakening to our shared vulnerability. These were riches hidden in secret places, glimpses of grace in the shadows.

Advent invites us to reflect in the same way. It is the season of watching in the darkness for treasures of hope, waiting for the light to dawn. Israel, in exile, longed for deliverance; we too wait for Christ to come make all things new. The treasures of darkness are signs that God is already at work, shaping us for the future. The question is: have we held on to them? Advent asks us to remember, to hope, and to trust that the riches of God's purposes will not be lost.

> Almighty God,
> as your kingdom dawns,
> turn us from the darkness of sin to the
> light of holiness,
> that we may be ready to meet you
> in our Lord and Saviour, Jesus Christ.

COLLECT

Reflection by **Esther Prior**

Advent

Monday 7 December

Psalm **44** *or* 27, **30**
Isaiah 45.14-end
1 Thessalonians 1

Isaiah 45.14-end

'Turn to me and be saved, all the ends of the earth!' (v.22)

Here I hear the anguish of the God who loves all that he has made. He declares himself Creator of the heavens and the earth, and yet what he intended for order and goodness we have filled with chaos. Israel, will you be saved? Yours is salvation. But God's heart stretches far beyond Israel. His salvation is for all the ends of the earth.

So, in love he even calls to Babylon: Will you turn and be saved? Will you stop clinging to idols that cannot rescue? God declares: 'To me every knee shall bow, every tongue shall swear' (confess). This is not the cry of an egotist, but of a loving God who longs for his creation to be restored. One day this posture will be inevitable; some will bow in joy, others in shame. But the invitation is for now: Turn to me and live.

This is the voice of Advent. The child of Bethlehem is the Creator come in flesh, the Saviour whose cross has opened salvation to Jew and Gentile alike. And Advent also points us forward to the day when every knee will bow before Christ the King. The invitation is urgent and tender: do not wait until it is too late. How might you help others to step into his mercy today, and to discover the joy of a salvation that stretches to the ends of the earth?

COLLECT

O Lord, raise up, we pray, your power
and come among us,
and with great might succour us;
that whereas, through our sins and wickedness
we are grievously hindered
in running the race that is set before us,
your bountiful grace and mercy
may speedily help and deliver us;
through Jesus Christ our Lord.

Reflection by **Esther Prior**

Advent

Psalms **56**, 57 *or* 32, **36**
Isaiah 46
1 Thessalonians 2.1-12

Tuesday 8 December

Isaiah 46

'... even when you turn grey I will carry you' (v.4)

What do you believe about God? This is a vital question in a world filled with voices competing for our attention. It is easy to hedge our bets, like supporting two football clubs; yet faith calls us to nail our colours to the mast.

Isaiah 46 opens with a pathetic picture of Babylon's idols: carried away on carts, powerless to save. And then God speaks: 'I have made, and I will bear; I will carry and I will save.' Here is no fragile idol, but the incomparable God: Creator, Sustainer, the one who is from everlasting to everlasting.

If God is truly the source and sustainer of all things, then there cannot be two of him. To compare him to anything else would be to diminish what it means to be God. And this one God has revealed himself not as vague or distant but as one who speaks, acts and saves.

Advent anchors us in this truth. The one God we worship has entered history in the person of Jesus Christ, the promised 'Man' who brings righteousness and salvation. Advent points us to his coming again, when every rival will be shown as nothing and every heart will know there is one Lord. And so we stand firm, placing our confidence in him, and we wait with hope.

COLLECT

Almighty God,
purify our hearts and minds,
that when your Son Jesus Christ comes again as
judge and saviour
we may be ready to receive him,
who is our Lord and our God.

Reflection by **Esther Prior**

Wednesday 9 December

Psalms **62,** 63 *or* **34**
Isaiah 47
1 Thessalonians 2.13-end

Isaiah 47
'I will take vengeance, and I will spare no one' (v.3)

When I was a team vicar, my rector would often say: 'Justice says, this far and no further.' Those words lodged deeply in me. As the leaders of this world strut about as if they are invincible, as if they own the earth, I am grateful to serve a God who is not shy about saying: 'Vengeance is mine.' He is clothed in justice, and his judgements can be trusted.

We sometimes feel God waits too long before he speaks that boundary word, no further! But Isaiah reminds us that his thoughts are higher than ours. We may not understand the delay, but we can trust that evil will not endure forever. Babylon's power looked overwhelming, its oppression unbearable. Babylon herself was deceived, imagining her rule was unshakable. Yet the day of reckoning came suddenly, and there was no one to save her.

This is the hope of Advent. The child born in Bethlehem is not weak or sentimental but the Judge of all the earth. Advent reminds us that injustice, cruelty and oppression will not have the final word. God has already said 'this far and no further' in Christ's cross and resurrection, and one day he will say it again with finality when Christ returns. For now, we wait and watch, holding onto hope: Babylon falls, but God's kingdom endures forever.

COLLECT

O Lord, raise up, we pray, your power
and come among us,
and with great might succour us;
that whereas, through our sins and wickedness
we are grievously hindered
in running the race that is set before us,
your bountiful grace and mercy
may speedily help and deliver us;
through Jesus Christ our Lord.

Reflection by **Esther Prior**

Advent

Psalms 53, **54**, 60 *or* 37*
Isaiah 48.1-11
1 Thessalonians 3

Thursday 10 December

Isaiah 48.1-11

'... invoke the God of Israel, but not in truth or right' (v.1)

Do you despair when people invoke the name of the Lord, but not in truth or right? Does it sometimes feel like a disease particular to our generation? Take some comfort – there is nothing new under the sun. It was ever thus. Yet Isaiah 48 reminds us: God will not be mocked.

God sees the arrogance of those who act as though they have full knowledge, as though their pronouncements must be right. Into this, God calls us back to the ancient path: to walk in the ways he has revealed and to give him glory for what he has done. But he also humbles us, doing a new thing we could not have imagined. Christ's coming was such a new thing, confounding the wise and making wise the simple.

Advent takes us into this tension. We look back to Bethlehem, to the astonishing moment when the Word became flesh, and we look forward to the day when Christ will return, and all pride and falsehood will be silenced. In the meantime, God keeps calling us away from hollow words and shallow claims, into lives that reflect his truth.

Ultimately, as Isaiah declares, God's righteousness will shine like the dawn. In Advent, we rehearse that hope, lighting candles against the dark, lifting prayers of longing and trust, gathering around Scripture and the Lord's table. In these small but steady acts, we live towards the day when all glory will be his alone, as his truth is revealed to every nation, every people and every heart.

COLLECT

Almighty God,
purify our hearts and minds,
that when your Son Jesus Christ comes again as
judge and saviour
we may be ready to receive him,
who is our Lord and our God.

Reflection by **Esther Prior**

Advent

Friday 11 December

Psalms 85, **86** *or* 31
Isaiah 48.12-end
1 Thessalonians 4.1-12

Isaiah 48.12-end

'I am the first, and I am the last' (v.12)

Here is a wonderful declaration of God's eternal sovereignty. Long before creation, God was. Long after the fading of empires and nations, God will be. God is the beginning, the source of all life, and God is the end, the one toward whom all history moves. In a world of constant change, God anchors us with his unchanging presence.

Israel needed to hear this as they faced exile, confusion and the loss of all security. Their story looked like it was ending, but God reminded them: I am the first and the last. I am still writing the story.

Advent takes up this same theme. Christ is the Alpha and the Omega, the child born in Bethlehem who is also the Lord of history. He stands at the beginning and will stand at the end, bringing justice, peace and renewal. Advent reminds us we live in the 'in-between', held by the God who is both first and last, origin and completion.

That means our present struggles are not the final word. The pain, injustice and weariness of this age will pass. The final word belongs to Christ, who will come again to bring freedom. Isaiah reminds us that for those who trust in him, there is an everlasting peace.

In these in-between times, we live as people of hope: choosing forgiveness when resentment would be easier, practising generosity in a world of scarcity, lifting our voices in prayer when despair presses in. We keep watch together, waiting not passively, but with active trust in the One who was, and is, and is to come.

COLLECT

O Lord, raise up, we pray, your power
and come among us,
and with great might succour us;
that whereas, through our sins and wickedness
we are grievously hindered
in running the race that is set before us,
your bountiful grace and mercy
may speedily help and deliver us;
through Jesus Christ our Lord.

Reflection by **Esther Prior**

Advent

Psalm **145** *or* 41, **42**, 43
Isaiah 49.1-13
1 Thessalonians 4.13-end

Saturday 12 December

Isaiah 49.1-13

'... he made me a polished arrow, in his quiver he hid me away'
(v.2)

Isaiah 49 speaks of a servant prepared for just the right time. To a nation crushed under the weight of exile, this is a word of hope: you are not forsaken but purposed. And that purpose is far greater than Israel's own deliverance. God's dream is much bigger.

In one astonishing phrase God declares: 'It is too light a thing.' Too light! Too small! Israel's restoration alone is not enough. God's people were never meant to exist for themselves; nor is their healing an end in itself. God gathers his people into his life for one purpose: the salvation of the world. 'I will give you as a light to the nations.'

This is where Advent lifts our eyes. Just as Israel's exile was not the end of the story, neither is their restoration. At just the right time, the Servant came, Jesus Christ, born in Bethlehem, the true light of the world. His mission was not for one people only but for all peoples.

And still Advent points us forward. The Servant will come again to complete the mission, to gather every nation, tribe and tongue into the joy of God's kingdom. Until then, we live in hope, called not to turn inward, but outward, bearing witness to the One who is light and life for the world.

COLLECT

Almighty God,
purify our hearts and minds,
that when your Son Jesus Christ comes again as
judge and saviour
we may be ready to receive him,
who is our Lord and our God.

Reflection by **Esther Prior**

Advent

Monday 14 December

Psalm **40** or **44**
Isaiah 49.14-25
1 Thessalonians 5.1-11

Isaiah 49.14-25

'... these may forget, yet I will not forget you' (v.15)

A voice speaks, and then another voice. Have we joined a play halfway through? Every word resonates, but who is speaking? It's a play about heartbreak, abandonment, longings, questions: that's what keeps us listening. It lingers in our minds. That's the mystery and joy of this book of Isaiah.

From the first word, we're drawn in. But Zion said, 'the Lord has forsaken me ...' I recognize this feeling. Even though everything is going well, isn't there always a 'but'? A nagging fear, an impostor syndrome, a note of uncertainty? Has the Lord forsaken us? Are we forgotten? And then the voice of God speaks: 'I will not forget you.'

To me, Isaiah's God sounds like a mother, or a father, holding a baby, singing a lullaby. We sing jingles to our children, full of dreamy promises: 'Hush little baby ... Papa's gonna buy you a mockingbird.' Impossible dreams, but the fitful baby relaxes into sleep, held in love.

Isaiah tells of dazzling visions, wonderful futures. It's gloriously, crazily over the top. It's unbelievable. But isn't this more about love than facts? Yes, there will be an end to exile, a bright future, but the real story is an outpouring of love. You are, says Isaiah, a child in the arms of God, whose only desire is to be with you. You are not forgotten.

COLLECT

O Lord Jesus Christ,
who at your first coming sent your messenger
to prepare your way before you:
grant that the ministers and stewards of your mysteries
may likewise so prepare and make ready your way
by turning the hearts of the disobedient to the wisdom of the just,
that at your second coming to judge the world
we may be found an acceptable people in your sight;
for you are alive and reign with the Father
in the unity of the Holy Spirit,
one God, now and for ever.

Reflection by **Andrew Rudd**

Advent

Psalms **70**, 74 *or* **48**, 52
Isaiah 50
1 Thessalonians 5.12-end

Tuesday 15 December

Isaiah 50

'Morning by morning he wakens – wakens my ear' (v.4)

I really can't make out a storyline when I listen to Isaiah. But then a phrase seems to swim into focus. Striking, relevant, familiar words. Words that the first Christians took to their hearts and quoted in the Gospels. Words that seem to belong in the mouth of Jesus. 'I did not hide my face from shame and spitting' (NKJV) or 'I have set my face like a flint'. Maybe Jesus himself, as he grew up, as he listened in the synagogue, was formed by these images conjured by Isaiah.

We know little about the author, but we recognize someone in touch with his heart, his feelings, his spirit. Someone who listens to his suffering community and puts into words the whisper of God.

And amid a lot of dark questioning, seemingly out of nowhere, comes this little gem about teaching and listening; about our daily reflection. And it turns out to be all about, not what I do, but what God does. God has given me a voice; God awakens me every morning; God opens my ear, and helps me.

This is the kind of treasure we discover in Isaiah. It reminds us to wait each day and listen for God's word, where we encounter something active, active in a way that is beyond ourselves. We cannot initiate or control it. We cooperate with God. God wakens us to the new day.

COLLECT

God for whom we watch and wait,
you sent John the Baptist to prepare the way of your Son:
give us courage to speak the truth,
to hunger for justice,
and to suffer for the cause of right,
with Jesus Christ our Lord.

Reflection by **Andrew Rudd**

Advent

Wednesday 16 December

Psalms **75**, 96 *or* **119.57-80**
Isaiah 51.1-8
2 Thessalonians 1

Isaiah 51.1-8

'Listen … Listen … Listen' (vv.1, 4, 7)

Listening – that's the whole point of lectionaries and daily readings, isn't it? Listening opens the way to looking, beholding and understanding. Isaiah gets to the heart of what doing a morning reflection is all about. 'Morning by morning he wakens my ear.' Every day, a simple practice reminds us of what we need to know: we keep on remembering, unforgetting. And so we begin to hear, not just words, but the voice of God.

Listen, says Isaiah, to your deep inheritance, the stories of where you came from, the rock from which you were carved out. Beyond the illusions and fashions of whatever culture we happen to live in, this listening shows us the deep connections that make us who we are. The Scriptures give us roots, a history in time and place.

Listen, says Isaiah – here's the big picture. This is a teaching for everybody, a teaching that leads to freedom: my own personal freedom, and the freedom of everybody else, across the whole world.

Listen, says Isaiah. With this teaching in your heart, you will start to lose your fear. You have found a source you can trust. In the midst of chaos, you can begin to live in safety and compassion. That's the joy of listening!

COLLECT

O Lord Jesus Christ,
who at your first coming sent your messenger
to prepare your way before you:
grant that the ministers and stewards of your mysteries
may likewise so prepare and make ready your way
by turning the hearts of the disobedient to the wisdom of the just,
that at your second coming to judge the world
we may be found an acceptable people in your sight;
for you are alive and reign with the Father
in the unity of the Holy Spirit,
one God, now and for ever.

Reflection by **Andrew Rudd**

Advent

Psalms **76**, 97 *or* 56, **57** (63*)
Isaiah 51.9-16
2 Thessalonians 2

Thursday 17 December

Isaiah 51.9-16
'Awake ... arm of the Lord!' (v.9)

With an image of astonishing physicality, Isaiah sees a great arm, as if somebody was asleep, but their arm was draped over the edge of the hammock or stretched out on the ground. A huge power, but apparently oblivious and unresponsive. This power used to operate in history, but nowadays seems to have gone to sleep. So here is this extraordinary prayer. 'Awake ... arm of the Lord!' It's a prayer of trust. This God of power is committed to these fearful people, to open a way forward, sweep away whatever hinders and bring them home.

There is no hand like this. Awake, it stretches out the heavens, as if pitching a tent. It builds the earth, as if that were just a little bit of digging. And yet, says Isaiah, you don't recognize it. This hand reaches out, moves on your behalf, pours gladness on your heads, puts new words in your mouths, protects you in its shadow.

All that is needed is to wake up. It's not God's hand that is asleep, but we ourselves who don't understand what is happening. We need to wake from sleep and open our eyes to reality. Is this what Isaiah calls 'comfort'?

You are in my hands, says God, my arm is round about you. I am the one who finally speaks the deepest word of love and relationship; you are my people.

> God for whom we watch and wait,
> you sent John the Baptist to prepare the way of your Son:
> give us courage to speak the truth,
> to hunger for justice,
> and to suffer for the cause of right,
> with Jesus Christ our Lord.

COLLECT

Reflection by **Andrew Rudd**

Advent

Friday 18 December

Psalms 77, **98** *or* **51**, 54
Isaiah 51.17-end
2 Thessalonians 3

Isaiah 51.17-end

'... there is no one to take her by the hand' (v.18)

Isaiah follows songs of affirmation with this poem of pure pain. It's comforting to read about peace and hope, a little oasis in a challenging world, but in this reading, there's scarcely a glimpse of goodness. We are invited into that most difficult of spiritual practices: staying, remaining, not looking away.

Jerusalem, an abused and wounded woman, lies in wrack and ruin. She has been forced to drink a chalice of poison, all the way to the dregs. Her children lie strewn along the streets. There are violent bootsteps along the roadway of her back: oppressors have walked all over her. She has nobody to help, no one to take her by the hand.

But already Isaiah starts to reframe this situation. It is not just physical disaster or political calamity, he asserts, but the 'wrath of God'. That is not immediately reassuring, except that Isaiah begins to see right through this crisis to something worse: the loss of relationship with God. 'Nothing is disastrous', said brother Roger of Taizé, 'except the loss of love.' And if our 'disaster' is situated in our relationship with God, then might there just be hope? Even if love seems lost, if God is infinitely merciful, couldn't love be restored?

COLLECT

O Lord Jesus Christ,
who at your first coming sent your messenger
to prepare your way before you:
grant that the ministers and stewards of your mysteries
may likewise so prepare and make ready your way
by turning the hearts of the disobedient to the wisdom of the just,
that at your second coming to judge the world
we may be found an acceptable people in your sight;
for you are alive and reign with the Father
in the unity of the Holy Spirit,
one God, now and for ever.

Reflection by **Andrew Rudd**

Advent

Psalms 144, **146**
Isaiah 52.1-12
Jude

Saturday 19 December

Isaiah 52.1-12
'How beautiful ... are the feet ...' (v.7)

In these chapters of Isaiah, we are ambushed by song. Out of the darkness, we suddenly find ourselves singing along with an aria from Handel's *Messiah*, or an exuberant and endlessly repeated charismatic hymn: 'Our God reigns!' In a series of striking images and surprising verses, Isaiah has created ancient memes that still seem to touch our hearts, generation after generation.

Treasures of darkness, flashes of light, little moments when ultimate meaning shines through the fog and chaos: Isaiah catches these in precious and physical images. Beautiful feet on the mountains; those left for dead shaking themselves out of the dust; the sleeves of God being rolled up; watchmen singing on the city walls. These pictures, once seen, never go away. And Isaiah is the seer, the one who sees. He is a true prophet. It's not so much that he looks into the future and sees what is to come; rather he sees what is, and his metaphors still land with us, fresh and alive, over such great distances, over so many years.

The song does not resolve the crisis, or fix the problem. But the song, as it rises in our hearts, reconnects us with the source of life, the love of God. We are awake!

COLLECT

God for whom we watch and wait,
you sent John the Baptist to prepare the way of your Son:
give us courage to speak the truth,
to hunger for justice,
and to suffer for the cause of right,
with Jesus Christ our Lord.

Reflection by **Andrew Rudd**

Advent

Monday 21 December

Psalms **121**, 122, 123
Isaiah 52.13 – end of 53
2 Peter 1.1-15

Isaiah 52.13 – end of 53
'… like a lamb that is led to the slaughter' (53.7)

Now Isaiah leads us into the heart of darkness. Why does a loving God seem to turn away from a beloved child? Why do bad things happen even to those who are good? Why do these exiles suffer such undeserved pain? In describing a 'servant', Isaiah personifies his people. The servant suffers, and he sees this suffering happening in relationship with God. Isaiah begins to see this pain – is it also his own personal pain? Is it something he endures on behalf of others? Is it possible that love can assimilate even the most intense suffering?

As we read this chapter, the melodies of Handel's *Messiah* rise again into our ears: 'He was despised and rejected', 'Surely he has borne our griefs', 'All we like sheep have gone astray'. In these words, the first Christians found a profound template for their understanding of the death of Jesus, so now it's hard to read the Jewish text without inscribing the story of Good Friday, where Jesus, only for love, goes voluntarily into the deepest suffering. He ends the cycle of violence by taking it into his own body. He transmutes darkness into meaning, and finally into the light of resurrection.

For Isaiah, suffering is reframed within the realm of God. We no longer see the righteous flourishing or the wicked suffering, but a servant of God whose glory shines in the midst of suffering, because that suffering is out of love for others. In the heart of darkness, there is love.

COLLECT

God our redeemer,
who prepared the Blessed Virgin Mary
to be the mother of your Son:
grant that, as she looked for his coming as our saviour,
so we may be ready to greet him
when he comes again as our judge;
who is alive and reigns with you,
in the unity of the Holy Spirit,
one God, now and for ever.

Reflection by **Andrew Rudd**

Advent

Psalms **124**, 125, 126, 127
Isaiah 54
2 Peter 1.16 – 2.3

Tuesday 22 December

Isaiah 54

'... with everlasting love I will have compassion on you' (v.8)

Something has changed. There is a sense that the storm has blown itself out, and the landscape settles into a kind of stillness. And in this peace a song begins that can no longer be silenced, an unexpected song of gladness.

Isaiah returns, as he must, as we all must, to his great theme of comfort. This comfort is only to be discovered in the heart of God, the *hesed,* which is the Hebrew word for kindness, and love, and faithfulness. The loving kindness of God lies underneath all the events and crises, the twists and turns of history, as a bedrock beneath the soil. The love of God finally turns out to be the deepest reality. Compared with this love, everything else is a blip, a brief moment of disturbance; ultimately, even shame, disgrace or hopelessness cannot resist its flow. Even the breakdown of relationship, forsaking, anger, rejection cannot stem this loving kindness. Love is stronger than death.

Centuries later, the New Testament letter of John is able to speak the majestic, simple summary of our faith and theology: 'God is love' – but the idea is already present in the vision of Isaiah. Nothing is beyond the restoring, rebuilding, reconciling love of God.

COLLECT

> Eternal God,
> as Mary waited for the birth of your Son,
> so we wait for his coming in glory;
> bring us through the birth pangs of this present age
> to see, with her, our great salvation
> in Jesus Christ our Lord.

Reflection by **Andrew Rudd**

Advent

Wednesday 23 December

128, 129, **130**, 131
Isaiah 55
2 Peter 2.4-end

Isaiah 55

'For you shall go out in joy, and be led back in peace' (v.12)

You might have imagined that God was the hardest of taskmasters, demanding that you get things right, but, in fact, to those who have no money at all, God offers a feast. Blessed are those who are hungry or thirsty, because with God is nothing but grace, unearned, freely given.

You might have imagined that God was hiding away from you, but God is near, exactly where you are. For everyone who seeks or calls, God is here.

You might have imagined that God had forgotten you, but God is waiting to revive you and to make with you an everlasting covenant relationship.

You might have imagined that you understood the work of God, that your theology was adequate to your life, but it turns out that God's love, God's grace, God's provision will always be greater than we can imagine, a mountain whose summit remains invisible. God's ways and God's thoughts are as high and unreachable as the bright sky.

You might have imagined that joy had gone for good, but God leads you into life: you shall go out with joy. There will be new life. There will be a future.

COLLECT

God our redeemer,
who prepared the Blessed Virgin Mary
to be the mother of your Son:
grant that, as she looked for his coming as our saviour,
so we may be ready to greet him
when he comes again as our judge;
who is alive and reigns with you,
in the unity of the Holy Spirit,
one God, now and for ever.

Reflection by **Andrew Rudd**

Advent

Psalms **45**, 113
Isaiah 56.1-8
2 Peter 3

Thursday 24 December

Christmas Eve

Isaiah 56.1-8

'… a house of prayer for all peoples' (v.7)

It's beautiful to see this brief prophecy of inclusion and welcome placed after the song of joy and restoration. This was a section of Isaiah known and loved by Jesus, who imagined the temple – with all its obvious faults – as a house of prayer 'for all peoples'. Such a welcome is easily forgotten by the institutions and structures of religion. We can often turn inwards, hold on to our power, and build walls to exclude any kind of outsider. But already, in the book of Isaiah, a wider vision is dawning. 'God is with us' was never just a privilege of a chosen people, but God loves every person that God has created: the whole world.

The unstoppable love of God is always flowing into the whole world, the world loved by God. The joy of God, discovered by Isaiah at the heart of exile, pain and suffering, springs up unexpectedly in every corner of the world. In this dawning love, there are no foreigners, no Jew or Greek, a family with no barriers to inclusion. The infinite love of God appears among us, in a suffering servant, in the news of hope, in the flowering of new life, and at last, in the Christian story, a baby in a manger, a child for the world, born to accompany every human being. God with us.

COLLECT

Almighty God,
you make us glad with the yearly remembrance
of the birth of your Son Jesus Christ:
grant that, as we joyfully receive him as our redeemer,
so we may with sure confidence behold him
when he shall come to be our judge;
who is alive and reigns with you,
in the unity of the Holy Spirit,
one God, now and for ever.

Reflection by **Andrew Rudd**

Christmas Season

Friday 25 December
Christmas Day

Psalms **110,** 117
Isaiah 62.1-5
Matthew 1.18-25

Matthew 1.18-25
'God is with us' (v.23)

This text might be so familiar that we no longer notice its strangeness. There's an engagement, a couple not yet living together. And then there's an unexpected pregnancy, an embarrassing scene. A bit of domestic conflict. In the middle of it all there's a good-hearted man wanting to keep everything quiet. It could be a soap-opera story, apart from one less usual character. 'The Holy Spirit' is dropped into the narrative as if it was somebody who happened to be living next door.

The stories of the birth of Jesus are full of such a mixture of the prosaic and the supernatural, because isn't that what the incarnation is all about? It is the beginning of the gospel, the good news, of Jesus Christ: that in the ordinary mess, the confusion and conflict of families, the ups and downs of village life, something new is already occurring. This familiar space, a place we all inhabit and know so well, is already visited by angels.

In this space where we live, something new is coming to birth. There's a process already underway that will change everything. Unexpectedly, astonishingly, just where we live, in the everyday, ordinary detail of our lives, 'God is with us'.

COLLECT

Almighty God,
you have given us your only-begotten Son
to take our nature upon him
and as at this time to be born of a pure virgin:
grant that we, who have been born again
and made your children by adoption and grace,
may daily be renewed by your Holy Spirit;
through Jesus Christ our Lord.

Reflection by **Andrew Rudd**

Christmas Season

Psalms 13, 31.1-8, 150
Jeremiah 26.12-15
Acts 6

Saturday 26 December
Stephen, deacon, first martyr

Acts 6
'... they saw that his face was like the face of an angel' (v.15)

The carols are still resounding in our ears, but on Boxing Day, between the turkey and the leftovers, comes this Feast of Stephen. No sooner have we celebrated the birth of Jesus, than we remember Stephen, the first martyr of the Church. But as the American theologian and civil rights leader Howard Thurman said, this is where the work of Christmas begins.

In the community of the first Christians, Stephen is busy organizing the food bank, handling complaints. He is trying to operate with sensitivity in a whirlpool of race, gender and religious difference. For this kind of work, says Luke, the apostles need somebody full of the Holy Spirit, and that phrase takes us right back to Luke's Christmas story. It was the Holy Spirit who brought Jesus into the world, into the everyday.

Stephen is full of grace and power. His speech is full of the wisdom of the Spirit. Stephen is doing the work of Christmas, giving himself for others. And now Luke, who introduced us to angels at the nativity, gives us a hint of what those angels might have looked like. Confronted by the furious crowd, bent on his destruction, Stephen shows us the shining face of a servant of God: 'his face was like the face of an angel.' We might see some of those angels. We might even become one!

COLLECT

Gracious Father,
who gave the first martyr Stephen
grace to pray for those who took up stones against him:
grant that in all our sufferings for the truth
we may learn to love even our enemies
and to seek forgiveness for those who desire our hurt,
looking up to heaven to him who was crucified for us,
Jesus Christ, our mediator and advocate.

Reflection by **Andrew Rudd**

Christmas Season

Monday 28 December
The Holy Innocents

Psalms **36**, 146
Baruch 4.21-27
or Genesis 37.13-20
Matthew 18.1-10

Matthew 18.1-10

'... unless you change and become like children' (v.3)

Children had little status in the ancient world. They were vulnerable in ways it is hard for us to imagine. On Holy Innocents Day, we remember how helpless those children were who were murdered by Herod and how deeply their parents must have mourned their loss. The vulnerability of children moves the heart, which is why we feel such outrage at those who exploit or cause hurt to children.

Jesus was particularly harsh to those who damaged 'little ones'. We should not be harming children but learning from them. When Jesus urges his disciples to become like children, he was inviting them to experience life without the weapons of power and persuasion, open only to the protection God gives.

We will only understand the mission and the call of Jesus if we ourselves are prepared to live towards God from a place of vulnerability. This is why Jesus insists that we change from adult habits of self-assertion and self-defence, and learn once again to experience life with the curiosity and spontaneity of children. If we want to follow Jesus, we must re-evaluate our attitudes to power, authority and wealth. God wants real human beings not self-made ones – humans who can respond to him and to one another from a place of wonder and welcome.

COLLECT

Heavenly Father,
whose children suffered at the hands of Herod,
though they had done no wrong:
by the suffering of your Son
and by the innocence of our lives
frustrate all evil designs
and establish your reign of justice and peace;
through Jesus Christ our Lord.

Reflection by **Angela Tilby**

Christmas Season

Psalms **19**, 20
Isaiah 57.15-end
John 1.1-18

Tuesday 29 December

Isaiah 57.15-end

'Peace, peace to the far and the near, says the Lord' (v.19)

These final chapters of the book of Isaiah begin to strike a universal tone as the prophet, most probably a disciple of the 'Isaiah' who composed Chapters 40–55, looks beyond the traumas of the Jewish exile and the difficult return from exile to blessings in the future. These readings from the end of the book resonate with Christmas and Epiphany in their proclamation of God's goodwill to all humanity.

The leading theme here is of reassurance. It is the sheer majesty of God that guarantees his mercy. He has a particular care for those who have in the past suffered from his anger, who are genuinely humble and sorry for their sins. To them, he promises healing, peace and new life. It is an encouraging message for all of us at a time when the world seems so divided, and there is so much anger and aggression in our common life, in the Church and all too often, in our own hearts.

The peace God promises is not without cost and we do not receive it without making an effort. Worship is costly, requiring a commitment of our time and attention when we are all too often distracted by the anger and turbulence around and within us. Before we can become peacemakers and peacekeepers, we must receive God's peace, with humility and thankfulness.

COLLECT

Almighty God,
who wonderfully created us in your own image
and yet more wonderfully restored us
through your Son Jesus Christ:
grant that, as he came to share in our humanity,
so we may share the life of his divinity;
who is alive and reigns with you,
in the unity of the Holy Spirit,
one God, now and for ever.

Reflection by **Angela Tilby**

Christmas Season

Wednesday 30 December

Psalms 111, 112, **113**
Isaiah 59.1-15*a*
John 1.19-28

Isaiah 5 9.1-15*a*

'... our sins testify against us' (v.12)

God has promised his peace, but this does not mean we have truly received it or understand its implications. This is a time of year when it is not always easy to find space for Scripture reading and prayer, but it is important to attend to our inner lives as we 'wait for light', even if our new year expectations may be more of the same, 'Lo! There is darkness'.

So often it is our own attitudes that keep God's peace from us. Those of us who live in societies that have become indifferent to Christianity can find it hard to stand up for moral values that are more than well-meaning aspirations. 'Truth is lacking' proclaims Isaiah, and without truth, corruption festers. There is a moral lostness about the world we inhabit where 'truth stumbles in the public square'.

As individuals, we may often feel we can do nothing to counter or reverse negative trends in society. But that is not true. The repentance we offer for our personal failings has a vicarious element; Christianity is infectious when it spreads compassion, hope and joy. The peace of God is stronger than our sinfulness, and we should not be too alarmed when the purposes and promises of God for the world are kept alive only by a minority.

COLLECT

Almighty God,
who wonderfully created us in your own image
and yet more wonderfully restored us
through your Son Jesus Christ:
grant that, as he came to share in our humanity,
so we may share the life of his divinity;
who is alive and reigns with you,
in the unity of the Holy Spirit,
one God, now and for ever.

Reflection by **Angela Tilby**

Christmas Season

Psalm 102
Isaiah 59.15b-end
John 1.29-34

Thursday 31 December

Isaiah 59.15b-end

'... he will come to Zion as Redeemer' (v.20)

The end of a year is potentially a time of spiritual renewal. This is not about making the kind of resolutions that we always tend to make at this time of year – losing weight, exercising more, spending less time on our smartphones. It's about renewing our trust in the love and mercy of God.

Today's reading is a prophecy, that God, seeing 'that there was no justice' among his people, takes the cause of justice on himself and comes to Zion as a warrior to defeat his enemies and save his people. God also promises that the words of warning and blessing he has given through his prophets will remain with his people from generation to generation.

For us today, that means resting in the confidence that God's cause is not lost. He has indeed come to us and will continue to fulfil his promise among us. In the light of Christ, we now know that this coming is not as a mighty warrior, but as the child of the manger, who judges our hearts with more kindness and accuracy than we can imagine. So today is a day to rest on the promises of God and to trust in his mercy, whatever 2027 may bring.

> COLLECT
>
> God in Trinity,
> eternal unity of perfect love:
> gather the nations to be one family,
> and draw us into your holy life
> through the birth of Emmanuel,
> our Lord Jesus Christ.

Reflection by **Angela Tilby**

Christmas Season

Friday 1 January
Naming and Circumcision of Jesus

Psalms **103**, 150
Genesis 17.1-13
Romans 2.17-end

Genesis 17.1-13
'This is my covenant, which you shall keep' (v.10)

The covenant with Abraham is the foundation of faith for Jews, Muslims and Christians. Abraham is the spiritual ancestor for believers in all three traditions because he is the first to acknowledge the true God. We can all learn from Abraham's persistence in faith, his willingness to trust God and the long journey of faith that brought him to the Promised Land. As we start a new year, we should give thanks that God is a God who wants to be known, and who wants to be known not just by a few, but by many. Abraham was called to be the father of many nations, and this should show us the expansive breadth of God's appreciation of human variety and diversity.

The sign of circumcision marks those who follow in Abraham's faith, and Jesus shared that mark when he was circumcised. It is the first wound on his body. As baptized Christians, our version of that marking and wounding is baptism, where we are marked with the sign of the cross. The baptismal water stands for our identification with Christ in his death and resurrection.

God also asks of us what he asked of Abraham, a readiness to receive the future as a gift. So today, as children of God's promise, we look forward to another year of God's guidance and blessing, and pray that we may grow, not only in faith, but also in hope and charity.

COLLECT

Almighty God,
whose blessed Son was circumcised
in obedience to the law for our sake
and given the Name that is above every name:
give us grace faithfully to bear his Name,
to worship him in the freedom of the Spirit,
and to proclaim him as the Saviour of the world;
who is alive and reigns with you,
in the unity of the Holy Spirit,
one God, now and for ever.

Reflection by **Angela Tilby**

Christmas Season

Psalm 18.1-30
Isaiah 60.1-12
John 1.35-42

Saturday 2 January

Isaiah 60.1-12

'Arise, shine; for your light has come' (v.1)

Isaiah's message to the returned exiles was one of much-needed hope. As we saw in earlier readings, the hard lessons of exile had not been fully learnt in spite of the ongoing threat of divine judgement, there was widespread corruption and injustice among God's people. And yet here the prophet proclaims that God has once again taken the initiative and is preparing a future in which Israel will indeed fulfil its vocation to be 'a light to the nations' (Isaiah 49.6).

Israel's true vocation is to make God known by becoming a moral and spiritual beacon to the world. The gates to Zion will remain open perpetually and the surrounding nations shall bring their wealth as an acknowledgement of the true God. This theme is taken up in Luke's Gospel as the aged Simeon takes the child Jesus in his arms, and sees in him 'a light for revelation to the Gentiles and the glory of your people Israel' (2.12).

The Church of England's baptismal liturgy ends with the giving of a lighted candle to the newly baptized with the words: 'Shine as a light in the world to the glory of God the Father.' What will you do today to ensure your light shines out? And what will you do to bring new hope to your home, your workplace, your church, your community?

COLLECT

Almighty God,
who wonderfully created us in your own image
and yet more wonderfully restored us
through your Son Jesus Christ:
grant that, as he came to share in our humanity,
so we may share the life of his divinity;
who is alive and reigns with you,
in the unity of the Holy Spirit,
one God, now and for ever.

Reflection by **Angela Tilby**

Christmas Season

Monday 4 January

Psalm **89.1-37**
Isaiah 61
John 2.1-12

Isaiah 61

'… he has clothed me with the garments of salvation' (v.10)

This chapter begins with words that Jesus would later proclaim in the synagogue at Nazareth, words he chose deliberately to describe his mission from the Father. We should remember that Isaiah originally addressed these words to profoundly disillusioned people. The return from exile had not brought the benefits they had looked forward to. They were disappointed, cynical and angry. Yet it was at just such a point that God called them to look beyond themselves and their despair and to recognize that 'they are a people whom the Lord has blessed'.

It is easy for those of us who live in once-Christian nations to hunker down to a minority existence, giving up on missionary hope. Yet our integrity as Christians is not measured by our success but by our faithfulness. When Jesus read Isaiah's words in his home town, he was initially greeted with enthusiasm (Luke 4.22), but this turned to rage when he challenged them. They initially took his words as flattery, but then recognized he was calling them out of complacency.

We latter-day Christians should not be disheartened at this manifesto, but galvanized. The oppressed are all around us, as are the broken-hearted, the imprisoned and those who mourn. Pray today that we may hear the gospel for ourselves and be empowered by God's Holy Spirit to share it with others.

COLLECT

Almighty God,
in the birth of your Son
you have poured on us the new light of your incarnate Word,
and shown us the fullness of your love:
help us to walk in his light and dwell in his love
that we may know the fullness of his joy;
who is alive and reigns with you,
in the unity of the Holy Spirit,
one God, now and for ever.

Reflection by **Angela Tilby**

Christmas Season

Psalms 8, **48**
Isaiah 62
John 2.13-end

Tuesday 5 January

Isaiah 62

'Say to daughter Zion, "See your salvation comes: his reward is with him ..."' (v.11)

These are beautiful verses to ponder and enjoy. God's relationship with his people is that of bridegroom to bride. 'Your land shall be married.' This deep covenantal love of God is applied by the prophet to Israel. But in the Christian era, it also interprets and reflects God's relationship with the Church. It also speaks on an individual level of God's relationship with the human soul.

At each point it is clear that the marriage God intends is in no way a marriage of equals. God knows his people are grieving, ashamed and troubled. They have failed to live up to their vocation; their enemies have ruined them and remain a threat. Yet God will not abandon his covenant people. He rejoices over them; he protects them; he seeks them out and renews his vows to them.

Reflecting on this, we Christians should not despair of the Church, however grievous its failures. Nor should we despair of ourselves, however much we have failed to live up to our ideals, however broken we have been by our own mistakes and the wounds inflicted by others. Whatever our circumstances, whether in sickness or in health, in prosperity or poverty, God has a purpose for us and guards us until that purpose is fulfilled. We are not forsaken.

COLLECT

God our Father,
in love you sent your Son
that the world may have life:
lead us to seek him among the outcast
and to find him in those in need,
for Jesus Christ's sake.

Reflection by **Angela Tilby**

Epiphany Season

Wednesday 6 January
Epiphany

Psalms **132**, 113
Jeremiah 31.7-14
John 1.29-34

John 1.29-34

'I myself have seen and have testified that this is the Son of God'
(v.34)

Today's feast day, the Epiphany, means 'manifestation', hence its longer title 'The Manifestation of Christ to the Gentiles', which is associated with the story of the Magi coming to Jesus with their gifts. In John's Gospel, though, the first manifestation of Christ is to John the Baptist, the one who proclaimed his coming. Here, Jesus is revealed first to Israel, to God's own much-loved covenant people. It is important to remember this because the Christian Church has not always been faithful to its Jewish roots and has often been actively hostile to Jews. Yet John and Jesus were both Jews, and our faith is built on the faith that goes back to Abraham.

Often in the Christian life, we need to recognize Jesus in a new way and to receive the gospel afresh. Baptism is an immersion in the life, death and resurrection of Jesus, and a call to join in his transforming mission. This immersion only happens once, and yet, as an English bishop once put it, 'The water of baptism never quite dries off'. As we have received so we are called to give. John the Baptist reminds us that our call is always to proclaim the way of the Lord, the same Lord who loved Israel into being and called Abraham to live by faith. This is an opportunity to reflect on how we might offer our gifts to Jesus and let him use them in the cause of the gospel of forgiveness and reconciliation.

COLLECT

O God,
who by the leading of a star
manifested your only Son to the peoples of the earth:
mercifully grant that we,
who know you now by faith,
may at last behold your glory face to face;
through Jesus Christ our Lord.

Reflection by **Angela Tilby**

Epiphany Season

Psalms **99**, 147.1-12 *or* **78.1-39***
Isaiah 63.7-end
1 John 3

Thursday 7 January

Isaiah 63.7-end

'... you, O Lord, are our Father; our Redeemer from of old is your name' (v.16)

This passage reflects the extraordinary intimacy between God, his deeds of grace and his covenant people. God's being, God's nature and God's actions are all consistent. God is boundlessly gracious to his covenant people; the covenant relationship implies that even their rebellion and his subsequent punishment reveal his mercy. It was he who brought them through the Red Sea, he who brought them into the Promised Land. He is immediately present to those who seek him. This is consoling for all who feel that the Christian Church has lost its way in recent times, that its leadership is lacking and its future uncertain. We are bound to ask questions about what may or may not have gone wrong, but these can be a spur to a search for a deeper intimacy with God, who alone knows the ways of the human heart.

If the beginnings of a new year bring anxiety, remember that God has been faithful in the past and remains faithful now. He knows our weakness and infidelity. Part of his faithfulness to us is in showing us the truth. We may be faithless, but he remains faithful. Even among the ruins of our history and our belief, we are called to faith and worship.

> Creator of the heavens,
> who led the Magi by a star
> to worship the Christ-child:
> guide and sustain us,
> that we may find our journey's end
> in Jesus Christ our Lord.

COLLECT

Reflection by **Angela Tilby**

Epiphany Season

Friday 8 January

Psalms **46**, 147.13-end *or* **55**
Isaiah 64
1 John 4.7-end

Isaiah 64

'... we are the clay and you are our potter; we are all the work of your hand' (v.8)

It is fascinating to watch a potter at work, moulding the clay, attending to its texture, casting it on the wheel while still shaping it into the form it will eventually take – a vessel that can be used, an object that is both functional and beautiful. The potter must work fast and use the skill of their hands.

Through this powerful image, the prophet is attempting to restore his people's confidence. They long for a definitive revelation of God's presence, but God appears to have hidden himself as the reality of the people's unfaithfulness is breaking in. They are suffering because of their unrighteousness and they are experiencing God as hidden or absent. What is needed is a return to the true dependence of faith, the recognition that even though Jerusalem is a ruined desolation, God has not abandoned his people. He is still waiting to shape, form and rebuild them.

In the Christian life, most of us go through phases when we feel we have lost our way, that the closeness we once felt we had with God has become empty and distant. Meditating on the image of the clay and the potter may be an opportunity to realize how our heavenly Father continues to shape our lives in spite of our faithlessness and fragility.

COLLECT

O God,
who by the leading of a star
manifested your only Son to the peoples of the earth:
mercifully grant that we,
who know you now by faith,
may at last behold your glory face to face;
through Jesus Christ our Lord.

Reflection by **Angela Tilby**

Epiphany Season

Psalms 2, **148** *or* **76**, 79
Isaiah 65.1-16
1 John 5.1-12

Saturday 9 January

Isaiah 65.1-16

'I said, "Here I am, here I am"' (v.1)

In the early verses of this chapter, the destiny of God's covenant people has been one destiny, whether for good or evil. Now from verse 8, we begin to see a distinction being made between those who have abandoned God in various ways and those who have remained faithful. These faithful ones are known to God and protected by him. The ultimate fate of the whole people now depends on the continuing faithfulness of a minority. The passage suggests that many people have adopted a variety of pagan and superstitious practices and have abandoned the Jewish food laws, a visible proof of their infidelity.

In our time, many in society appear to have abandoned faith, adopting a range of spiritual and quasi-spiritual beliefs and practices that help them to feel, perhaps, more comfortable with themselves. Yet there are those of us who continue to look beyond ourselves to the love and mercy of God. It may be helpful to reflect that your commitment is not for yourself alone, but helps to carry others into the scope of God's mercy.

As the *Book of Common Prayer* puts it, following 1 Timothy 2.1, it is a Christian duty to 'make prayers and supplications and give thanks for all men'. God is ready to hear our prayer on their behalf and 'to be found by those who did not seek me'.

> COLLECT
>
> Creator of the heavens,
> who led the Magi by a star
> to worship the Christ-child:
> guide and sustain us,
> that we may find our journey's end
> in Jesus Christ our Lord.

Reflection by **Angela Tilby**

Epiphany Season

Monday 11 January

Psalms **2**, 110 *or* **80**, 82
Amos 1
1 Corinthians 1.1-17

1 Corinthians 1.1-17

'... you were called into the fellowship of his Son' (v.9)

At the beginning of his first letter to the Corinthians, Paul reminds his readers that God's faithfulness is not short-lived or only for a specific time, but for eternity. God has called us to share in Christ's saving work, and he will faithfully enable us to enjoy this fellowship until Jesus returns.

Throughout Scripture, we see God's faithfulness in his interactions with different people or in specific narratives of guidance and redemption. Here again, Paul reminds us of God's faithfulness in his eternal plan of salvation in Christ Jesus. God's faithfulness is seen both in the weft and warp of the daily or seasonal detail of life's patchwork, and in the overarching and eternal picture of salvation. This faithfulness is in stark contrast to the Corinthians, whose loyalty to their earthly teacher is leading to quarrels and divisions.

At times, the trials and tribulations of life can lead us to focus only on the immediate picture of life in which we stand. God's faithfulness will be found here in the detail, but sometimes we need to be reminded to look up and see the wonderful, reassuring grand picture of God's salvation. God called you to share in Christ's miracle of love overcoming death, of grace overcoming sin, of joy overcoming despair. God will make sure that this is always the bigger picture over you, regardless of what happens in the detail of today or tomorrow. Take heart; God is faithful.

COLLECT

Eternal Father,
who at the baptism of Jesus
revealed him to be your Son,
anointing him with the Holy Spirit:
grant to us, who are born again by water and the Spirit,
that we may be faithful to our calling as your adopted children;
through Jesus Christ our Lord.

Reflection by **Emma Parker**

Epiphany Season

Psalms 8, **9** *or* 87, **89.1-18**
Amos 2
1 Corinthians 1.18-end

Tuesday 12 January

1 Corinthians 1.18-end

'Let the one who boasts, boast in the Lord' (v.31)

Different societies and subcultures often have their own unspoken rules about publicly proclaiming our worth or achievements (or what we think they are). There are different rules about how to boast and who can boast. How we spend our money on items that are publicly visible (clothes, cars, jewellery) can be an attempt to construct our own non-verbal narrative for all to see. We might try to influence other's opinions of us by our social media posts. Alternatively, some of us might have grown up where naming our skills was socially frowned upon, and we might now find it difficult to receive praise.

The Corinthians were part of a society where reputation was everything, public boasting was an art, and esteem was based on culturally defined notions of success. In this passage, we circle around themes of wisdom and strength, and with one swift move, Paul demolishes any reason to boast in such things. In the presence of God, all perceived wisdom and strength pale into insignificance. In Christ alone we find ultimate power and wisdom. Echoing Jeremiah 9.24, Paul says that our boasting must only point to the greatness of the Lord.

To some of us this is a challenge, requiring transformation in how we navigate culture's expectations of self-promotion and ideas of worth. To others, it is an encouragement to see Christ's power and wisdom at work in us, to find our confidence in this and to rejoice!

> COLLECT
>
> Heavenly Father,
> at the Jordan you revealed Jesus as your Son:
> may we recognize him as our Lord
> and know ourselves to be your beloved children;
> through Jesus Christ our Saviour.

Reflection by **Emma Parker**

Epiphany Season

Wednesday 13 January

Psalms 19, 20 *or* 119.105-128
Amos 3
1 Corinthians 2

1 Corinthians 2

'… we have received … the Spirit … so that we may understand'
(v.12)

Having made a commitment to continue following Christ as a teenager, I then felt overwhelmed at how little I knew about my faith. A few years later at a student-focused church, I always wanted the ground to swallow me up as my peers around me adeptly found the Bible reference in record time, and I was left doing the flick of shame to the contents page. Fast forward several years and, although I now have a PhD in theology, the realization of how much I do not understand has grown, as my appreciation of the mystery of God has deepened.

Wherever we are on our faith journey, we can sometimes feel out of our depth trying to understand the merciful works of God, or absorb his amazing promises, or receive his abundant gifts. Sometimes our health can hinder this. Dementia, for example, can invite confusion into previous places of clarity. Memory loss can sweep away our mental library of pictures and knowledge, leaving gaping spaces and silence. Sometimes, difficult circumstances can try to rob us of everything we thought we knew. However, Paul tells us that God's Spirit works to help us grasp that which we so desperately need.

Today, be encouraged that whatever happens, we have the certainty that God's Spirit will always work to help us keep hold of God's gifts, even if we do not yet fully understand.

COLLECT

Eternal Father,
who at the baptism of Jesus
revealed him to be your Son,
anointing him with the Holy Spirit:
grant to us, who are born again by water and the Spirit,
that we may be faithful to our calling as your adopted children;
through Jesus Christ our Lord.

Reflection by **Emma Parker**

Epiphany Season

Psalms **21**, 24 *or* 90, **92**
Amos 4
1 Corinthians 3

Thursday 14 January

1 Corinthians 3

'... and you belong to Christ, and Christ belongs to you' (v.23)

'But where are you *really* from?' he asked for a third time, clearly not accepting that my answer accounted for my accent. His curiosity was rooted in a question of belonging: my accent clearly showed him that I did not belong to his community, so where else did I belong?

We can often look for indicators of belonging in ourselves and others, such as accents or fashion. The Corinthians looked to their leaders for their sense of belonging, but Paul passionately argues that they belong to no one else but Christ! They are *God's* field, they are *God's* building, they are *God's* temple. Their growth is down to God alone; others may help with this, but ultimately all life and all growth is from God.

It is wonderful to know that we need not look to any place or person to give us our primary sense of belonging: first and foremost, we belong to Christ. Places and people, cultures and heritage are all important; but above all, we belong to Christ. Accents and dress, stories and experiences are all important; but above all, we belong to Christ. We may traverse continents, move home, change job, wander among different social circles and churches, journey from one post to another; but our roots remain in Christ, for we belong to him. Nothing can change this wonderful, freeing, eternal, beautiful belonging. Where are you from? I am from Christ.

COLLECT

Heavenly Father,
at the Jordan you revealed Jesus as your Son:
may we recognize him as our Lord
and know ourselves to be your beloved children;
through Jesus Christ our Saviour.

Reflection by **Emma Parker**

Epiphany Season

Friday 15 January

Psalms **67**, 72 *or* **88** (95)
Amos 5.1-17
1 Corinthians 4

1 Corinthians 4

'... the kingdom of God depends not on talk but on power' (v.20)

Some members have been criticizing Paul by their worldly standards rooted in pride and superficial appearances. It is easy to talk behind a person's back and create division and uncertainty. It is easy to use words to discredit someone or create a sceptical view of them. But it is not as easy to follow the ways of Christ Jesus. Hence, Paul says that there is no place for words of arrogance when shaping our life after Christ. He appeals to the congregation to imitate him, as he in turn tries to imitate Christ, for the kingdom of God is not built up by empty talk but by the power that is released when we live and breathe Jesus.

In a world where words intended to spark fear, division and suspicion are launched into crowds or onto social media, it is challenging and inspiring to hear Paul's words. His words intend to spark humility and action rooted in Christ. God's kingdom is built up when we truly seek to behave like Jesus, who showed us how to serve and how to receive from those who are snubbed; who showed us how to love God unreservedly and offer him everything; who showed us how to recognize hypocrisy and seek holiness; who showed us how to tear down walls and create peace.

In all that we do and say today, let us build up God's kingdom with this kind of power.

COLLECT

Eternal Father,
who at the baptism of Jesus
revealed him to be your Son,
anointing him with the Holy Spirit:
grant to us, who are born again by water and the Spirit,
that we may be faithful to our calling as your adopted children;
through Jesus Christ our Lord.

Reflection by **Emma Parker**

Epiphany Season

Psalms 29, **33** *or* 96, **97**, 100
Amos 5.18-end
1 Corinthians 5

Saturday 16 January

1 Corinthians 5

'And you are arrogant! Should you not rather have mourned ...?'
(v.2)

This chapter probably raises more questions than the number of its verses! Although these verses need prayerful attention, it is easy to become lost in the detail and lose sight of the bigger picture. The detail here is the specific question of a man living with his father's wife. The bigger picture is our attitude towards transformation in Christ. Paul is frustrated with the congregation for not challenging this man's behaviour. In their arrogance, they seem to feel that anyone can do whatever they like, showing little gratitude for Christ's sacrifice and eschewing the call of transformation.

The refrain, 'Don't worry, it's just his way of dealing with things', or 'It's just how she is', can often be the commentary accompanying certain behaviours. With a wave of a hand, a sweep under the rug, a roll of the eyes, we permit damaging patterns of behaviour to weave their way even through the church. Instead, Paul says we should mourn.

Mourning is a deep response of the heart, soul, body and mind to loss: it is heartfelt, sincere and often overwhelming. We should mourn the loss of Jesus-shaped behaviour, the loss of kingdom values. The call to transformation is so vital in who we are as a Christian community that we should mourn when we see apathy and disregard in the face of this call. Let us pray that our communities long for transformation in Christ – starting with ourselves.

COLLECT

Heavenly Father,
at the Jordan you revealed Jesus as your Son:
may we recognize him as our Lord
and know ourselves to be your beloved children;
through Jesus Christ our Saviour.

Reflection by **Emma Parker**

Epiphany Season

Monday 18 January

Psalms 145, **146** *or* **98**, 99, 101
Amos 6
1 Corinthians 6.1-11

1 Corinthians 6.1-11

'… no one among you wise enough to decide' (v.5)

With every chapter, we see another layer of this chaotic Corinthian community. This time, Paul reveals that among the members, there is trickery and dishonesty, where believers unfairly treat each other. What Paul seems to find worse is that they are incapable of sorting this behaviour out: there is no one wise enough to name the bad behaviour, to challenge its nature as being contrary to all that Christ stands for, and to redirect the people involved to a better way. Wisdom is the ability to discern what is good and true, and to make fair decisions based on knowledge and understanding. For those who have been washed, sanctified and justified, peeling back the layers of complexity to reveal reality and then acting accordingly should be a prophetic work of wisdom.

There can often be many instances in our lives when we stumble across intensely complex situations, whether to do with relationships, processes, systems or forms. Such situations can be made more complex because of historic threads of injustice, unkindness or ignorance running through them. Trying to unravel these situations can seem overwhelming. But our transformation in the name of Christ and in the Spirit of our God can help us to find the wisdom needed to see clearly enough to respond to what is wrong.

Let us pray for wisdom in our churches, that together we can discern truth and hold fast to what is good.

COLLECT

Almighty God,
in Christ you make all things new:
transform the poverty of our nature by the riches of your grace,
and in the renewal of our lives
make known your heavenly glory;
through Jesus Christ our Lord.

Reflection by **Emma Parker**

Epiphany Season

Psalms **132**, 147.1-12 *or* **106*** *(or* 103*)*
Amos 7
1 Corinthians 6.12-end

Tuesday 19 January

1 Corinthians 6.12-end

'… your body is a temple of the Holy Spirit within you' (v.19)

'What do you get if you squeeze a lemon?' the preacher asked. 'Lemon juice' came a few voices from the congregation. 'What do you get if you squeeze a tomato?' the preacher continued. 'Tomato juice' answered a few more, with some laughter. 'What do you get if you squeeze a Christian?' asked the preacher, who then answered as he saw confused faces: 'the Spirit!' I suspect this worked better in his thoughts as he crafted it earlier, but it has always stayed with me because I was struck by the thought that, not only is God in me, but that this should be obvious to anyone who interacts with me.

This is one of the most wonderful aspects of our faith: God has always desired to dwell with his people, from walking with Adam and Eve in the first garden to the promise in Revelation that he will be with his people in the 'new heaven and new earth'. In our passage today, we are told that God dwells with us now in such an intimate and relational way.

It would be good to pause and ponder on this amazing truth, and consider how we let God's Spirit in us shine through the whole of our lives to reveal God's holiness, mercy and justice. When others encounter us, by the grace of God, we hope and pray that in some way they truly taste the Spirit of God.

> Eternal Lord,
> our beginning and our end:
> bring us with the whole creation
> to your glory, hidden through past ages
> and made known
> in Jesus Christ our Lord.

COLLECT

Reflection by **Emma Parker**

Epiphany Season

Wednesday 20 January

Psalms **81**, 147.13-end
or 110, **111**, 112
Amos 8
1 Corinthians 7.1-24

1 Corinthians 7.1-24

'... obeying the commandments of God is everything' (v.19)

The Corinthians have written to Paul asking him about marriage, and in this chapter, we have some of Paul's responses, which cover an array of ideas and thoughts. These verses move from one situation to another: being married, unmarried, widowed, married to unbelievers; being circumcised, being uncircumcised; being a slave, being free. Many commentators believe that Paul is writing from a perspective of hoping for an imminent return of Christ, and so is encouraging the believers that the situation they find themselves in now will not last too long.

But at the heart of these verses, we suddenly see a glimpse of Paul's concern: making sure that we can still follow the commandments of God regardless of our relationships and social situations. Each circumstance can bring its difficult questions, and we might find ourselves longing to move from one situation to another.

What is important is that we don't permit these questions and longings to take our eyes off God, and from our ultimate call to be with him, to follow in his ways and to participate in his story of salvation for the whole world. Living according to God's commandments brings joy and strength to the soul and transformation to all our relationships. Our social situations may change through life, bringing us joy or grief, but let us pray that we can always remain faithful to our primary calling, which will never change: keeping company with God and following in God's ways.

COLLECT

Almighty God,
in Christ you make all things new:
transform the poverty of our nature by the riches of your grace,
and in the renewal of our lives
make known your heavenly glory;
through Jesus Christ our Lord.

Reflection by **Emma Parker**

Epiphany Season

Psalms **76**, 148 *or* 113, **115**
Amos 9
1 Corinthians 7.25-end

Thursday 21 January

1 Corinthians 7.25-end
'... unhindered devotion to the Lord' (v.35)

The boilers in our church are no longer able to heat both the church and the hall simultaneously; we now must flip a valve in the boiler room to direct heat one way or the other. Perhaps Paul is concerned that the Corinthians have hearts like these inefficient boilers, where they can be devoted *either* to God or to their family.

In contrast, I have witnessed my parents being devoted both to God *and* to each other. As more strokes took away my mother's speech and movement, my father sat holding her hand, for hours every day. And at the end of each day, he would lead their prayers together. Devotion looked very different in this season of life, but ill health could not touch the boiler in their hearts that was still very much on fire with love for the Lord and for each other.

For those of us who balance many responsibilities and commitments, it can be difficult knowing how not to flip a valve, but keep up devotion to all. Let us remember: devotion to God opens all the valves so that we are able to love and care for others God has given us. In our devotion to the Lord, we will find the grace to have hearts on fire with love for all. Devotion to God never shuts down; rather, it opens new ways of loving service.

COLLECT

Eternal Lord,
our beginning and our end:
bring us with the whole creation
to your glory, hidden through past ages
and made known
in Jesus Christ our Lord.

Reflection by **Emma Parker**

Epiphany Season

Friday 22 January

Psalms **27**, 149 *or* **139**
Hosea 1.1 – 2.1
1 Corinthians 8

1 Corinthians 8

'Knowledge puffs up, but love builds up' (v.1)

It is clear from reading Paul's letters that he is a teacher: he loves imparting knowledge, trying to help the congregations deepen their understanding of their faith and see how it shapes their lives. For Paul, knowing about God the Father, Jesus our Lord and the Holy Spirit brings freedom and opens the door to conversion and transformation. Paul is clearly not against knowledge. But here in this chapter, he reveals how dangerous knowledge can be when it is not partnered with love. Those Corinthians who know the truth about idols have not been sensitive to those who have not shaken off their previous conditioning and convictions about food offered to idols. They have not linked their knowledge with the selfless way of love, and so have harmed the faith of 'those weak believers'.

Knowledge without love can be dangerous and selfish, and it can feed into harmful games of power where the intent can be to divide and exclude. True knowledge is only ever that when it partners with love. When knowledge and love work together, then all are edified.

It is worth reflecting on how we and our churches use knowledge, and who benefits from it. Pray about this today and see if there are any areas where you might need to join your knowledge more intentionally with love to encourage all believers in their walk of faith.

COLLECT

Almighty God,
in Christ you make all things new:
transform the poverty of our nature by the riches of your grace,
and in the renewal of our lives
make known your heavenly glory;
through Jesus Christ our Lord.

Reflection by **Emma Parker**

Epiphany Season

Psalms **122**, 128, 150
or 120, **121**, 122
Hosea 2.2-17
1 Corinthians 9.1-14

Saturday 23 January

1 Corinthians 9.1-14

'Are you not my work in the Lord?' (v.1)

There is clearly a complex relationship between Paul and the Corinthians. Some of the believers are examining him, and he feels compelled in this passage to set out his defence. After reminding them of his status as an apostle, he argues that he has every right to be materially supported by the Corinthians, although he is not making use of this right. In the previous chapter, he challenged some of the believers not to use their freedom to eat idol meat, and here he states that he is not using his freedom to benefit from his own work in planting the gospel in Corinth.

It is difficult not to hear sadness and frustration in Paul's letter at this point. The relationship between Paul and the Corinthians has become one marked by mistrust and sacrifice, and it is unmistakably costly for Paul. He appears to receive little thanks or encouragement, and his work seems to be mostly about correcting bad behaviour or unholy attitudes. This type of service is about grasping hold of nettles, which can leave your hands stinging and your soul deflated. Despite this, however, Paul perseveres in serving the Corinthians. They are his 'work in the Lord', and he will not abandon his calling to proclaim the gospel. In our own discipleship, we might also face difficult relationships and challenges. Pray for courage, grace and wisdom as you persevere in living out God's calling on your life.

COLLECT

Eternal Lord,
our beginning and our end:
bring us with the whole creation
to your glory, hidden through past ages
and made known
in Jesus Christ our Lord.

Reflection by **Emma Parker**

Epiphany Season

Monday 25 January
Conversion of Paul

Psalms 66, 147.13-end
Ezekiel 3.22-end
Philippians 3.1-14

Philippians 3.1-14

'... the righteousness from God based on faith' (v.9)

At a Confirmation service recently, a man in his eighties shared his journey to faith. As part of his preparation, he had joined a small group. He told us about a physical exercise the group of four had done together. Standing upright, arms folded across his chest, facing away from the other three behind him, he had been invited to fall backwards towards them. He had been asked to trust that he would be caught (which, thankfully, he was!).

He shared how, in his previous life, he had found it exceptionally hard to trust. Being 'caught' that day had enabled him to begin a journey of trust. It had proved to be an early step along the road to entrusting the whole of his days – past, present and future – to the God who is Christ-like.

Saul's change of mind began with a blinding light, the voice of Christ, and by falling off his horse. It continued as Saul, becoming Paul, learned to entrust ever more of his life to Christ, this world's life and centre. Conversion for Paul was a process. It was a learning not to fall back upon his own right-ness, reputation or religious credentials, but rather to receive in faith that which he could never achieve for himself, the gift of being put right with God in Christ.

What might being 'unseated from your horse' begin for you today?

COLLECT

Almighty God,
who caused the light of the gospel
to shine throughout the world
through the preaching of your servant Saint Paul:
grant that we who celebrate his wonderful conversion
may follow him in bearing witness to your truth;
through Jesus Christ our Lord.

Reflection by **Jonathan Frost**

Epiphany Season

Psalms 34, **36** *or* 132, 133
Hosea 4.1-16
1 Corinthians 10.1-13

Tuesday 26 January

1 Corinthians 10.1-13
'God is faithful' (v.13)

How do Christians learn to be more Christ-like? The early part of today's passage, addressed to the spiritually wayward Corinthians, proposes an answer: by keeping the severity and judgement of God before our eyes.

Paul points to God's judgements upon Israel's unfaithfulness as 'examples' and 'warnings'. He includes the body count: sexual immorality (23,000 dead), putting the Lord to the test (mass death by snake bite) and grumbling (death at the hands of 'the destroying angel').

But does recollection of divine judgement – in our own experience, in the record we possess of the life of Israel or of the early Church – secure deeper faithfulness to Christ? Perhaps, in some circumstances, a person's behaviour might be restrained by fear of the consequences. On balance, however, I sense this approach casts God's people in the role of anxious children, who find they need to tiptoe around a violent and unpredictable parent.

Wonderfully, three words towards the end of the passage propose a more promising way forward. 'God is faithful': this affirmation opens the way to joyful thanksgiving, calls forth our responding love and opens the way to personal and communal transformation. For it is not the threat of divine judgement that transforms or heals, but rather, the good news of God in Christ: that in Christ, God has loved us, met our deepest need and now longs to love us into life.

> Almighty God,
> whose Son revealed in signs and miracles
> the wonder of your saving presence:
> renew your people with your heavenly grace,
> and in all our weakness
> sustain us by your mighty power;
> through Jesus Christ our Lord.

COLLECT

Reflection by **Jonathan Frost**

Epiphany Season

Wednesday 27 January

Psalms 45, **46** *or* **119.153-end**
Hosea 5.1-7
1 Corinthians 10.14 – 11.1

1 Corinthians 10.14 – 11.1

'Be imitators of me, as I am of Christ' (11.1)

As a university chaplain, I had been invited to a lunchtime gathering of our physics department. I recall the joy of being with that dynamic group as we explored the deceptively simple question: 'At what point can a person describe themselves (legitimately) as a physicist?'

Like me in early years, perhaps you imbibed over-individualistic accounts of how knowledge, wisdom, learning and genius are acquired. By contrast, three things came through in our discussion: the formative role of supervisors and mentors; the need for graft and for students to engage with a body of knowledge *and* practice; and the way individual endeavour is set relationally within a community of practice. Far from being a *gulf* between learning in scientific and Christian communities, we found analogies, resonances and interconnections.

'Be imitators of me' urges Paul, 'as I am of Christ' – in whose ascended life Christians participate through baptism and their sharing in the Lord's body and blood.

Like a wise supervisor, Paul steers the Corinthians away from spiritual dead ends towards faithfulness to Christ. They are to flee idolatry, to seek God's glory rather than their own advantage. Transformation will take patience and faithful imitation, but eventually, the Corinthians – and even we ourselves – will learn to live, speak and act as Christians.

So, who are *your* role models?

COLLECT | Almighty God,
whose Son revealed in signs and miracles
the wonder of your saving presence:
renew your people with your heavenly grace,
and in all our weakness
sustain us by your mighty power;
through Jesus Christ our Lord.

Reflection by **Jonathan Frost**

Epiphany Season

Psalms **47**, 48 *or* **143**, 146
Hosea 5.8 – 6.6
1 Corinthians 11.2-16

Thursday 28 January

1 Corinthians 11.2-16

'Judge for yourselves' (v.13)

It is vital, in wrestling with Scripture (not least when we find a passage problematic), to remain attentive to cultural difference: to engage fully in the communal work of biblical interpretation, to read texts in their contexts and to seek cross-cultural translation.

Women had been praying with their heads uncovered. Paul describes it as a disgrace. In the culture of Corinth, head coverings served to differentiate, subordinate and control women. A married or young woman with her head uncovered might be considered sexually forward – a matter of shame for the man under whose authority she lived.

We are not entirely sure why these sisters of ours threw off their hats. They might have expected Paul's approval. For, surely, he would see their 'hats off' policy as a bold, countercultural expression of a woman's freedom in Christ – a freedom in which conventional hierarchies and imposed gender distinctions are being set aside (cf. Galatians 3.28). But Paul condemns the practice and seeks to reimpose, on Christian sisters then and still in certain places now, a head-covering rule he argues is of universal application in the churches.

With few exceptions in Christian history, subsequent generations have tended to follow their sisters' boldness rather than Paul's command. To those who found courage to disobey, we might well want to use a phrase once used quite frequently in English culture to express respect: 'Hats off to them!'

COLLECT

God of all mercy,
your Son proclaimed good news to the poor,
release to the captives,
and freedom to the oppressed:
anoint us with your Holy Spirit
and set all your people free
to praise you in Christ our Lord.

Reflection by **Jonathan Frost**

Epiphany Season

Friday 29 January

Psalms 61, **65** *or* 142, **144**
Hosea 6.7 – 7.2
1 Corinthians 11.17-end

1 Corinthians 11.17-end

'Do you ... humiliate those who have nothing?' (v.22)

Blind spots are those areas of personal reality we cannot (or will not) see or recognize about ourselves or our community, without the assistance of another. Their prevalence supports the wisdom of choosing to put ourselves into relationship with a trusted spiritual director, soul friend or accountability group.

It is Gaius, the host of the church in Corinth, who is having a blind spot removed in today's passage. The Corinthians are divided between wealthy Christians of high standing and their poorer brothers and sisters. Unlike our own symbolic meal, with its piece of bread and sip of wine, the 'Lord's Supper' in Corinth would involve the sharing of bread and wine as a centrepiece within a fuller meal.

In the Graeco-Roman world, it was customary for hosts to provide better food for their more distinguished guests. But Paul is scandalized that the meal that proclaims the reconciling work of Christ crucified continues this custom unchallenged: the wealthy are amply filled, eat before others and keep back the best for themselves. Paul's critique is searing: '... do you show contempt to the church of God and humiliate those who have nothing?' Unthinkingly and without theological critique, Gaius has followed the cultural norms of his day. Gaius and I have our blind spots.

What will you put in place to address yours?

COLLECT

Almighty God,
whose Son revealed in signs and miracles
the wonder of your saving presence:
renew your people with your heavenly grace,
and in all our weakness
sustain us by your mighty power;
through Jesus Christ our Lord.

Reflection by **Jonathan Frost**

Epiphany Season

Psalm **68** *or* **147**
Hosea 8
1 Corinthians 12.1-11

Saturday 30 January

1 Corinthians 12.1-11
'... for the common good' (v.7)

The Corinthians were spiritually gifted, yet failed to grasp the basics of life in the Church, so Paul offers them an introductory course 'Spiritual Matters 101'.

Far from turning the spiritual spotlight onto *us* or onto *our* spiritual giftedness, the Holy Spirit leads us to confess Jesus as Lord: the go-between-God connects us to Christ. To be filled with the life of the Holy Spirit is to be *ec-centric*: literally meaning to be liberated from a centre in ourselves, into a centre outside of ourselves in Christ.

Paul develops a Spirit-driven, Christ-oriented and God-activated theological vision in one of his earliest 'trinitarian' writings. Who is the source of the varieties of gift? The Spirit is. Who is the source of the varieties of service you give and receive in community? Christ is. The source and true end of every Christian endeavour? It is God in and through it all. And for what *purpose* are the Spirit's gifts so freely given – gifts that tempt some to a sense of spiritual superiority? Each gift is bestowed 'for the common good'.

To have grasped 'Spiritual Matters 101' is not only to be led out of self-absorption into the life of God, but also, through the same Spirit, to live in love and mutual concern for one another in community: to participate in that form of existence called forth (the *ecclesia* – the gathered community of the Church) to proclaim and reflect the reconciling love of God in Christ.

> God of all mercy,
> your Son proclaimed good news to the poor,
> release to the captives,
> and freedom to the oppressed:
> anoint us with your Holy Spirit
> and set all your people free
> to praise you in Christ our Lord.

COLLECT

Reflection by **Jonathan Frost**

Epiphany Season

Monday 1 February

Psalms **57**, 96 *or* 1, 2, 3
Hosea 9
1 Corinthians 12.12-end

1 Corinthians 12.12-end

'Now you are the body of Christ' (v.27)

Paul continues his 'Spiritual Matters 101', which we looked at last week.

He is disturbed by reports from Corinth. There, the gift of tongues is being misused – by some at least – as a sign of personal achievement and superiority over others. Paul responds with a theological framework for navigating the spiritual gifts. Love, expressed in mutuality and interdependence, is to come first in everything. Love, as a reflection of God's love (chapter 13) guides the use of tongues within worship (chapter 14).

Paul writes: 'Now you are the body of Christ and individually members of it.' Like parts of the human body, each person '… made to drink of one Spirit' has an indispensable contribution to make to the Church. As God has arranged the members of a human body 'as he chose', so God gives gifts to the Church. In conscious reference to the self-promoters, Paul accords a higher priority to spiritual gifts that build up the body in love.

Paul's choice of the word 'gift' provides a critique of spiritual elitism. For gifts are neither achievements nor grounds for superiority. Rather, they reflect the overflow of God's abundant love and are to be welcomed with gratitude expressed in love. For, as Paul says, gifts are freely given, that all the baptized may learn to 'care for one another'.

COLLECT

God our creator,
who in the beginning
commanded the light to shine out of darkness:
we pray that the light of the glorious gospel of Christ
may dispel the darkness of ignorance and unbelief,
shine into the hearts of all your people,
and reveal the knowledge of your glory
in the face of Jesus Christ our Lord.

Reflection by **Jonathan Frost**

Presentation

Psalms **48**, 146
Exodus 13.1-16
Romans 12.1-5

Tuesday 2 February
Presentation of Christ in the Temple

Romans 12.1-5

'Do not be conformed to this age' (12.2, CSB)

When I was a child, my siblings and I were taken on summer holidays to a run-down bed and breakfast hotel. The place was nice enough and close to the beach. But to our horror over the years, every week would end up with a dance or 'discotheque', as my late father would call it. And how he would dance!

Two or three steps off the beat, and quite unaware of his children's embarrassment, my father would dance the evening away. Caught up in the music, my father was seemingly unhindered by the judgement of his children.

I freely admit that it has taken a while (and some therapy!) to appreciate the memory for the gift it has become. For today, my father's dancing and attention to the music point me (however inadequately) to our calling as a community of disciples: to dance to the music of God's kingdom, whatever anyone thinks, or however out of step we may seem to those in the culture or society around us.

Today, the Church recalls the presentation of Christ in the temple. Anchored firmly in their own age, Simeon and Anna recognize the dawning presence of the new age of God's reign in the Christ-child. Our calling is the same: with Anna and Simeon, perhaps even with my late father, to dance to the same kingdom-music wherever we find ourselves today.

COLLECT

Almighty and ever-living God,
clothed in majesty,
whose beloved Son was this day presented in the Temple,
in substance of our flesh:
grant that we may be presented to you
with pure and clean hearts,
by your Son Jesus Christ our Lord,
who is alive and reigns with you,
in the unity of the Holy Spirit,
one God, now and for ever.

Reflection by **Jonathan Frost**

Ordinary Time

Wednesday 3 February

Psalms 119.1-32
Hosea 11.1-11
1 Corinthians 14.1-19

1 Corinthians 14.1-19

'Pursue love and strive for the spiritual gifts' (v.1)

Paul's focus takes a practical turn.

His 'Spiritual Matters 101' course has laid the pastoral foundation for what he has to say, through a vision of the Church as the Body of Christ.

In the Body of Christ, there are no spiritual elites. The wisdom of the world is being turned upside down by the foolishness of what is preached (1 Corinthians 1.26–29). By contrast, a spiritually wise and gifted Christian community lives from God's grace and learns together (however slowly or fitfully) what it means to put love and a concern for the needs of others first. God gives gifts to all his people, valuing the lowly or foolish in human reckoning, so that 'the Church may be built up'.

For Paul, speaking five intelligible words that build up, encourage or console others is worth 'ten thousand words in a tongue', for 'Those who speak in a tongue build up themselves, but those who prophesy build up the Church.'

Reflecting on your experience, can you identify those whose contribution is to build others up or to walk with those who weep? Those who encouraged you in the faith, lifted you when you fell and kept you seeking Christ and God's kingdom? Perhaps you might give thanks for them now.

COLLECT

Almighty God,
by whose grace alone we are accepted and called to your service:
strengthen us by your Holy Spirit
and make us worthy of our calling;
through Jesus Christ your Son our Lord,
who is alive and reigns with you,
in the unity of the Holy Spirit,
one God, now and for ever.

Reflection by **Jonathan Frost**

Ordinary Time

Psalms 14, **15**, 16
Hosea 11.12 – end of 12
1 Corinthians 14.20-end

Thursday 4 February

1 Corinthians 14.20-end

'God is really among you' (v.25)

Love for others can manifest itself in the care we give to the preparation and planning of worship. For Paul, this care extends to those on the fringe or margins of the Church.

In my teenage years and seeking faith, a friend invited me to a service. I was unprepared for what happened. That evening, during worship, the gathering began to sing loudly in strange languages. Overwhelmed, uncomfortable and confused, I did not stop for coffee. Perhaps it would have helped clarify things if I had.

Undoubtedly, I had sensed something of the reality of God's presence. However, the weirdness of that seemingly chaotic experience put me off God's people for a while. Paul addresses a comparable situation when he writes: 'if ... the whole Church comes together and all speak in tongues, and outsiders or unbelievers enter, will they not say that you are out of your mind?'

Paul gives guidance about the use of the gifts of the Holy Spirit and the conduct of worship, believing 'all things should be done decently and in order'. I read this as Paul's concern for liturgy. Far from constraining the Holy Spirit's freedom, good order – expressed in thought-through common worship – creates a structured space within which to welcome God's presence. For, as Paul puts it, 'God is a God not of disorder but of peace'.

COLLECT

God of our salvation,
help us to turn away from those habits
which harm our bodies and poison our minds
and to choose again your gift of life,
revealed to us in Jesus Christ our Lord.

Reflection by **Jonathan Frost**

Ordinary Time

Friday 5 February

Psalms 17, **19**
Hosea 13.1-14
1 Corinthians 16.1-9

1 Corinthians 16.1-9

'… if the Lord permits' (v.7)

The closing verses of Paul's letter call to mind a prayer of the twelfth-century mystic Hildegard of Bingen. With her, Paul longs to be 'a feather on God's breath'.

As the passage opens, we note Paul's dynamism and purpose: giving direction, offering solutions, raising funds, seizing opportunities and dealing with adversaries.

And yet for Paul, everything is qualified by four words that disclose Paul's life posture and deepest desire. Words that reflect Paul's relationship with the One in whom he trusts. Four words: '… if the Lord permits'. Paul's life, with its plans and proposals, inner conflicts and personality, is an offered life.

These four words, written almost as an aside, recall the prayer of Jesus in Gethsemane: 'Yet not what I want, but what you want' (Mark 14.36). They are words that express Paul's desire to be led in all things by the Spirit, for Paul's will to reflect and serve God's will.

But in no sense is Paul's freedom of action, intelligence or personality bypassed or undervalued. For he, and we in our day, are called to respond for ourselves with all of ourselves to God's grace in Christ and the Holy Spirit. For ourselves, but never by ourselves or apart from the prompting of the Holy Spirit who fills, guides and leads God's people.

'If the Lord permits.' What would being 'a feather on God's breath' look like for you, today?

COLLECT

Almighty God,
by whose grace alone we are accepted and called to your service:
strengthen us by your Holy Spirit
and make us worthy of our calling;
through Jesus Christ your Son our Lord,
who is alive and reigns with you,
in the unity of the Holy Spirit,
one God, now and for ever.

Reflection by **Jonathan Frost**

Ordinary Time

Psalms 20, 21, **23**
Hosea 14
1 Corinthians 16.10-end

Saturday 6 February

1 Corinthians 16.10-end

'Keep alert' (v.13)

Perhaps you have a rule of life already or are thinking of developing one. A rule can help to sustain Christian life and discipleship. Hidden in plain sight, amid closing farewells and travel updates, two exhortations provide inspiration to get started on a rule or to review what we have in place. With simplicity, Paul offers to Christian imagination a whole way of being in the world:

> Keep alert.
> Stand firm in your faith.
> Be courageous, be strong.
> Let all that you do be done in love.

One could memorize these verses as a basis for a rule of life. A rule will identify the practices, the actions and attitudes that enable us to live the vision we have glimpsed for ourselves. So, for example, we might ask: 'How am I to keep spiritually alert?' And we might write into our rule a daily practice of silence before God. Or we might ask: 'How am I to stand firm in my faith?' We might express commitment to a practical service, joining a home group or to receiving Holy Communion more regularly.

And where will I need courage? As I adopt a daily practice of facing my fears or of turning towards God's world in its need. And how can I be strong? Through the practice of asking for help. You will know what properly belongs within your rule.

Is it time to get started?

> God of our salvation,
> help us to turn away from those habits
> which harm our bodies and poison our minds
> and to choose again your gift of life,
> revealed to us in Jesus Christ our Lord.

COLLECT

Reflection by **Jonathan Frost**

Ordinary Time

Monday 8 February

Psalms 27, **30**
Jeremiah 1
John 17.1-5

Jeremiah 1

'I have put my words in your mouth' (v.9)

In the person of Jeremiah, we are met by a prophet who, like Moses before him, has been seized by the sovereign word of God – a word that will compel him over a period of 40 years to speak to a nation heading for disaster: towards 'the captivity of Jerusalem', the destruction of the temple and the end of Israel as an independent kingdom. It's a harsh word that Jeremiah is called to proclaim – 'to pluck up and to pull down, to destroy and to overthrow' as well as 'to build and to plant'. More than any other of the Hebrew prophets, Jeremiah's identity is shaped by the word he has been called to proclaim – a word for which he will get no thanks; a word that will be strongly opposed by the powerful and for which he will have to suffer.

Where are the prophetic voices for our world today – the voices through which God's word in history is made present to us? Hailing from the small village of Anathoth four miles to the north of the city of Jerusalem, Jeremiah was an outsider to the establishment – the ruling class of temple priests and the royal house of David. It is often one who is 'other' than us and who sees differently who can break open our settled ways of seeing and hearing. How can we both hear God's prophetic word and also speak, live and act that word for our time?

COLLECT

Almighty Father,
whose Son was revealed in majesty
before he suffered death upon the cross:
give us grace to perceive his glory,
that we may be strengthened to suffer with him
and be changed into his likeness, from glory to glory;
who is alive and reigns with you,
in the unity of the Holy Spirit,
one God, now and for ever.

Reflection by **Brother Samuel SSF**

Ordinary Time

Psalms 32, **36**
Jeremiah 2.1-13
John 17.6-19

Tuesday 9 February

Jeremiah 2.1-13

'I remember the devotion of your youth, your love as a bride' (v.2)

Many will have memories of the tenderness and generosity of the early days of falling in love, a time when all we wanted to do was to be with our beloved. The word spoken through Jeremiah is a passionate appeal to Israel's imagination: to remember the halcyon days of rescue from slavery in Egypt, of dependence on God in the wilderness and of the gift of a rich and fruitful land.

In contrast to that time, the present reality of Israel is of a love gone cold. The nation is accused of abandoning the source of its abundant life in order to seek other lovers. The people have forsaken the nation's foundation story and the intimate relationship at its heart. Jeremiah speaks of the deep pathos of God as a confused, deserted spouse. 'What did I do wrong?'

When we as humans no longer remember our dependence on the God who out of love has called us into being, and when we lose our essential relationship with the rest of creation, then our world is in danger of dismemberment. Likewise, when we, the Church, are distracted by the allure of power, possession and popularity, forgetting our rootedness in Jesus Christ, then we become 'a cracked cistern' unable to hold the water of life, which alone provides nourishment for ourselves and for the world. Here is a call for the renewal of our early love.

> Holy God,
> you know the disorder of our sinful lives:
> set straight our crooked hearts,
> and bend our wills to love your goodness and your glory
> in Jesus Christ our Lord.

COLLECT

Reflection by **Brother Samuel SSF**

Lent

Wednesday 10 February
Ash Wednesday

Psalm **38**
Daniel 9.3-6, 17-19
1 Timothy 6.6-19

Daniel 9.3-6, 17-19

'We have sinned and done wrong' (v.5)

The call to 'turn away from sin and be faithful to Christ' on Ash Wednesday is a call to get real about ourselves and about our world. The undeniable fact is that we all 'mess up'. Relationships go wrong; we often act selfishly and unkindly; we make unwise decisions; we find it hard to be merciful; we are forgetful of our dependence on the abundant graciousness of God. We are members of the human community, which the philosopher Iain McGilchrist declares is experiencing a crisis of meaning on account of its divorce from nature, its alienation from the structures and traditions of a stable society, and its indifference to the divine.

Sin is a word that has gone out of fashion, yet we are all to a greater or lesser extent caught up in sin, prone to thinking, living and acting sinfully. The line between good and evil runs through every heart. The words used at the ashing in today's liturgy – 'Remember you are dust and to dust you shall return' – may seem dour, but they bring us back to the human situation and to our relationship with the earth from which we are made. They are also words of hope because it is into dust that God has breathed life. We are beloved dust, dust that is capable of receiving God's transforming mercy; dust that is called to share God's glory.

COLLECT

Almighty and everlasting God,
you hate nothing that you have made
and forgive the sins of all those who are penitent:
create and make in us new and contrite hearts
that we, worthily lamenting our sins
and acknowledging our wretchedness,
may receive from you, the God of all mercy,
perfect remission and forgiveness;
through Jesus Christ our Lord.

Reflection by **Brother Samuel SSF**

Lent

Psalm **77** or **37***
Jeremiah 2.14-32
John 4.1-26

Thursday 11 February

Jeremiah 2.14-32

'But where are your gods that you made for yourself?' (v.28)

The religious sceptic Voltaire remarked that: 'If God created us in his own image, we have returned the compliment.' There is a strong tendency to create the gods we want to rule over us and to choose those before whom we bow down in worship – not just idols of wood or stone, but the gods of power, wealth, status and fear.

In one poetic image after another – Israel drinking the waters of the Nile and Euphrates, Israel as a wild ass on heat, a vine that has lost the purity of its original stock – the prophet mocks the foolish choices that the nation's leaders have made. He tells them to call upon those they have 'run after' to serve to get them out of the present crisis. The problem, of course, is that these gods are no God; they are powerless. They can bring only shame.

The whole prophetic work of Jeremiah is to bring us back to the God who is other than us, who cannot be shaped by our fantasies or manipulated according to our own desires. The God of Israel and of Jesus Christ is over all, through all and in all, present to us both in judgement and in mercy, who alone has power to save. Today and every day, we are called to discern our choice of whom we will serve.

COLLECT

Holy God,
our lives are laid open before you:
rescue us from the chaos of sin
and through the death of your Son
bring us healing and make us whole
in Jesus Christ our Lord.

Reflection by **Brother Samuel SSF**

Lent

Friday 12 February

Psalms **3**, 7 *or* **31**
Jeremiah 3.6-22
John 4.27-42

Jeremiah 3.6-22
'Return, faithless Israel' (v.12)

The break-up of a committed relationship is never without cost to the parties concerned, and in the case of Israel's lusting after other gods, the land itself has become polluted. It's a remarkable image of the soil itself having been made noxious by the poison of unfaithfulness seeping into the lifeblood of the nation.

And yet despite his huge hurt over this desertion, the Lord has not given up his love for Israel nor the hope of reconciliation with his beloved. The heartfelt cry for return is made three times in these verses, with the promise of mercy rather than anger, of healing rather than revenge, and the opportunity of a better future together.

The God who speaks to us through the words of Jeremiah and throughout the Scriptures is a 'stayer'. God doesn't give up on his world, his Church, or on us as individuals, however toxic things have become. God is always longing for a return of his love, always seeking our reconciliation with the source of our life. The question to us is whether or not we are open to responding to God's appeal, both personally and also as the world community. Do we recognize the need for repentance – not just a patching-up after the occasional tiff, but a daily turning back to the one who is eternally seeking us, fervently longing for us and graciously desiring the intimacy of our love?

COLLECT
Almighty and everlasting God,
you hate nothing that you have made
and forgive the sins of all those who are penitent:
create and make in us new and contrite hearts
that we, worthily lamenting our sins
and acknowledging our wretchedness,
may receive from you, the God of all mercy,
perfect remission and forgiveness;
through Jesus Christ our Lord.

Reflection by **Brother Samuel SSF**

Lent

Psalm **71** *or* 41, **42**, 43
Jeremiah 4.1-18
John 4.43-end

Saturday 13 February

Jeremiah 4.1-18

'Your ways and your doings have brought this upon you' (v.18)

The word of the Lord in today's reading proclaims a harsh reality, the hurricane-like terror of an invading army on its way, bringing siege, destruction and ruin. The nation is doomed. This is a self-inflicted disaster brought on by Israel's rebellion against her true partner and Lord, and by her complacent attitude that, despite her unfaithfulness and her 'evil schemes', all shall be well. Actions have consequences.

The conditions for averting the catastrophe are spelled out: '… if you return to me', '… if you remove your abominations', '… if you swear "As the Lord lives!"'. God's love for the world is unconditional, but for that to be effective, our cooperation is required. Jesus in John's Gospel speaks the same language: 'If you keep my commandments, you will abide in my love' (15.10); 'You are my friends if you do what I command you' (15.14). It takes two to tango. God's love is unable to operate outside of 'truth, justice and uprightness'. The theological reality is that when these are not present, then love itself works as judgement.

We live in a world that seems perennially engulfed by crises – of war, famine, economic collapse and social upheaval – brought about by human hubris, selfishness and ignorance. The words of Jeremiah can be heard as a call for us to recognize our responsibility and to return to the One who is continually at work to bring the world back to the fullness of his justice, mercy and peace.

COLLECT

Holy God,
our lives are laid open before you:
rescue us from the chaos of sin
and through the death of your Son
bring us healing and make us whole
in Jesus Christ our Lord.

Reflection by **Brother Samuel SSF**

Lent

Monday 15 February

Psalms 10, 11 *or* 44
Jeremiah 4.19-end
John 5.1-18

Jeremiah 4.19-end

'I looked on the earth ... it was waste and void' (v.23)

The barrenness that is exposed by the felling of rainforest, the devastation of the landscape after the extraction of oil from tar-shale, and the catastrophic collapse of biodiversity among species of plants and animals are all foreshadowed in Jeremiah's ominous vision of the unmaking of creation, a return to the primeval chaos of the opening verses of Genesis. The prophet cries out in agony at the vast loss that he sees as impending.

The environmental crisis that the world faces today, if not met with outright denial, tends to be approached simply as a technological problem that can be solved by more technology. Jeremiah urges us to look deeper. For him, both the desolation of the land and the destruction of the nation are the result of human stupidity – the desertification of the heart. The nation, oblivious to the warnings of catastrophe, parties on, 'dressed in crimson' and 'decked with ornaments of gold'. The ecological crisis is social, ethical and spiritual as well as technological.

When we treat the world as a giant warehouse of stuff simply there for our convenience and exploitation – forgetting that we are part of a community of creatures living in relationship with the giver and sustainer of all life – then disaster will inevitably follow. The caveat 'I will not make a full end' gives hope that there is yet time for us to come to our senses.

COLLECT

Almighty God,
whose Son Jesus Christ fasted forty days in the wilderness,
and was tempted as we are, yet without sin:
give us grace to discipline ourselves in obedience to your Spirit;
and, as you know our weakness,
so may we know your power to save;
through Jesus Christ our Lord.

Reflection by **Brother Samuel SSF**

Lent

Psalm **44** *or* **48**, 52
Jeremiah 5.1-19
John 5.19-29

Tuesday 16 February

Jeremiah 5.1-19

*'... see if you can find one person who acts justly
... that I may pardon Jerusalem' (v.1)*

The opening verse of today's passage brings to mind Abraham's haggling with God over the destruction of the city of Sodom (Genesis 18.16–33) in which he beats down the condition for averting the disaster to there being just ten righteous people in the city. Here, it is only one citizen of Jerusalem acting justly that is needed to make room for the Lord's forgiveness. However, the community remains gripped by the deathly pathologies of injustice, stupidity and apostasy. All this is supported by windy-worded prophets who deny that there is any sickness, saying that evil will not happen, that sword and famine hold no threat. We can sense the frustration of God desperately seeking a way out of the looming crisis in which the life of the nation will be devoured. The search is among both the poor and the rich, but neither make any response. 'How can I pardon you?'

We ourselves can be lulled into complacency about our own lives, our communities and our world. If we shut our eyes and ears to truth, if we ignore injustice and the anguish of those who suffer, if our hearts remain hardened against reality, then we carry on as though all is well and no radical change is necessary. But God continues to batter away at human resistance, his love and mercy searching for a chink in our defensive armour and withholding 'a full end'.

COLLECT

Heavenly Father,
your Son battled with the powers of darkness,
and grew closer to you in the desert:
help us to use these days to grow in wisdom and prayer
that we may witness to your saving love
in Jesus Christ our Lord.

Reflection by **Brother Samuel SSF**

Lent

Wednesday 17 February

Psalms **6**, 17 *or* **119.57-80**
Jeremiah 5.20-end
John 5.30-end

Jeremiah 5.20-end

'Hear this ...' (v.21)

The appeal to 'hear' echoes the '*Shema*' – the central declaration of Jewish faith that begins 'Hear, O Israel' (Deuteronomy 6.4–5). The sickness of the nation, according to Jeremiah, is that the people can no longer hear the word of the Lord: to 'love the Lord your God with all your heart, and with all your soul and with all your might'. Without such loving desire, the heart itself has become hardened, not just towards the One who gives rain for the land but also towards the neighbour. Goods are stolen, riches have been accumulated, and the cause of the orphan has been ignored. Because the nation's ear has become closed to the relationship at the heart of its life, the bonds of communal life have been weakened. Injustice has taken over. A caring ethos without attention to the core covenantal commitment is not possible. Jesus, when asked what is the greatest commandment, similarly links the love of God with the love of neighbour (Mark 12.28-31).

The root meaning of the English word 'obedience' is to listen or hear. Our obedience to God involves an attentive ear and an open heart – to the words of Scripture, to the daily life of the world, to voices from the margins, to the groaning of creation, to the inner voice of the heart. For the early monks of the desert, '*nepsis*', meaning watchfulness or vigilance, was a fundamental virtue and a repeating call: 'Pay attention, pay attention, pay attention.'

COLLECT

Almighty God,
whose Son Jesus Christ fasted forty days in the wilderness,
and was tempted as we are, yet without sin:
give us grace to discipline ourselves in obedience to your Spirit;
and, as you know our weakness,
so may we know your power to save;
through Jesus Christ our Lord.

Reflection by **Brother Samuel SSF**

Lent

Psalms **42**, 43 *or* 56, **57** (63*)
Jeremiah 6.9-21
John 6.1-15

Thursday 18 February

Jeremiah 6.9-21

'See, their ears are closed' (v.10)

For a nation heedless of the word of the Lord, Jeremiah can see only disaster. It's a disaster that he himself understands and feels as God's wrath poured out on the people who are greedy for unjust gain and who are led by rulers careless of the deep wound of the broken relationship with their passionate, sovereign Lord. The prophet foresees the innocent as well as the culpable caught up in the suffering; whole families, young and old, will be led into captivity.

Agonizing disasters continue today. In several parts of the world, land is laid waste by war and ecological collapse, cities are devastated, roads and boats are filled with refugees. As always, it's the children and the elderly who bear the brunt of the suffering. Wrath is not the angry emotion of a hard-hearted dictator who needs to be placated, but is the inevitable consequence when our relationship with the love that, as Dante wrote, 'moves the Sun and the other stars', and that sustains all life in gracious mercy and wisdom, is forgotten or denied.

Like the people in Jeremiah's time, we stand daily at the crossroads with a choice of ways to follow. The appeal to 'ask for the ancient paths' is not a nostalgic hankering after past glories, but a call to return to the One who longs for our wellbeing, who 'loves the world so much …'.

COLLECT

Heavenly Father,
your Son battled with the powers of darkness,
and grew closer to you in the desert:
help us to use these days to grow in wisdom and prayer
that we may witness to your saving love
in Jesus Christ our Lord.

Reflection by **Brother Samuel SSF**

Lent

Friday 19 February

Psalm **22** *or* **51**, 54
Jeremiah 6.22-end
John 6.16-27

Jeremiah 6.22-end

'O my poor people, put on sackcloth, and roll in ashes' (v.26)

As well as being an outpouring of grief and great sadness, lament is an expression of love over someone or something that has been lost. The death of a person dear to us, the destruction of a community, the collapse of a cherished hope, the failure of a relationship, the image of a starving child, the suffering of a mistreated animal – all these may bring forth tears. Throughout the book of Jeremiah, the prophet calls his people to lament on account of their stubborn refusal to see their true situation. Within his words, we hear the grief of the One whose Son in his ministry wept over the city of Jerusalem – God lamenting in sorrow over his beautiful and beloved world.

We live in a society in which public shared lament is usually avoided; grief tends to be kept at a personal level or sometimes even buried. However, at the time of the Covid pandemic, when during its initial phase we were shocked into the recognition of our powerlessness in face of the rapid spread of the virus, many discovered the power of lament to question their values and the values of society. It was a shame that churches had to remain locked. The church fathers spoke of 'the gift of tears' that exposes the truth about ourselves and about our world with its false comforts and delusions. Lament can leverage sorrow towards repentance.

COLLECT

Almighty God,
whose Son Jesus Christ fasted forty days in the wilderness,
and was tempted as we are, yet without sin:
give us grace to discipline ourselves in obedience to your Spirit;
and, as you know our weakness,
so may we know your power to save;
through Jesus Christ our Lord.

Reflection by **Brother Samuel SSF**

Lent

Psalms 59, **63** *or* **68**
Jeremiah 7.1-20
John 6.27-40

Saturday 20 February

Jeremiah 7.1-20

*'Do not trust in these deceptive words:
"This is the temple of the Lord ..."' (v.4)*

Sometimes religion gets in the way of our relationship with God and with each other. The Jerusalem temple, the 'dwelling place of God', was at the heart of the nation's life and the guarantor of its security. Yet, surrounded by a culture of injustice and unfaithfulness, its holiness and its power had become compromised – the place had become 'a den of robbers', the saying taken up by Jesus in the Gospels. The building itself had supplanted the God whom it was supposed to host.

It's not just a building that can take the place of God. The institution of the Church, its management culture, its divisive conflicts over Scripture, doctrine and practice, its anxiety about its finances and its future, can squeeze God out, hindering relationship with the One who in Jesus has come to dwell with us, who himself has become our temple. The words of Jeremiah lead us to question the temples that we build for ourselves: the places, organizations, programmes and possessions in which we put our faith for a security that is other than God. Institutions, structures of government, finance and buildings are a necessary part of life in community, but we need to remember what they are for and not mistake them for what they are not. Truly holy lives, holy communities and holy places direct attention away from themselves towards the One who alone is holy.

> Heavenly Father,
> your Son battled with the powers of darkness,
> and grew closer to you in the desert:
> help us to use these days to grow in wisdom and prayer
> that we may witness to your saving love
> in Jesus Christ our Lord.

Reflection by **Brother Samuel SSF**

Lent

Monday 22 February

Psalms 26, **32** *or* **71**
Jeremiah 7.21-end
John 6.41-51

Jeremiah 7.21-end
'... and looked backwards rather than forwards' (v.24)

Walking while looking backwards is a risky business. With our eyes fixed on what has already been, we might miss the hole that we are about to fall into, the tree that we are about to bump into.

Walking while looking backwards is also impoverishing. The views that otherwise open up to us are lost to us; possibility and choice – right or left? – are closed off to us. The promise of the horizon, the question of what might lie around the next corner or over the summit of the next hill is obscured by our attachment to the familiar, to what has been.

And walking while only looking backwards is a kind of blasphemy, denying the forward trajectory of our faith, where we hope for – look to – things promised and as yet unseen. To look only backwards is to deny all that God might do, the future that God is unfolding before us.

In Lent, the temptation is to walk while looking backwards: to shape our observation of this season by focusing on our failures that we must atone for; on our habitual weaknesses that we need to correct.

What might it be, instead, to look forwards in Lent to future possibility; to draw on the Old English root of 'Lent' and to see this as a time of 'lengthening', of moments to pay special attention, not to the less of ourselves, but to the more of God?

COLLECT

Almighty God,
you show to those who are in error the light of your truth,
that they may return to the way of righteousness:
grant to all those who are admitted
    into the fellowship of Christ's religion,
that they may reject those things
    that are contrary to their profession,
and follow all such things as are agreeable to the same;
through our Lord Jesus Christ.

Reflection by **Mary Gregory**

Lent

Psalm **50** *or* **73**
Jeremiah 8.1-15
John 6.52-59

Tuesday 23 February

Jeremiah 8.1-15
'... saying, 'Peace, peace', when there is no peace' (v.11)

To begin, we might look with gentleness on our reluctance to confront a painful reality. To name what is broken, or distorted, or dis-eased, is to make suffering present – to look it in the eye. Once we have named it, we are compelled to respond, and this might be costly; it might disrupt our own ease, challenge our relationships or our reputation. Perpetuating comfortable myths is seductive – it enables us to remain as we are.

We will, then, need to be courageous if we are to bring ourselves to name situations where there is no peace, or justice, or love; we will need compassion, to privilege others over self; we will need imagination, to see how things might be different so that naming isn't the deadening definition of what 'is' but the opening up of what 'might be'.

Colluding with the myth that there is peace when there is none is to treat the wounds of others carelessly, to keep them in the place of conflict and of vulnerability, to sentence them to life without reprieve. But compassion weighs suffering, counts its cost, demands its healing. 'There is no peace,' compassion says.m And imagination refuses to be held by 'no peace'; instead, it sketches what peace might look like and then charts a path towards it.

Today, where might we need courage to name what has been denied, compassion to outweigh the cost of confrontation, and imagination to forge a better future?

COLLECT

Almighty God,
by the prayer and discipline of Lent
may we enter into the mystery of Christ's sufferings,
and by following in his Way
come to share in his glory;
through Jesus Christ our Lord.

Reflection by **Mary Gregory**

Lent

Wednesday 24 February

Psalm **35** *or* **77**
Jeremiah 8.18 – 9.11
John 6.60-end

Jeremiah 8.18 – 9.11

'Take up weeping and wailing for the mountains ...' (9.10)

For too long, too many of us have cast ourselves as actors, and the natural world as the stage on which we perform, even as we pillage the very platform beneath our feet. We are nature's myopic mathematicians – always subtracting, rarely adding, never multiplying.

Jeremiah, uncompromising as ever, punctures our complacency, reanimates the mountains and the wilderness as creatures that suffer loss, like us, and experience our neglect as pain. He insists that we recognize the wild not as the dramatic backdrop to the performance of our lives but, like us, as beings shaped by God, for whom we should weep, wail, lament.

If recognizing our relationship with the earth from which we were shaped (Genesis 2.7) is an ancient way, insisted on here by Jeremiah and lyricized by St Francis in his Canticle of the Sun, it is also the focus of contemporary worldwide activism. There are movements to give rivers and woodland the legal status of personhood, to insist that the streams and the coastlands have rights beyond – even in opposition to – our own.

Lamentation begins by looking, by bearing witness, by crying out that the rainforests are as compromised as a punctured lung, that the ground beneath our feet is flailed with dryness as dehydrated skin. Lamentation alone becomes self-indulgence. We must also recover our vocation as custodians of creation; create the conditions for abundance and then delight in it. Time is short. What can you do today?

COLLECT

Almighty God,
you show to those who are in error the light of your truth,
that they may return to the way of righteousness:
grant to all those who are admitted
    into the fellowship of Christ's religion,
that they may reject those things
    that are contrary to their profession,
and follow all such things as are agreeable to the same;
through our Lord Jesus Christ.

Reflection by **Mary Gregory**

Lent

Psalm **34** *or* **78.1-39***
Jeremiah 9.12-24
John 7.1-13

Thursday 25 February

Jeremiah 9.12-24

'I act with steadfast love, justice, and righteousness ...' (v.24)

This final verse of today's reading from Jeremiah is as incongruous as a ballerina's tutu stitched onto the fatigues of a battle-weary soldier. For what does this assurance of God's steadfast love have to do with God's stated intent of poisoning God's people, of summoning women to lament the corpses piling up in the streets? In such a context, this avowal of steadfast love is confusing, disquieting, for how can love preside over such devastation?

There are theological gymnastics we could engage in as we stretch for an answer. We could cite the ancient understanding that God is the sole actor and so all things are attributed to God, even if, actually, humankind has been the author of its own devastation.

Maybe. But doesn't the season of Lent ask something else of us? Doesn't it call us out beyond the easy answer? Doesn't Jesus, who spent 40 days and nights in the wilderness, model something different for us: that there is a place for struggle, for emptying out? That from hunger and vulnerability, a deeper understanding can be born, even if only of our own unknowing? Perhaps, like Jacob, it is in wrestling that we see God, even if our questions remain unanswered (Genesis 32.22-32).

Ultimately, the contradictions of this passage coalesce not in complex argument, but in the person of Jesus, who, for love, drinks deeply of the bitterness of existence, as he hangs on the cross.

> COLLECT
>
> Almighty God,
> by the prayer and discipline of Lent
> may we enter into the mystery of Christ's sufferings,
> and by following in his Way
> come to share in his glory;
> through Jesus Christ our Lord.

Reflection by **Mary Gregory**

Lent

Friday 26 February

Psalms 40, **41** *or* **55**
Jeremiah 10.1-16
John 7.14-24

Jeremiah 10.1-16

'Their idols are like scarecrows in a cucumber field' (v.5)

There is something playful about this image of a scarecrow. Immediately, we step into the pictures of a storybook, where we encounter a straw-stuffed figure, dressed in a farmer's cast-offs – bright plaid shirt, patched jeans, floppy sun hat – with a slightly baffled smile embroidered onto its face.

From a distance, the scarecrow towers above the field, presides with authority over all that grows and all that would disrupt it. Move in closer and we see that a crow has settled on the scarecrow's head. The deterrent has become a perch; the scarecrow more friend than foe. With only the *illusion* of life, the scarecrow is unfit for purpose.

Today, we might draw closer to the idols that we have created, those props we rely on to forestall collapse, those practices we have adopted to pattern our lives, those promises that have been peddled to us and on which we have set our hope. Zoom in; examine these idols. Is there truth and life in them, or are they as redundant as a scarecrow with a bird balancing on its sun hat?

We should also zoom out on the majesty of God; recognize that, as we have made our idols too big, we have made God too small. We have failed to recognize God's wild, free life, where God holds wind in storehouses and creates lightning in a workshop. It's time to reset our perspective and relocate our hope.

COLLECT

Almighty God,
you show to those who are in error the light of your truth,
that they may return to the way of righteousness:
grant to all those who are admitted
    into the fellowship of Christ's religion,
that they may reject those things
    that are contrary to their profession,
and follow all such things as are agreeable to the same;
through our Lord Jesus Christ.

Reflection by **Mary Gregory**

Lent

Psalms 3, **25** *or* **76**, 79
Jeremiah 10.17-24
John 7.25-36

Saturday 27 February

Jeremiah 10.17-24

'Correct me, O Lord, but in just measure' (v.24)

'Correct me, O Lord' is a strikingly courageous prayer. Even hedged about with its caveat – 'but in just measure'. It is an invitation to God, who is Almighty, to intervene in our lives not with blessing, mercy or love, but to change us.

This, then, is of a different order to a prayer for forgiveness, where God might wipe the slate clean, and we might begin afresh, before diverting again from the course God has set for us, and returning for forgiveness. This is a cycle made virtuous by the grace of God, but one that might leave us fundamentally unchanged.

To invite God to correct us is to ask God to reset us: like realigning a supermarket trolley whose wheels veer in all directions and make steering impossible; like trimming a sail to make it catch the wind; like cracking open the sternum to access the very heart of us and make us beat to God's rhythm. Correction is invasive. It might hurt before it heals us. Correction makes us more than we have been – it might be as costly as it is expansive. Are we ready for more? Dare we pray, 'Correct me, O Lord'?

The rich young ruler finds the correction that Jesus asks of him – to sell his possessions and become a disciple – too high a price to pay (Matthew 19.21-22). He walks away grieving. When God sets out our correction, will we walk with God, or walk away?

> Almighty God,
> by the prayer and discipline of Lent
> may we enter into the mystery of Christ's sufferings,
> and by following in his Way
> come to share in his glory;
> through Jesus Christ our Lord.

COLLECT

Reflection by **Mary Gregory**

Lent

Monday 1 March

Psalms **5**, 7 *or* **80**, 82
Jeremiah 11.1-17
John 7.37-52

Jeremiah 11.1-17

'What right has my beloved in my house …?' (v.15)

We can be preoccupied by rights. Sometimes this is good and life-giving, a matter of honouring ourselves as children of God; a fulfilment of our calling to amplify the voices of those who otherwise go unheard. We should feel able to say when something has diminished us. We must raise our voices to rail against the oppression of others, even if we are voices crying in the wilderness.

We would be wise to be cautious, though, about introducing the language of rights into our spiritual life, into the ebb and flow of our relationship with God. If we did, we would find the answer to the question posed here by God to be always, ever, the same: 'What right has my beloved in my house?' 'None. No *rights* at all', we would have to answer.

The covenant between God and God's people suggests that we *are* in this sort of territory, but even here, writ large, is boundless gift, eternal generosity on God's part and, on humanity's, simply a walking in the ways that will bring us life (not that we have ever found it simple). It is as if God knows that humanity will never quite grasp amazing grace and needs something that looks like a contract to make the gift acceptable.

In your approach to God, set aside any thoughts of rights. It has never been about that. This has always been about the Lover pursuing you, the beloved.

COLLECT

Almighty God,
whose most dear Son went not up to joy
    but first he suffered pain,
and entered not into glory before he was crucified:
mercifully grant that we, walking in the way of the cross,
may find it none other than the way of life and peace;
through Jesus Christ our Lord.

Reflection by **Mary Gregory**

Lent

Psalms 6, **9** *or* 87, **89.1-18**
Jeremiah 11.18 – 12.6
John 7.53 – 8.11

Tuesday 2 March

Jeremiah 11.18 – 12.6

'Why does the way of the guilty prosper?' (12.1)

We have lost the language of complaining to God in our worship and liturgy. In other situations, we have no such reticence. In church, we feel able to express clear views to other people on the hymns: the wrong hymn, or the right hymn with the wrong tune, or the hymn no one knew, or the sermon (too long). We protest against politicians, rail at retailers, leave poor reviews for restaurants — but we feel coy about calling out the Almighty.

What accounts for our departure from the freedom of our ancestors of faith, of Jeremiah, Isaiah and Job, who summon God to trial, complain that God is being grindingly slow in the sort of decisive action demanded, and mark God's end-of-term report as 'Could do better'?

Are we afraid that to complain to God is a kind of heresy – a calling into question of God's power or goodness? Or that if we voice our questions, make our doubts present, we might undermine our already fragile faith?

In fact, to lament, to complain, to interrogate God about the aching brokenness of the world, is not heresy. Quite the opposite: it is a form of creed founded on the faith that God is just and true and that God loves God's people beyond any limit. It is this belief – not doubt – that prompts the questions 'Why?', 'Why not?', 'When?' We complain not because we think that God is indifferent, but because we trust that God listens and responds. Complaint is rich worship.

COLLECT

Eternal God,
give us insight
to discern your will for us,
to give up what harms us,
and to seek the perfection we are promised
in Jesus Christ our Lord.

Reflection by **Mary Gregory**

Lent

Wednesday 3 March

Psalm **38** *or* **119.105-128**
Jeremiah 13.1-11
John 8.12-30

Jeremiah 13.1-11
'But they would not listen' (v.11)

God's indictment of Israel and Judah – 'But they would not listen' – stands in stark contrast to Jeremiah, who listens attentively and, presumably, with some bewilderment to what God asks of him. For beyond all apparent reason, and just as he is told, Jeremiah buys a linen loincloth, wears it, puts it beside the Euphrates and removes it again. This is radical listening – attending to what seems nonsensical without any sense of outcome and without an audience who might be challenged or changed by Jeremiah's performance – except, of course, they probably would not listen.

Jeremiah listens with openness to something that, at the outset, at least, makes no sense to him. How rare this is. All too often we put ourselves only in the way of listening to what we already think and, if we *are* exposed to something that challenges us, listen only to rebut with our well-worn arguments, from our settled sense of self and world.

This failure to listen impoverishes and polarizes; it keeps us at a distance from the other: from the divine Other, and from people not like us. But reconciliation, coming closer, will only be born through courageous listening; that is, by listening in such a way that we might be changed by what we hear.

How might we listen to the other today; seek out voices that surprise and discomfort us; follow their baffling narrative until we find ourselves somewhere new?

COLLECT

Almighty God,
whose most dear Son went not up to joy
    but first he suffered pain,
and entered not into glory before he was crucified:
mercifully grant that we, walking in the way of the cross,
may find it none other than the way of life and peace;
through Jesus Christ our Lord.

Reflection by **Mary Gregory**

Lent

Psalms **56**, 57 *or* 90, **92**
Jeremiah 14
John 8.31-47

Thursday 4 March

Jeremiah 14
'We acknowledge our wickedness, O Lord' (v.20)

How tempting to rest in the words in today's reading that might give us comfort: 'Yet you, O Lord are in the midst of us, and we are called by your name'; 'We set our hope on you'. Instead, it is our task, in these shadowlands of Lent, to bring to light the things hidden in darkness and to disclose the purposes of the heart (1 Corinthians 4.5). And so, we acknowledge our wickedness, O Lord.

This is much more than we habitually do. We might be far more ready to name our weakness, our frailty, the ways in which our story and our society has mis-shaped us. 'Wickedness' is of a different order; it is something we struggle to own, reserving it instead for the real villains, for those who inhabit the headlines.

Perhaps we have set the bar too high; exonerated ourselves by way of comparison with those we consider extreme other. Instead, we are to name the darkness we have preferred (John 3.19) and move beyond it to be illumined by 'the true light' who is Jesus (John 1.9).

Moving ourselves into the light, acknowledging our wickedness, is not to flog ourselves. It is to know our need of God, to call upon God to re-orient us, to renew God's life within us. Naming our wrongdoing is not a confession that leads to conviction, but the gateway to grace, the moment of our liberation. It is hiding that holds us captive.

> Eternal God,
> give us insight
> to discern your will for us,
> to give up what harms us,
> and to seek the perfection we are promised
> in Jesus Christ our Lord.

COLLECT

Reflection by **Mary Gregory**

Lent

Friday 5 March

Psalm **22** *or* **88** (95)
Jeremiah 15.10-end
John 8.48-end

Jeremiah 15.10-end

'And I will make you to this people a fortified wall of bronze' (v.20)

Among the ways in which Jeremiah's contemporaries might have described him, it seems unlikely that 'a fortified wall of bronze' would have featured. More likely, they would have called him an outlier with the most tenuous grip on reality; a vessel as shattered as the jug he breaks (19.10); one stuck in the mud of his despondency and doom-saying (38.6).

God sees him differently. This broken man becomes as inviolable as a fortified wall of bronze through his steadfastness before God; his courageous, faithful sounding out of the words of God. Falteringly, then, Jeremiah points to Christ, who conquers in defeat, makes whole through brokenness, and at the point of greatest weakness is the strongest he has ever been.

Here is consolation and challenge. The consolation is familiar *and* elusive: that God sees beyond our outer appearance to the very heart of us (1 Samuel 16.7); that God chooses the weak and the foolish (1 Corinthians 1.27-28); that in this weakness that makes space for God, we are strong (2 Corinthians 12.10). Beleaguered though we be, in aligning ourselves with God we are fortified, like bronze.

The challenge is a sharp one: that we remain radically open to the 'Jeremiahs' around us; those with whom we profoundly disagree; who disturb and disrupt us; who show us a version of life that is unpalatable, even unbearable. Might they be voicing God's words to us? In silencing them, do we mute God?

COLLECT

Almighty God,
whose most dear Son went not up to joy
   but first he suffered pain,
and entered not into glory before he was crucified:
mercifully grant that we, walking in the way of the cross,
may find it none other than the way of life and peace;
through Jesus Christ our Lord.

Reflection by **Mary Gregory**

Lent

Psalm **31** *or* 96, **97**, 100
Jeremiah 16.10 – 17.4
John 9.1-17

Saturday 6 March

Jeremiah 16.10 – 17.4

'For my eyes are on all their ways ...' (16.17)

In Psalm 139, the assurance that God is our witness and companion is deeply consoling. Anywhere we go, God goes with us. God charts the minutiae of our lives. In the darkest place, where the very memory of light is extinguished, even there God is with us. We are never lost because God ever finds us.

In today's reading, this assurance of God's attentiveness sounds a different note; it feels less like that of a besotted lover, more like the relentless surveillance of an intrusive state. Here, God sees us, catalogues our wrongdoing with forensic attention, and unflinchingly sentences us. Suddenly, being watched at every moment is far less beguiling. We are fatally exposed.

This is the God whom Amos hears roaring out of Zion (Amos 1.2); the God of Isaiah's vision whose holiness shakes the temple (Isaiah 6.4). This is the God of C.S. Lewis' *The Lion, the Witch and the Wardrobe* – Aslan, the lion who is not tame, but who is good. This is our God: uncompromisingly holy, ever present, fierce in the pursuit of right.

Our task is to resist privileging the God who consoles us over the God who confronts us, as if God could be subdivided to suit us. Instead, we are to wrestle with God's complexity, to understand how God's refusal to compromise on holiness is an expression of enduring love; that God's irresistible power, which we can so fear, is what raises us to new life.

COLLECT

Eternal God,
give us insight
to discern your will for us,
to give up what harms us,
and to seek the perfection we are promised
in Jesus Christ our Lord.

Reflection by **Mary Gregory**

Lent

Monday 8 March Psalms 70, **77** or **98**, 99, 101
Jeremiah 17.5-18
John 9.18-end

Jeremiah 17.5-18

'They shall be like a tree planted by water' (v.8)

As the flourishing of a tree is reliant upon a regular supply of water, so, according to Jeremiah, the nation depends for its survival on trust in its life-giving source. Yet this is what has been neglected by placing trust in the uncertain security of unjustly gained wealth and the fickle human heart.

It's generally recognized that in our world today, there's a crisis of trust. Many no longer have confidence in the institutions that once held communities together – the government, the press, the banks, the police, the Churches. Those who are experts in their field are often accused of concealing the truth when something goes wrong. The use of social media encourages a culture of suspicion among us. Who can be trusted? There needs to be a confidence deeper than in 'mere mortals' who, like ourselves, are fragile human beings with hearts prone to deceit and misunderstanding.

Jeremiah appeals to the nation to trust in the One who is the 'hope of Israel', who is its 'fountain of living water', the same image used by Jesus in John's Gospel (John 7.38). The recovery of a relationship of trust in the overflowing and gushing source of life poured out for the life of others is the only hope for a society that is thirsting for meaning and purpose, but which is losing confidence that there is security to be found in its markets, media and management structures.

COLLECT

Merciful Lord,
absolve your people from their offences,
that through your bountiful goodness
we may all be delivered from the chains of those sins
which by our frailty we have committed;
grant this, heavenly Father,
for Jesus Christ's sake, our blessed Lord and Saviour.

Reflection by **Brother Samuel SSF**

Lent

Psalms 54, **79** or **106*** (*or* 103)
Jeremiah 18.1-12
John 10.1-10

Tuesday 9 March

Jeremiah 18.1-12

'... go down to the potter's house' (v.2)

Clay is such a wonderful material with which to work, sensitive and responsive to the fingers of the potter, capable of being shaped into something that is both useful and beautiful. Jeremiah's image draws upon clay's plasticity, which allows it to be refashioned when the first attempt on the wheel goes wrong. Don't be ignorant, says the prophet, that God can do this with his people.

However, there is not just threat to be found in this image. The potter doesn't discard the clay when the pot goes out of shape between their hands, continually reusing it until the desired form is found. In the same way, God is constantly at work with and in us – forming us into the likeness of his Son. The God of Jesus Christ is a God of infinite artistry and ingenuity when it comes to his creation.

Such work requires the cooperation of the clay in the hands of the potter. The spiritual practices of prayer and worship, reflection on Scripture, the celebration of the liturgy, our attention to creation and to each other, and our life in the community of the Church, are all for the purpose of formation – of our becoming who we already are in the heart of God – God's most beloved. 'When God looks at each one of us' said Karl Barth, 'he sees only Jesus.' We are not yet finished pots – the potter's wheel is still spinning!

> Merciful Lord,
> you know our struggle to serve you:
> when sin spoils our lives
> and overshadows our hearts,
> come to our aid
> and turn us back to you again;
> through Jesus Christ our Lord.

COLLECT

Reflection by **Brother Samuel SSF**

Lent

Wednesday 10 March

Psalms 63, **90** or 110, **111**, 112
Jeremiah 18.13-end
John 10.11-21

Jeremiah 18.13-end

'Is evil a recompense for good?' (v.20)

Why do bad things happen to good people? Why do well-intentioned efforts to heal get rejected? Why are people slandered and peaceful words distorted? Why, why, why? We share Jeremiah's anguished questioning, his argument with God, similar to that of Job and of the psalmist in Psalm 88 with its unrelieved despair. We may also feel the prophet's cry for payback on his persecutors, that they may get their full desert. All of us have probably had these conversations in our hearts at some point in our lives.

And God keeps silent. Right at the beginning of his call 'to pluck up and to pull down, to destroy and overthrow', Jeremiah was warned of the opposition he would face and was told that he must stand as a 'fortified city'. Here, he is experiencing the cost of that commission.

At his trial before the Sanhedrin, before Herod, before Pilate and the tormenting crowd, Jesus kept silent, bearing the mockery, the insults and the brutality. There's no cry for revenge. We remember the persecuted Church in different parts of the world – Christians who have been murdered or imprisoned on trumped-up charges, congregations that have been forbidden to meet for worship, and buildings that have been wrecked. At times, they must ask the same question as Jeremiah. We give thanks for their faithfulness, we pray for their protection and we trust in God's righteousness.

COLLECT

Merciful Lord,
absolve your people from their offences,
that through your bountiful goodness
we may all be delivered from the chains of those sins
which by our frailty we have committed;
grant this, heavenly Father,
for Jesus Christ's sake, our blessed Lord and Saviour.

Reflection by **Brother Samuel SSF**

Lent

Psalms 53, **86** *or* 113, **115**
Jeremiah 19.1-13
John 10.22-end

Thursday 11 March

Jeremiah 19.1-13

'Go and buy a potter's earthenware jug' (v.1)

Here is a very different purpose for a visit to the potter than that in chapter 17. There it was to speak of reformation; here it illustrates another message. Jeremiah smashes an earthenware jar – a symbolic act to pronounce the inevitability of Jerusalem's destruction.

You could call it 'direct action' – on a par with toppling the statue of a wealthy ship-owner to protest against the continuing legacy of the slave trade or lying in the road to 'Just Stop Oil'. To some, these actions may be questionable; for others, there comes a point when words alone are not sufficient for the urgency of the times.

The Church itself is, or should be, 'an action', a sign of radical contradiction amid the chaos and craziness of the present world order. At the heart of our life is the cross of Christ – God's direct action of love, mercy and compassion. By welcoming the stranger in an otherwise hostile environment, by standing beside and speaking for those whose voice is not heard, and by passionate engagement in care for creation, we may articulate both God's mercy and also God's judgement. The Franciscan brothers serving in a mission church in East London at the end of the nineteenth century, and protesting against the poverty and unjust working conditions of the time, used to speak of the Sunday Mass as 'the weekly gathering of rebels'.

COLLECT

Merciful Lord,
you know our struggle to serve you:
when sin spoils our lives
and overshadows our hearts,
come to our aid
and turn us back to you again;
through Jesus Christ our Lord.

Reflection by **Brother Samuel SSF**

Lent

Friday 12 March

Psalm **102** *or* **139**
Jeremiah 19.14 – 20.6
John 11.1-16

Jeremiah 19.14 – 20.6

'I am making you a terror to yourself' (20.4)

In a diary entry for 27 February 1943, written in the Westerbork transit camp before she and her family were transported to Auschwitz, the Dutch Jewish woman, Etty Hillesum, recorded the abuse, verbal and physical, that she and other internees had received that day at the hands of a young Gestapo officer. Rather than being afraid of him, she saw in him just a pitiable and weak young man. 'Such men are dangerous,' she wrote.

Violence, as that received by Jeremiah at the hands of the temple priest Pashhur, springs not from strength but weakness. Jeremiah's words and actions, exposing the vulnerability of Jerusalem and its temple before the might of the Babylonian Empire, which was swallowing up the independent city-states of the region, provoked in Pashhur the fear that led to his aggression against the prophet. His violence revealed both his own vulnerability and the fear that went with it. He was, indeed, already a 'terror to himself'.

How do we respond to the aggression and violence that we see around us and sometimes experience in the world today? The knee-jerk reaction of 'locking them up and throwing away the key', of punishing violence with more violence, may calm our fear and satisfy our outrage for a time, but it does little to address the root causes of violence in others and in ourselves. 'Do not be afraid' is probably the most frequently repeated injunction in the Scriptures.

COLLECT

Merciful Lord,
absolve your people from their offences,
that through your bountiful goodness
we may all be delivered from the chains of those sins
which by our frailty we have committed;
grant this, heavenly Father,
for Jesus Christ's sake, our blessed Lord and Saviour.

Reflection by **Brother Samuel SSF**

Lent

Psalms **32** *or* 120, 121, 122
Jeremiah 20.7-end
John 11.17-27

Saturday 13 March

Jeremiah 20.7-end

'Cursed be the day on which I was born!' (v.14)

Jeremiah is at breaking-point. He is caught between, on the one hand, his need to speak a message of violence and destruction, a compulsion so strong that it feels like a burning fire within him, and, on the other, the denunciation he receives from those around him, the taunts and mockery of even his closest friends.

For those who are impelled to speak truth to power today – whistleblowers, investigative journalists, opponents of oppressive regimes – the tension between what feels like a vocation and its consequences can be overwhelming. Have I got it all wrong? Have I been deceived? Have I been enticed into a cause that can never succeed? At the extremity of this tension, a political prisoner, held for years without hope of release, may well, like Jeremiah, curse the day they were brought into the world.

Yet in the midst of this chapter of Jeremiah's anguish, there is in verse 13 a hymn of defiant praise. Despite the bleakness of the situation, the prophet sings out God's promise of deliverance that has echoes of Job 19.25, 'I know that my Redeemer lives', and of Psalm 22, which, beginning with the words, 'My God, My God, why have you forsaken me', then moves into a song of confidence in God's blessing. We give thanks for those who endure the darkness of great hardship, suffering and death for the cause of truth and righteousness.

COLLECT

Merciful Lord,
you know our struggle to serve you:
when sin spoils our lives
and overshadows our hearts,
come to our aid
and turn us back to you again;
through Jesus Christ our Lord.

Reflection by **Brother Samuel SSF**

Passiontide

Monday 15 March Psalms **73**, 121 *or* 23, 124, 125, **126**
Jeremiah 21.1-10
John 11.28-44

Jeremiah 21.1-10

'I am setting before you the way of life and the way of death' (v.8)

Many of us live with the availability of multiple choices – we are used to choosing the food we eat, the places we live, the education pathways we take, the careers we follow. The freedom of the individual to choose has become a pillar of our way of life. Such belief in freedom of choice includes the practice of faith; we tend to choose the church where we feel at home, the spirituality that suits our personality and the truth we wish to live by. Israel suffered from the same compulsion, choosing its gods and its allies, drinking alternately from the Nile and the Euphrates.

However, according to the word of the Lord in Jeremiah, there are just two choices to be made – between the way of life and the way of death. The latter is the consequence of the nation's false choices; the former is the offer of the One who long ago chose Israel.

For us to choose God in our lives means recognizing that we are already chosen by the One who has known us before we were born and who has loved us from all eternity – our name written on the palm of God's hand. When the overriding priority is to find life with the One who has chosen us, then our desire to make choices that fit our own fancies, preferences and self-interest becomes less urgent.

COLLECT

Most merciful God,
who by the death and resurrection of your Son Jesus Christ
delivered and saved the world:
grant that by faith in him who suffered on the cross
we may triumph in the power of his victory;
through Jesus Christ our Lord.

Reflection by **Brother Samuel SSF**

Passiontide

Psalms **35**, 123 *or* **132**, 133
Jeremiah 22.1-5, 13-19
John 11.45-end

Tuesday 16 March

Jeremiah 22.1-5, 13-19
'Are you a king because you compete in cedar?' (v.15)

Throughout history, from before the time of the Pharaohs to the present day, 'building big' has been a means of projecting power, of overawing a population and of guaranteeing a legacy. The foolishness of such projects is demonstrated by their ruins. In Bob Gilbert's book, *Ghost Trees*, about the trees to be found around his area of London, he includes a chapter on 'The Post-human Tree', the buddleias and willows that spring up on and around those buildings that have become empty and derelict in today's cities – a witness to human hubris. Cities can very quickly become uninhabitable deserts.

It's not only power-crazed rulers who are prone to 'competing in cedar'. The market economy urges all of us to imagine that bigger is better, that more is necessary and that progress involves the accumulation of possessions. We usually ignore the unsafe and unjust working conditions of those engaged in the production of our excess and the widening gap of inequality that often comes with striving for growth above all else.

The word of the Lord through Jeremiah is that Israel had abandoned the Torah with its demand for justice for the oppressed and care for the orphan and widow, and that therefore the Lord was abandoning the nation as it was then constituted. Any society built upon inequality and injustice, relying upon coercive control for its stability, is bound eventually to collapse.

COLLECT

Gracious Father,
you gave up your Son
out of love for the world:
lead us to ponder the mysteries of his passion,
that we may know eternal peace
through the shedding of our Saviour's blood,
Jesus Christ our Lord.

Reflection by **Brother Samuel SSF**

Passiontide

Wednesday 17 March

Psalms **55**, 124 *or* **119.153-end**
Jeremiah 22.20 – 23.8
John 12.1-11

Jeremiah 22.20 – 23.8

'I myself will gather the remnant of my flock' (23.3)

In the midst of lament and the warnings of doom, there comes a voice of hope, not as a result of the political machinations of the neglectful shepherds who are ruling the nation, but from the one whose name is 'The Lord is our righteousness'. It's a promise – 'the days are surely coming' – of a remnant rescued from the tragedy that is unfolding and of a return to land that has been lost.

Within the multiple crises of our world – environmental, social, economic and spiritual – we live with a fierce hope in the power of God to rescue and renew. Hope is not the same as optimism – the assumption that things will somehow get better – but a radical stripping back of false expectations about ourselves and the world, and a reorientation of our trust towards the creative love and mercy that hold the world in being.

The gathering of communities of prayer and stillness, small actions of kindness, compassion and forgiveness that sow the seeds of peace, generous hospitality to strangers, the planting of a tree and the recycling of waste are just a few of the small signs that witness to hope in God's future for a land restored. Such hope depends upon the faithful care, the sensitive creativity and the sacrificial service of a 'shepherding Church' that is itself shaped by the life, death and resurrection of the one Good Shepherd.

COLLECT

Most merciful God,
who by the death and resurrection of your Son Jesus Christ
delivered and saved the world:
grant that by faith in him who suffered on the cross
we may triumph in the power of his victory;
through Jesus Christ our Lord.

Reflection by **Brother Samuel SSF**

Passiontide

Psalms **40**, 125 *or* **143**, 146
Jeremiah 23.9-32
John 12.12-19

Thursday 18 March

Jeremiah 23.9-32
'Do not listen to the words of the prophets ...' (v.16)

We tend to listen to the words of those who agree with us and who reinforce our own worldview. The algorithms set up within internet search engines feed us into a network of similarly minded explorations, which in turn seek our money, our action or our vote. The conspiracy theories that flourish are today's false prophecies.

In contrast, the prophetic word of the Lord through Jeremiah is 'like fire', which consumes vain hopes, a hammer that shatters human complacency and self-reliance. It disturbs settled securities and opens us to the strange anarchic God who upends our plans and will not be moulded into human images of power and glory.

Discerning true from false prophecy requires a willingness to repent, to question fixed and cherished ways of thought and to learn from those who are other than us. It calls for an inner silence that is not diverted by the latest crisis or new idea away from attention to the mysterious presence of God in the world around us – in the daily lives of people, in creation, in the Scriptures and in the life of the Church. The collected sayings of the early monks and nuns of the desert reveal a wisdom learnt in withdrawal from the clamour of world voices, able to distinguish demons from angels and truth from falsehood. Authentic prophecy usually comes to us from one or other kind of wilderness.

COLLECT

Gracious Father,
you gave up your Son
out of love for the world:
lead us to ponder the mysteries of his passion,
that we may know eternal peace
through the shedding of our Saviour's blood,
Jesus Christ our Lord.

Reflection by **Brother Samuel SSF**

Passiontide

Friday 19 March
Joseph of Nazareth

Psalms 25, 147.1-12
Isaiah 11.1-10
Matthew 13.54-end

Isaiah 11.1-10

'A shoot shall come out from the stock of Jesse' (v.1)

There's a picture by the Pre-Raphaelite painter, John Everett Millais, in the Tate Britain Gallery in London, titled *The Carpenter's Shop*, which portrays the Holy Family in Nazareth with Jesus at the side of Joseph, who is working at his bench. We know little of the man from 'the stock of Jesse' apart from his obedient response to the angel's message to take Mary as his wife and his presence at Jesus' birth, yet Joseph must have had a formative influence on the developing child well into Jesus' adulthood. By his example, Jesus will have learned to be a faithful Jew. Through him, Jesus will have received the wisdom of craft, recognizing the grain and smell of wood and the values of different types of timber. Living in the security of his Nazareth home, Jesus would have grown up within a wider community that practised its religion not just in synagogue and temple but as the warp and weft of daily life.

We grow into a trusting relationship with God not only by studying the Scriptures and worshipping with other believers, but by learning from those close to us the virtues of kindness, thankfulness, humility, generosity and truthfulness. 'Where did this man get all this?' was the question asked when, later in life, Jesus came back to teach and heal in Nazareth. The answer was or had been among them: the Holy Spirit working through the village carpenter.

COLLECT

God our Father,
who from the family of your servant David
raised up Joseph the carpenter
to be the guardian of your incarnate Son
and husband of the Blessed Virgin Mary:
give us grace to follow him
in faithful obedience to your commands;
through Jesus Christ our Lord.

Reflection by **Brother Samuel SSF**

Passiontide

Psalms **23**, 127 *or* **147**
Jeremiah 25.1-14
John 12.36*b*-end

Saturday 20 March

Jeremiah 25.1-14

'I am going to send for ... King Nebuchadrezzar ... my servant' (v.9)

A stone tablet on display at the British Museum in London is inscribed with an account of the achievements of the King of Babylon, who in Jeremiah's time destroyed Jerusalem and took its citizens into captivity. The remarkable thing about Jeremiah's prophecy of this national disaster is that Nebuchadrezzar, who worshipped the god Marduk, is named as God's servant, the agent of God's purpose in bringing to an end Solomon's temple and the line of Davidic kings. Seventy years later, the Babylonian empire itself would be brought to an end by an invading army. The Lord's hand is truly at work to 'destroy and overthrow, to build and to plant'.

How do we see God at work in the world today? While many would be cautious in ascribing particular historical events to God's direct involvement, the God of Abraham, Isaac and Jacob, the God of Moses and the prophets, is one who is passionately concerned for and engaged with the lives of people and the affairs of nations. The true sovereignty of God is established through the one who has shared our humanity in all its fragility and suffering, and who, through death and resurrection, has revealed the fulfilment of God's purpose for the whole of creation. More than ever today, amid the struggle of conflicting 'empires', we call upon the Holy Spirit for the gift of discerning God's hope for the world's future.

> Most merciful God,
> who by the death and resurrection of your Son Jesus Christ
> delivered and saved the world:
> grant that by faith in him who suffered on the cross
> we may triumph in the power of his victory;
> through Jesus Christ our Lord.

COLLECT

Reflection by **Brother Samuel SSF**

Holy Week

Monday 22 March
Monday of Holy Week

Psalm 41
Lamentations 1.1-12a
Luke 22.1-23

Luke 22.1-23

'The teacher asks you …' (v.11)

Jesus had a habit of borrowing things: loaves and fishes, a donkey, an upper room. The God who brought the world into existence and could commandeer everything, including the forces of nature, lived in Jesus with a light footprint, owning little and sharing in the resources that others were willing to offer.

What would our world be like if we held on to resources as lightly as the owner of this upper room? What if we opened our doors and hearts to strangers just as readily? Of course, some will say this is naive and misguided. Jesus was all but naive: he knew he would be betrayed and named the reality of betrayal at the Passover table, and yet, he did not expel the betrayer but remained in a posture of openness. Holy Week starts with a reminder that God's work includes an offer and an embrace for those who fall short, and an invitation to follow suit.

'The teacher asks you …' It is a wonder that the owner thought this was enough explanation. As we take part, again and again, in our own celebrations of the Last Supper, looking back to this meal of Jesus, what does the Teacher ask of us, in the symbol of this meal? What should our posture be in the world, and who are those we are called to welcome and embrace, and at what cost?

COLLECT

Almighty and everlasting God,
   who in your tender love towards the human race
      sent your Son our Saviour Jesus Christ
   to take upon him our flesh
and to suffer death upon the cross:
   grant that we may follow the example of his patience and humility,
   and also be made partakers of his resurrection;
through Jesus Christ our Lord.

Reflection by **Isabelle Hamley**

Holy Week

Psalm 27
Lamentations 3.1-18
Luke 22. [24-38] 39-53

Tuesday 23 March

Tuesday of Holy Week

Luke 22. [24-38] 39-53

'Pray that you may not come into the time of trial' (v.40)

Hollywood would struggle without great shows of strength. So would social media: tales of fighting and winning over adversity – whether the adversity is bad skin or the great trials of life – these tales are everywhere, and delight us. There is something comforting in the reassurance that it is possible to do great things and beat great odds. It is comforting to recast difficult moments as a great struggle within which we triumph, and we want to tell the world about it. Human dreams were not that different 2,000 years ago.

Jesus' words would have sounded just as odd back then as they do now: 'Pray that you may not come into the time of trial.' Not, 'Pray that you would triumph over adversity', or 'that you would have the strength to withstand trials', or 'that you would conquer temptation'. Strength and power are not glamourized. In real life, triumph in trials is much less glamorous than in the media and looks more like desperate survival with unlikely outcomes.

Jesus is preparing the disciples for what lies ahead. Peter thought he was strong enough to stand by Jesus, but failed. Jesus does not counsel them to strengthen themselves, but to be kept safe instead – and be sober in judging their own capacity. It goes against any glamourization of suffering and against the human tendency to rely on our own resources. It is the logic of the cross.

COLLECT

True and humble king,
hailed by the crowd as Messiah:
grant us the faith to know you and love you,
that we may be found beside you
on the way of the cross,
which is the path of glory.

Reflection by **Isabelle Hamley**

Holy Week

Wednesday 24 March
Wednesday of Holy Week

Psalm 102 [*or* 102.1-18]
Wisdom 1.16 – 2.1; 2.12-22
or Jeremiah 11.18-20
Luke 22.54-end

Luke 22.54-end

'Peter was following at a distance' (v.54)

Peter wanted to do the right thing. He cared about his friend and followed as far as he could – and discovered his limits. Jesus had counselled the disciples to pray that times of trial would be kept away. Today, trials come to Jesus and Peter alike, and within trials, character is revealed. Peter is brought face to face with the truth of who he is and the limits of his own strength.

He attempts to follow and finds out he is not Jesus; Peter is afraid, small and limited. He weeps bitterly, though we are not told whether he weeps over his shortcomings, or the fate of his friend, or both. Trials can bring us to greater self-awareness and truth about ourselves, but trials can also break us. At this point, it is not clear which it will be for Peter. Will he go back and follow Jesus despite his denial? Will he give up? Will he become permanently unsure of himself?

Of course, we know the end of the story, so it is easy to skip to it and see this Holy Week cameo as the story of grace and redemption that it becomes. But from within, as we trace Holy Week, we need to walk with Peter, with open-ended questions, and ask ourselves how we fare in trials, and whether past failures have enabled us to grow, or been more than we can bear.

COLLECT

Almighty and everlasting God,
who in your tender love towards the human race
    sent your Son our Saviour Jesus Christ
to take upon him our flesh
and to suffer death upon the cross:
grant that we may follow the example of his patience and humility,
and also be made partakers of his resurrection;
through Jesus Christ our Lord.

Reflection by **Isabelle Hamley**

Holy Week

Psalms 42, 43
Leviticus 16.2-24
Luke 23.1-25

Thursday 25 March
Maundy Thursday

Luke 23.1-25

'They began to accuse him' (v.2)

The scene that opens up this Maundy Thursday reading is depressingly familiar. People crowding in with accusations, eager to outdo one another, ganging up on one person regardless of the truth, with no one seeking to find right from wrong, yet simply letting the mob rule. I wonder what this scene would have looked like today?

Would we see a famed teacher, with a huge following on social media and TikTok videos from his followers showing him caring, loving, healing and breaking the boundaries that society and culture work so hard to maintain? It is not difficult to imagine accusations starting amid all the 'likes' and strident voices seeking to bring down this popular figure. It happens all the time.

It is easy, in modern democracies, to think ourselves far from lynching crowds, when in fact human instincts have changed little. Humans still delight in murky accusations, and human leaders are still tempted to give in to populist demands rather than seek truth, right and justice.

This Holy Week, let us examine our words and intentions, our care for the truth, and resist an easy slide into joining the accusing voices and crowds that forget the humanity of those they turn against. How can we be voices for truth and gentleness, for justice and kindness, so that our words and actions reflect the Christ who reached out to, rather than accused, those who fell short?

COLLECT

True and humble king,
hailed by the crowd as Messiah:
grant us the faith to know you and love you,
that we may be found beside you
on the way of the cross,
which is the path of glory.

Reflection by **Isabelle Hamley**

Holy Week

Friday 26 March
Good Friday

Psalm 69
Genesis 22.1-18
Hebrews 10.1-10

Hebrews 10.1-10

'... there is a reminder of sin year after year' (v.3)

Our fast-paced world is in love with innovation, new products, new films, new experiences. Western economies rely on disposable products, quickly broken or obsolete, quickly swapped for newer, more exciting models. Within this cultural logic, there is something odd about the insistence of the Christian tradition to put down anchors that call us back, year after year, century after century, to tell and retell the story. We can try and dress it up in slightly different clothes, use different media, but it is, fundamentally, the same story.

The story calls us back to who we are, and to who God is. It reminds us that all our 'new' is not 'better', but an incarnation of who we have always been, with glimpses of glory, reflecting the image of a creator God, alongside our fallenness and sin. The story calls us back to God and our responsibilities to care for the world and one another; it places us face to face with our failures to do so, individually and collectively.

Human beings have always needed reminders, long before industry and technology quickened the pace of change – hence the Hebrew Scriptures' festivals, because humans too quickly forget the truth of who they are and of who they are called to be. On Good Friday, we acknowledge the cost of Jesus' willingness to face the consequences of who we are and to open up a way for us to step into our calling once again.

COLLECT

Almighty Father,
look with mercy on this your family
for which our Lord Jesus Christ was content to be betrayed
    and given up into the hands of sinners
    and to suffer death upon the cross;
who is alive and glorified with you and the Holy Spirit,
one God, now and for ever.

Reflection by **Isabelle Hamley**

Psalm 142
Hosea 6.1-6
John 2.18-22

Saturday 27 March

Easter Eve

John 2.18-22

'After he was raised from the dead' (v.22)

Jesus has not been raised yet. The writer of John's Gospel wryly points out the difference that hindsight can make. After he was raised from the dead, Jesus' words about the temple not only made sense, but sounded like something that should have given them comfort. Did they not understand, or remember? On that day, when all hope had fled and the disciples could see no sign of resurrection, did they not remember the sayings of Jesus?

Hindsight is a wonderful thing. But there is no short-circuiting the process of grief, waiting, and struggling for meaning in the middle of desolation. There is no shortcut to resurrection, no shortcut to a better world. The disciples had to go through Holy Saturday before dawn could bring a new reality.

New realities can, at best, only be glimpsed. They are new precisely because there is discontinuity and something unpredictable about them. The struggle of Holy Saturday, therefore, is a struggle with knowing that only something truly new could bring relief, and yet not being able to imagine what this new thing can look like. No one imagines a butterfly if all they have ever seen is a caterpillar.

The call of Easter is a call to allow God to take us into something so new, so unthinkable that we could never do it ourselves – love, truth, justice beyond what we can control, imagine or, at times, even want.

COLLECT

Grant, Lord,
that we who are baptized into the death
of your Son our Saviour Jesus Christ
may continually put to death our evil desires
and be buried with him;
and that through the grave and gate of death
we may pass to our joyful resurrection;
through his merits,
who died and was buried and rose again for us,
your Son Jesus Christ our Lord.

Reflection by **Isabelle Hamley**

Easter Season

Monday 29 March
Monday of Easter Week

Psalms 111, 117, 146
Song of Solomon 1.9 – 2.7
Mark 16.1-8

Mark 16.1-8

'... the stone ... had already been rolled back' (v.4)

Did the stone need to be rolled away already? Sometimes we make it sound as if the stone was rolled away so Jesus could get out, though this is the Jesus who later appears in a locked room. The stone was not rolled away primarily because otherwise he was trapped. It was not rolled away so he could appear to disciples (given that disciples were about to roll the stone anyway, he could have met them there).

And yet the stone is a powerful symbol of Easter.

Because it is already rolled away, the women can come in. Had they needed a man/men to move it, the story of the witness to the resurrection would have unfolded differently and would have been told by different people. At Easter, this first precious glimpse of resurrection is given to those whose testimony would not have been seen as credible, because somehow, they were not deemed to be as equal, reliable or important. Easter morning cements what had characterized the ministry of Jesus: an attention to the least, the last and the lost, as the saying goes.

Yet more than this, the stone is rolled away so disciples can come in, so they can inhabit the place of death and know that death no longer reigns, and so they can learn to seek God where God is at work: among the living.

COLLECT

Lord of all life and power,
who through the mighty resurrection of your Son
overcame the old order of sin and death
to make all things new in him:
grant that we, being dead to sin
and alive to you in Jesus Christ,
may reign with him in glory;
to whom with you and the Holy Spirit
be praise and honour, glory and might,
now and in all eternity.

Reflection by **Isabelle Hamley**

Easter Season

Psalms **112**, 147.1-12
Song of Solomon 2.8-end
Luke 24.1-12

Tuesday 30 March
Tuesday of Easter Week

Luke 24.1-12
'... they did not believe them' (v.11)

Faith would not be faith if there were no room for doubt. It is easy to look back on this story and wonder how these disciples, who had spent time with Jesus, heard his teaching and witnessed his power, could possibly not believe. This initial unbelief however, is crucial to the witness of the gospel. If there had been no room for doubt, there would be no room for faith either. If there had been absolute proof of the resurrection, then accepting it would not be an act of faith, but an intellectual acceptance of facts.

The resurrection was such an unexpected, unprecedented, unbelievable event that it took time for the early Church to make sense of it and accept it. The different reactions – the women's, Peter's, other disciples' – are typical of human differences. They tell us that people react differently to what they hear and to the witness of others. Sometimes faith simply overwhelms; sometimes faith comes slowly. Sometimes faith looks like an obvious step; and sometimes faith comes out of ongoing struggle and wrestling, and feels tentative and risky.

The disciples are not berated for their initial reactions; Jesus, post-resurrection, works with human processes, foibles and struggles just as he did in his earlier ministry. He meets disciples where they are and invites them to take the next step on the journey – whether faith is only just starting or is part of the journey of a lifetime.

> God of glory,
> by the raising of your Son
> you have broken the chains of death and hell:
> fill your Church with faith and hope;
> for a new day has dawned
> and the way to life stands open
> in our Saviour Jesus Christ.

COLLECT

Reflection by **Isabelle Hamley**

Easter Season

Wednesday 31 March
Wednesday of Easter Week

Psalms 113, 147.13-end
Song of Solomon 3
Matthew 28.16-end

Matthew 28.16-end

'When they saw him, they worshipped him, but some doubted'
(v.17)

Most preachers, faced with the end of Matthew's Gospel, tend to go for one of two angles: either the 'Great Commission' – Jesus charging his followers to make disciples and baptize – or the promise of Jesus' presence 'to the end of the age'. Both are hugely important, and yet, we seldom hear about what comes just before commission and promise: some worshipped, and some doubted.

The best message in the world, the Word himself, was before them, and they doubted. In an era of Church decline and a wider disenchanted culture that rejects a lot of Christian faith, it is at times easy to forget that doubt is not new. Nor is it, necessarily, our fault as a Church. Learning from good practice in speaking, preaching and mission matters. Yet even if we do these things well, earnestly and to the best of our ability, some will still doubt. Not even God incarnate won everyone over, instantly.

This is hard teaching, because it forces us to accept that Church growth is not fully in our hands – and, to a degree, not fully in God's hands either, because God has given all human persons free will. Instead, we have to hold the 'results' of our efforts lightly, while still trusting in the promise and responding to Jesus' commission. Our task is to make the offer of life to those around us – not control their response.

COLLECT

Lord of all life and power,
who through the mighty resurrection of your Son
overcame the old order of sin and death
to make all things new in him:
grant that we, being dead to sin
and alive to you in Jesus Christ,
may reign with him in glory;
to whom with you and the Holy Spirit
be praise and honour, glory and might,
now and in all eternity.

Reflection by **Isabelle Hamley**

Easter Season

Psalms 114, 148
Song of Solomon 5.2 – 6.3
Luke 7.11-17

Thursday 1 April

Thursday of Easter Week

Luke 7.11-17

'... he had compassion' (v.13)

What motivates God to act? It is a pretty big question and one we cannot answer, because God is far beyond our patterns of thought. In common Christian parlance, however, we hear quite a lot about why God does things: because God loves, is angry, objects to sin, does justice ... All these are intimately related: challenging injustice and sin is loving because sin mars and impacts the whole of creation.

Scripture often comments on what moves God into action. Both Old and New Testaments regularly identify compassion as the reason for God's intervention in human affairs. Not God's response to prayer or requests or sin, or repentance, or human offers. Rather, the biblical writers tell us, again and again, that God acts out of compassion, because God sees suffering and hears the cries of earth's people. It is a reaction that brings God alongside humanity – in *com-* (with), *passion* (suffering). God suffers with God's creatures; whatever hurts and maims the world and its people causes God to suffer with them and alongside them – a response that finds its fulfilment in the incarnation.

To find that God acts out of compassion is an essential compass for our own engagement, so we can ask what the root of our own responses is, and whether we truly come *alongside* those around us, seeing them through the eyes of the God of compassion.

> God of glory,
> by the raising of your Son
> you have broken the chains of death and hell:
> fill your Church with faith and hope;
> for a new day has dawned
> and the way to life stands open
> in our Saviour Jesus Christ.

COLLECT

Reflection by **Isabelle Hamley**

Easter Season

Friday 2 April
Friday of Easter Week

Psalms 115, 149
Song of Solomon 7.10 – 8.4
Luke 8.41-end

Luke 8.41-end

'She came up behind him' (v.44)

How do you imagine yourself meeting Jesus? Would you be like Jairus, unafraid, with a request, knowing that Jesus' compassion will prevail? Or are you like the disciples, speaking easily to Jesus as companion on the road, and occasionally telling him what he already knows? Or maybe you are more like Jairus' daughter, finding that Jesus has come thanks to the faith of others? Many people surround Jesus in this story, all with a different posture, a different relationship. Some may feel almost entitled, or at least at ease with making requests; some are curious, some uncertain; and a woman clearly feels she is unworthy and only tentatively reaches out for his cloak, out of desperation.

Jesus meets the various characters differently. He makes Jairus wait, yet still heals his daughter; he exposes the trembling woman to the crowd, and declares she is entitled to his attention, love and healing, because she is a woman of faith. He makes her visible. He challenges the crowd and their gawking at human misery as spectacle, by refusing to perform the healing of the little girl in public; he challenges doubters who laugh, refusing to be distracted; and he cares for the little girl by giving her privacy and dignity.

Who might you be in this story – and how do you dare, and struggle, to come before God?

COLLECT

Lord of all life and power,
who through the mighty resurrection of your Son
overcame the old order of sin and death
to make all things new in him:
grant that we, being dead to sin
and alive to you in Jesus Christ,
may reign with him in glory;
to whom with you and the Holy Spirit
be praise and honour, glory and might,
now and in all eternity.

Reflection by **Isabelle Hamley**

Easter Season

Psalms 116, 150
Song of Solomon 8.5-7
John 11.17-44

Saturday 3 April
Saturday of Easter Week

John 11.17-44

'Could not he who opened the eyes of the blind man ...' (v.37)

Why does God fail to act in the face of such immense human misery as we see around us? The question onlookers ask – *Couldn't Jesus have saved Lazarus?* – does not go away with the happy resolution of this story. Yes, here we have a happy ending, and Lazarus comes out of the tomb and his family welcomes him back. This is a story of a miracle, and miracles, by definition, are not the rule. All of us will, at some point, ask the same question: *Why couldn't God ...* (fill in your own blank)? It's a question many of us ask even simply watching the news; it is a question that resists facile answers and that isn't answered by great intellectual concepts.

Jesus does not answer the question. Neither Jesus nor God really ever answers the question of why suffering is allowed by a good and loving God, and, if we are honest, no intellectual answer would make suffering acceptable. Instead, Jesus' reaction is to be 'again greatly disturbed'. He does not fight the question – because it is a fair question. Instead, he displays his own sorrow at the reality of suffering and death.

God's answer to the question is not intellectual; it does not make reasonable sense. God's only answer is one of presence alongside us, changing and transforming the world within, inhabiting with us the ongoing Holy Saturday of living in between the resurrection and the promise of all things being made new.

> God of glory,
> by the raising of your Son
> you have broken the chains of death and hell:
> fill your Church with faith and hope;
> for a new day has dawned
> and the way to life stands open
> in our Saviour Jesus Christ.

COLLECT

Reflection by **Isabelle Hamley**

Easter Season

Monday 5 April

Annunciation of Our Lord
to the Blessed Virgin Mary

Psalms 111, 113
1 Samuel 2.1-10
Romans 5.12-end

Romans 5.12-end

'... but where sin increased, grace abounded all the more' (v.20)

What has happened to sin and death? Think for a while about how they affect our lives, our societies, our world. They can shake or wreck whole families, communities and peoples, take the joy, peace and trust out of life, instil fear, drive to despair, set off devastating chain reactions and vicious cycles that can last centuries, and cause seemingly endless misery. Paul has no illusions about all this; he takes its measure. Then he announces something utterly astonishing: there is a new, overwhelmingly greater reality, freely given by God, available to all. Note the repeated waves of amazed gratitude as he faces the terrible reality of sin and death, but then says 'much more surely ...', 'much more surely ...', 'all the more ...'.

But the opening question is wrong. It should be, '*Who* has happened to sin and death?' The answer, a name, again comes in wave after wave, 'the one man, Jesus Christ', 'the one man, Jesus Christ ...', culminating in 'eternal life through Jesus Christ our Lord'. Sin and death happened to Jesus Christ. But he happened to sin and death, and overcame them. We need not fear them. We can trust in him on both sides of death. We can trust in his forgiveness and fresh starts after sin. We can rejoice *in him* whatever happens to us. As the angel said to Mary, 'Nothing will be impossible with God'.

COLLECT

We beseech you, O Lord,
pour your grace into our hearts,
that as we have known the incarnation of your Son Jesus Christ
　　by the message of an angel,
so by his cross and passion
we may be brought to the glory of his resurrection;
through Jesus Christ our Lord.

Reflection by **David Ford**

Easter Season

Psalms **8**, 20, 21 *or* **5**, 6 (8)
Deuteronomy 1.19-40
John 20.11-18

Tuesday 6 April

John 20.11-18

'Jesus said to her, "Do not hold on to me ..."'(v.17)

What a reunion! Is it this Gospel's most moving moment? Mary Magdalene saw Jesus crucified. Now the tomb is empty and the trauma is intensified. She weeps inconsolably, searching for the dead body. Then the supposed gardener asks her the crucial question: 'Whom are you looking for?' The very first words Jesus spoke to his first two disciples were: 'What are you looking for?' (John 1.38). He is asking them about their core desire. But now the 'what' changes to 'who'. Mary has been searching for a 'what', a dead body. What happens is the ultimate surprise, the unimaginable fulfilment of her deepest desire, as they address each other: '"Mary!" ... "Rabbouni!"'

Yet what a shock! 'Do not hold on to me ...' Why? '... because I have not yet ascended to the Father.' But what does that mean? It goes to the heart of what the resurrection of Jesus can mean for all of us. Jesus being with his Father is Jesus free to be present as God alone is present, anywhere and everywhere, for anyone and everyone. He will not be limited to a last supper, a cross, a tomb, a garden, a Sunday morning. Even more glorious, it will be a more fulfilling, more intimate, more permanent relationship. It is the fulfilment of his ultimate desire always to be with us – and ours for that presence – as, three days earlier, he had poured it out in prayer to his Father (17.20–26).

COLLECT

Almighty Father,
you have given your only Son to die for our sins
and to rise again for our justification:
grant us so to put away the leaven of malice and wickedness
that we may always serve you
in pureness of living and truth;
through the merits of your Son Jesus Christ our Lord.

Reflection by **David Ford**

Easter Season

Wednesday 7 April

Psalms 16, **30** *or* **119.1-32**
Deuteronomy 3.18-end
John 20.19-end

John 20.19-end

'As the Father has sent me, so I send you' (v.21)

'As' is one of the most dynamic, imagination-stretching and challenging words in this Gospel. Just try to fathom the meaning of 'For I have set you an example, that you also should do *as* I have done to you' (13.15); or 'Just *as* I have loved you, you also should love one another' (13.34). The climactic 'as' happens now, when the resurrected Jesus brings to his fearful disciples peace (repeated twice – how they and we need peace that has been through crucifixion for us all!), tangible proof that torture and death do not have the last word, joy at his presence, authority to forgive, and the supreme gift, breathed into them: 'Receive the Holy Spirit!' The Spirit and the Word come inseparably together. And the words that are carried by his breath give us, his followers, our vocation.

What a vocation! This is the ultimate spirituality. It has a triple thrust, putting three radical questions to us day after day. First, can we go deeper into that deepest of all love relationships between the Father and the Son, which is at the heart of the sending of Jesus in love for the world? Second, can we go deeper into the community of his followers and friends who are being sent together? (The 'you' in the Greek is plural.) Third, can we go deeper into the world God loves?

COLLECT

Almighty Father,
you have given your only Son to die for our sins
and to rise again for our justification:
grant us so to put away the leaven of malice and wickedness
that we may always serve you
in pureness of living and truth;
through the merits of your Son Jesus Christ our Lord.

Reflection by **David Ford**

Psalms **28**, 29 *or* 14, **15**, 16
Deuteronomy 4.1-14
John 21.1-14

Thursday 8 April

John 21.1-14

'... but the disciples did not know that it was Jesus' (v.4)

This final chapter of John feels like the transition from plainly seeing and touching the crucified and resurrected Jesus, as Thomas demanded, to something less obvious, more about spiritual discernment. The repeated verb *ephanerōthrē*, translated 'showed himself', need not mean being seen – it can also be translated 'was revealed' or, at a stretch, 'was recognized'. It is only the beloved disciple who has eyes to see who the figure some distance away on the beach is, and cries out: 'It is the Lord!' The Greek *ho kurios esti* is literally 'The Lord is!', echoing the 'I am' affirmations of Jesus, and of God in Exodus 3.14. Those three Greek words are repeated three times in this short passage.

John seems to be describing something more like the experiences of his readers. We are among those who have received the blessing of Jesus in the previous chapter: 'Blessed are those who have not seen and yet have come to believe' (20.29). This is the Jesus who is recognized through obeying what he says: 'Cast the net to the right side of the boat ...', or through sharing a meal: 'Come and have breakfast'. Here is *Word and sacrament*. The passage concludes with the disciples not talking about seeing Jesus, but somehow knowing *ho kurios esti* – 'The Lord is'. Then for the third time comes that verb of revelation or recognition, this time translated as 'appeared'.

COLLECT

Risen Christ,
for whom no door is locked, no entrance barred:
open the doors of our hearts,
that we may seek the good of others
and walk the joyful road of sacrifice and peace,
to the praise of God the Father.

Reflection by **David Ford**

Easter Season

Friday 9 April

Psalms 57, **61** *or* 17, **19**
Deuteronomy 4.15-31
John 21.15-19

John 21.15-19

'... and take you where you do not wish to go' (v.18)

The grace! The tact! Jesus does not even mention that Peter had denied he was his disciple. He simply gives him a completely fresh beginning, even calling him by his birth name. Not only that, he gives him his vocation, the responsibilities that will fill the rest of his life. Jesus has already laid down his life for Peter and all his other friends, including us. What is happening between him and Peter is that, after a bitterly regretted denial, their love becomes fully mutual again: 'Yes! ... Yes! ... You know that I love you!' It is what we long for after a close, desired relationship is damaged, and trust breaks down.

Love can be one-way without mutual trust, but two-way love needs that trust. This is what Jesus desires for us above all: utter unity in love and trust with himself and his Father, and with each other, for the sake of the world to which he and we are sent in love. He prayed for this (John 17.20–26). Pray that too!

It is a love supreme, fulfilling beyond anything we can imagine, and we may taste it in our closest relationships with our friends, our husbands or wives, our children, or dedicated partnerships of many sorts and in many spheres. And it is also such relationships that often, for love's sake, take us where we do not wish to go.

COLLECT

Almighty Father,
you have given your only Son to die for our sins
and to rise again for our justification:
grant us so to put away the leaven of malice and wickedness
that we may always serve you
in pureness of living and truth;
through the merits of your Son Jesus Christ our Lord.

Reflection by **David Ford**

Easter Season

Psalms 63, **84** *or* 20, 21, **23**　　　**Saturday 10 April**
Deuteronomy 4.32-40
John 21.20-end

John 21.20-end

'... what is that to you? Follow me!'(v.22)

How much trouble in the Church could be avoided if we took this scene seriously? If we could trust that Jesus can have very different plans, callings and relationships with different disciples? If we could ignore rumours, deny fake news, and not attempt to second-guess Jesus' verdict on each other, content that we are all *his* disciples, and he is the only one with an overview of us all?

How much fear and anxiety could be avoided if we were to take 'until I come' as the one sure thing we need to know about the future. *Jesus is our future*. So we can be at peace about it and get on with being disciples now. And, for each of us, Jesus has a will, a desire (the Greek *thelō* means both will and desire) that can be utterly trusted as we 'remain' – the Greek is *menein*, a favourite word of John, often translated 'abide', and used multiple times in the parable of the vine (John 15).

Where is the beloved disciple abiding? 'And from that hour the disciple took [the Greek verb is lambanein] her into his own home.' (19.27) With the mother of Jesus! Is this the first fulfilment of the astounding promise of Jesus, 'Very truly, I tell you, whoever receives (*lambanein*) one whom I send receives me; and whoever receives me receives him who sent me'? (13.20)

COLLECT

Risen Christ,
for whom no door is locked, no entrance barred:
open the doors of our hearts,
that we may seek the good of others
and walk the joyful road of sacrifice and peace,
to the praise of God the Father.

Reflection by **David Ford**

Easter Season

Monday 12 April

Psalms **96**, 97 *or* 27, **30**
Deuteronomy 5.1-22
Ephesians 1.1-14

Ephesians 1.1-14

'... in ... in ... in ... in ... in ... in ... in ... in ... in ... in ...'

'Blessed be the God and Father of our Lord Jesus Christ ... to the praise of his glory.' This in Greek is one 202-word sentence, exuberant in blessing and praise, opening up a God-centred worldview embracing the whole of reality. Through it all sounds the insistent drum-beat of 'in' – 'in Christ' (this most of all, ten times in various forms), 'in the heavenly places', 'in love', 'in the Beloved', and more. What is happening? We are being invited to inhabit a glorious, love-centred reality.

What a place! Here, we are adopted into a new family. We are forgiven and have a completely fresh start. Our minds are stretched, trying to take in 'all wisdom and insight'. We have hope, truth, salvation, and the Holy Spirit. And we glimpse what history is all about, oriented in hope towards 'the fullness of time'. This place is above all a person, 'our Lord Jesus Christ'. What does it mean to be 'in Christ'? Meditate on each 'in' to begin to comprehend it.

Meditating is just one way of inhabiting this reality. Full participation involves our whole selves, and openness to receiving more and more of 'the riches of his grace that he lavished on us', and more and more of his love, forgiveness and truth. And in response, we are inspired to give continual thanks and to 'live for the praise of his glory'.

COLLECT

Almighty Father,
who in your great mercy gladdened the disciples
    with the sight of the risen Lord:
give us such knowledge of his presence with us,
that we may be strengthened and sustained by his risen life
and serve you continually in righteousness and truth;
through Jesus Christ our Lord.

Reflection by **David Ford**

Easter Season

Psalms **98**, 99, 100 *or* 32, **36**
Deuteronomy 5.22-end
Ephesians 1.15-end

Tuesday 13 April

Ephesians 1.15-end

'... the fullness of him who fills all in all' (v.23)

Is that really a description of the Church? Yes! Paul is a realist about things that can go wrong with the Church – his letters are full of them. Like the first disciples of Jesus, the Church then, down the centuries and around the world now has at times failed him, denied him and betrayed him in terrible ways. But the secret of the Church – why it has survived both those who have failed it and betrayed it, and also those in every age who have tried to undermine or destroy it – is given here. It is *'the Lord Jesus Christ'*. He is One who, in the face of all that can go wrong, in the Church and the world, is immeasurably great, with all the greatness of God.

His greatness is of a radically surprising, even shocking, sort. It is the greatness of love, forgiveness, gentleness, service, and all the other things that Ephesians is about. These are the essence of true greatness and ultimate power, and need to become – more and more – our essence too.

'I have heard of your faith in the Lord Jesus Christ and your love toward all the saints.' These Ephesian Christians had learned the secret and were trying to live it. As the rest of the letter shows, they were far from perfect and had a great deal more to learn. But Jesus is Lord!

COLLECT

Risen Christ,
you filled your disciples with boldness and fresh hope:
strengthen us to proclaim your risen life
and fill us with your peace,
to the glory of God the Father.

Reflection by **David Ford**

Easter Season

Wednesday 14 April

Psalm **105** *or* **34**
Deuteronomy 6
Ephesians 2.1-10

Ephesians 2.1-10

'... and seated us with him' (v.6)

Paul has just prayed about how God has raised Jesus from the dead, 'seated him at his right hand in the heavenly places', and 'made him the head over all things for the church, which is his body' Now he pictures us, who trust in Jesus, sitting with him there. It is an image of being fully at home in the family, sitting together. The logic of the imagery is: if we are part of his body, of course we are seated with him. How can we ever adequately picture the astonishing gift of this utter intimacy, mutuality, and completely trustworthy relationship? And it gives us not only Jesus to sit with, but also all the others who sit with him, 'made alive together' (there'll be some surprises there!).

The Bible stretches our imaginations in one way after another about this amazing community with numerous images – vine branches, children in a family, a flock of sheep each called by name, different parts of a body, and many more, including, as we will reflect tomorrow, 'one new humanity' in Christ.

Extraordinary! Yes, we sit in his presence, we read the Bible, and are daily overwhelmed by who God is, who Jesus is, and what it means to be part of this family. But also ordinary. We get up from our chair and go about our daily lives. And we find God-given opportunities, one after another, for good works of all sorts.

COLLECT

Almighty Father,
who in your great mercy gladdened the disciples
  with the sight of the risen Lord:
give us such knowledge of his presence with us,
that we may be strengthened and sustained by his risen life
and serve you continually in righteousness and truth;
through Jesus Christ our Lord.

Reflection by **David Ford**

Easter Season

Psalm **136** *or* **37***
Deuteronomy 7.1-11
Ephesians 2.11-end

Thursday 15 April

Ephesians 2.11-end

'... that he might create in himself one new humanity' (v.15)

Gentiles and Jews together are all humanity. What has happened, through Jesus dying on the cross, in utter unity both with the Creator of all and with all of us, is that there is a new creation in him, 'one new humanity'. It is already a reality in him and is open to all. We now live in the same space as everyone else, a world where peace and reconciliation are the most fundamental realities because Jesus Christ sits at the right hand of God – even if not everyone recognizes this. Jesus Christ has died for all, has been raised from the dead, and is now 'our peace'. To trust this is to be a citizen of this new country, a participant in the family life of the new humanity, 'the household of God', and 'a dwelling place for God'.

To trust this is also to be given a ministry of reconciliation in the face of every 'dividing wall', both within and beyond the Church. What does it mean that Jesus himself is 'our peace' in situations and relationships of division and hostility? Can the Church become, more and more, a sign of this happening? Does our baptism into the death and resurrection of Jesus Christ open us to being at peace with 'strangers and aliens', based on the astonishing new reality of the dividing wall between us being already demolished?

COLLECT

Risen Christ,
you filled your disciples with boldness and fresh hope:
strengthen us to proclaim your risen life
and fill us with your peace,
to the glory of God the Father.

Reflection by **David Ford**

Easter Season

Friday 16 April

Psalm **107** or **31**
Deuteronomy 7.12-end
Ephesians 3.1-13

Ephesians 3.1-13

'… in whom we have access to God in … confidence through faith'
(v.12)

We can be confident in the new reality we are now part of, though it is always beyond our full comprehension. It is a bright mystery, something unprecedented, not known to previous generations; it comes as 'news of the boundless riches of Christ', a revelation from 'God who created all things'. We can wake up every morning to be amazed afresh at who and what we are part of. It is an astonishing privilege, a sheer undeserved gift, to be, with Paul, a servant (the Greek is *diakonos*, one who waits and serves at table and in other ways) entrusted with a part to play in this. And each of us does have a part to play, including those who think of themselves as 'the very least'.

How can we best serve in the Church? One way is to love God with all our minds and imaginations. Paul wants those receiving the letter to read attentively what he writes, so as to 'perceive my understanding of the mystery of Christ'. He wants 'everyone' to see what he means, and for his message to be as public and widely known as possible – even for it to impact powerful spiritual and cultural forces. So, service in the Church can be a passionate, confident yet humble searching for 'the wisdom of God in its rich variety' that can enable such impact.

COLLECT

Almighty Father,
who in your great mercy gladdened the disciples
    with the sight of the risen Lord:
give us such knowledge of his presence with us,
that we may be strengthened and sustained by his risen life
and serve you continually in righteousness and truth;
through Jesus Christ our Lord.

Reflection by **David Ford**

Easter Season

Psalms 108, **110**, 111 *or* 41, **42**, 43
Deuteronomy 8
Ephesians 3.14-end

Saturday 17 April

Ephesians 3.14-end

'... abundantly far more than all we can ask or imagine' (v.20)

This prayer is central to Ephesians, just as the Lord's Prayer is at the centre of the Sermon on the Mount – and they profoundly illuminate each other, just as both of them are illuminated by Jesus' prayer in John 17. Today's is a prayer that stretches our hearts, minds and imaginations, drawing us in all directions – wider, further, higher, deeper – in order to 'know the love of Christ that surpasses knowledge'. It is about our deepest identity ('rooted and grounded') as the Father's family, indwelt by both the Spirit and Christ.

Then, just when we might think God has been asked for the ultimate gift – 'that you might be filled with all the fullness of God' – comes a further stretch: God is able to do 'abundantly far more than all we can ask or imagine'. Like the love that surpasses knowledge, we are to expect things far surpassing anything we can imagine asking for. But it is not only 'things' that come: it is above all people – people to be loved and (sometimes) to love us. Who could ever have imagined in advance the key people – teachers, friends, mentors, partners, children, and more – who have meant most to us? God our Father, who wants us to be 'rooted and grounded in love', continually surprises us, above all through people. And some of them stretch our capacity to love.

COLLECT

Risen Christ,
you filled your disciples with boldness and fresh hope:
strengthen us to proclaim your risen life
and fill us with your peace,
to the glory of God the Father.

Reflection by **David Ford**

Easter Season

Monday 19 April

Psalm **103** *or* **44**
Deuteronomy 9.1-21
Ephesians 4.1-16

Ephesians 4.1-16

'... one ... one ... one ... one ... one ... one ... one ...'

This is as massive an imperative to be united with fellow Christians (and who should ever judge who are 'real' Christians if they trust in Jesus Christ?) as is the prayer of Jesus in John 17. How much energy today goes into considering, planning, organizing, advocating, financing or defending being or becoming divided from other baptized Christians? What might happen if, instead, the energy were spent seeking new ways to love them, to converse with them humbly, gently and patiently, to read Scripture with them (starting with Ephesians 4 and John 17), to pray with them, to 'bear with them' – in short, to 'make every effort to maintain the unity of the Spirit in the bond of peace'? How do you communicate across Christian divisions? How many friendships do you have with those of a very different Christian persuasion?

And would we ever divide the Church if we had met the requirement to have made 'every effort' before deciding to separate? How could we know we had made every conceivable effort? Jesus died to reconcile us with God and with each other: how far will we go to be reconciled? Christians differ from each other on each 'one' mentioned here: on the Church; the Holy Spirit; hope (eschatology); Jesus Christ; faith; baptism; and the unity of God. Yet God continually surprises us with the glorious gift of unity in Christ. Be open to those surprises!

COLLECT

Almighty God,
whose Son Jesus Christ is the resurrection and the life:
raise us, who trust in him,
from the death of sin to the life of righteousness,
that we may seek those things which are above,
where he reigns with you
in the unity of the Holy Spirit,
one God, now and for ever.

Reflection by **David Ford**

Easter Season

Psalm **139** *or* **48**, 52
Deuteronomy 9.23 – 10.5
Ephesians 4.17-end

Tuesday 20 April

Ephesians 4.17-end

'... but only what is useful for building up' (v.29)

What if it were to become an absolute imperative for everyone in the Church that, in all our communications, with others and about others, we had 'only' one aim: to build up a community of love? A community of loving and praising God? Of thanksgiving in everything? Of humble, gentle speech with and about each other? Of patience with those who irritate, anger, offend or even slander us? Of tenderheartedness and kindness? Of forgiveness of wrongs done to us? Of speaking the truth in love? Of words that 'give grace to those who hear'? What if ...?

But absolute imperatives are often disobeyed. Something deeper, more transformative and more effective is needed: to be renewed in the spirit of our minds, to have a radically new beginning, to be given the utterly free gift of a new self, 'created according to the likeness of God in true righteousness and holiness'. This self is who we are created to be, who, when we are liberated from all the false sorts of identity, we realize we are most fulfilled in being. Our deepest desires are fulfilled beyond anything we can ask or imagine. We are loved and freed to love in new ways. We are known deeply and opened up to the depths of God, of other people, of creation, of ourselves. And the absolute imperative becomes our absolute delight.

COLLECT

Risen Christ,
faithful shepherd of your Father's sheep:
teach us to hear your voice
and to follow your command,
that all your people may be gathered into one flock,
to the glory of God the Father.

Reflection by **David Ford**

Easter Season

Wednesday 21 April

Psalm **135** *or* **119.57-80**
Deuteronomy 10.12-end
Ephesians 5.1-14

Ephesians 5.1-14

'… as beloved children … as Christ loved us and gave himself' (vv.1–2)

As we noted earlier, one of the richest and most capacious words in scripture is 'as', inviting us to stretch our thoughts, desires and actions in new directions. What might it mean to 'be imitators of God, as beloved children'? Can we ever take in being loved by God, by one who is perfect love – wise, forgiving, creative, inspiring?

Growing up as God's children is about opening ourselves more and more, day after day, to that inexhaustibly deep love, wisdom, forgiveness, creativity and inspiration. Above all, there is 'as Christ', the beloved Son. He 'gave himself up for us' and said, 'Love one another as I have loved you', and, 'As the Father has sent me, so I send you'. Our vocation, like his, is love.

So, 'as Christ' opens up a way of wholehearted daily loving, though not as an impossible ideal or burdensome duty '… but instead, let there be thanksgiving'. That is the secret. As we appreciate more and more God's love for us, and the overwhelming gift of Jesus, and of the Holy Spirit he breathes into us, gratitude inspires our whole life. As in the best of families, gratitude for love inspires love in return. It overflows in all directions; it is the light of life; and it is the only truly effective counter to the many forms of darkness in ourselves, in our Church, and in our world.

COLLECT

Almighty God,
whose Son Jesus Christ is the resurrection and the life:
raise us, who trust in him,
from the death of sin to the life of righteousness,
that we may seek those things which are above,
where he reigns with you
in the unity of the Holy Spirit,
one God, now and for ever.

Reflection by **David Ford**

Easter Season

Psalm 118 *or* 56, **57** (63*)
Deuteronomy 11.8-end
Ephesians 5.15-end

Thursday 22 April

Ephesians 5.15-end

' ... because the days are evil' (v.16)

There is a widespread sense today too that 'the days are evil', that families and households, institutions, countries, alliances, international organizations, cultural norms, truth in the public sphere, and the very ecosystem we all depend on are being shaken, in danger, under massive strain and often under attack, and that divisions, enmities, and conflicts are intensifying. These are serious times. The first crying need is to live wisely, which means seeking to understand what God desires (the Greek for 'will', *thelēma*, also means 'desire').

And what does God desire? The first thing is to be attuned to who God is and to what God does, and so to praise, adore, rejoice, delight, give thanks and love with all our being. God is God, God is good, God is love, God is light, no matter what the state of the world. That gives us a sure, unshakeable place to stand. But, as the Psalms demonstrate, we are also to cry out in anguish, to lament, to take to heart what is happening, just as God does.

Then we do what we can. Especially, we nurture our relationships, our households and our Church communities. And the primary, all-encompassing, wise guideline (no matter what our line in the culture wars about gender roles) is an image of utter mutuality from making music in harmony together: 'Be subject to one another out of reverence for Christ.' A great mystery indeed!

> Risen Christ,
> faithful shepherd of your Father's sheep:
> teach us to hear your voice
> and to follow your command,
> that all your people may be gathered into one flock,
> to the glory of God the Father.

COLLECT

Reflection by **David Ford**

Easter Season

Friday 23 April

George, martyr,
patron of England

Psalms 5, 146
Joshua 1.1-9
Ephesians 6.10-20

Joshua 1.1-9

'... you shall meditate on it day and night' (v.8)

Reading and rereading 'all that is written in it', soaking ourselves in what God desires so that our desires are shaped by God's, organizing our time so that we are constantly reminded of what an amazing reality we are part of, and above all remembering continually who God is: that is the spring of true confidence, strength and courage. The meaning of 'the law', Torah, is far wider than what law means in our culture – it is more like a whole way of life. It is the way of life Jesus, who was steeped in Torah, summed up as loving God with all your heart, and with all your soul, and with all your mind, and with all your strength, and loving your neighbour as yourself (Mark 12.29–21). Perhaps the greatest text in the Bible on Torah-centred meditation is its longest chapter, Psalm 119. It deserves meditating on.

And 'do not be frightened'. This is repeated so many times in the Bible because fear and anxiety are at the root of so much misery, so many divisions and conflicts, so much prejudice and discrimination, so many unfulfilled lives, so many defeats, so much cowardice. Soldiers and martyrs can be icons of refusal to let fear dominate. St George was both. Tortured and beheaded for refusing to give up his faith, he slew the dragon of fear.

COLLECT

God of hosts,
who so kindled the flame of love
in the heart of your servant George
that he bore witness to the risen Lord
by his life and by his death:
give us the same faith and power of love
that we who rejoice in his triumphs
may come to share with him the fullness of the resurrection;
through Jesus Christ our Lord.

Reflection by **David Ford**

Easter Season

Psalm **34** *or* **68**
Deuteronomy 15.1-18
Ephesians 6.10-end

Saturday 24 April

Ephesians 6.10-end

'... able to withstand ... and having done everything, to stand firm'
(v.13)

Sit, Walk, Stand is a summary of Ephesians by the Chinese church leader Watchman Nee. First, we sit with Jesus in the presence of God, beloved members of an utterly loving family. We also walk the way of service, love and peace, deepening our relationships with God and with others. But, given the 'forces of evil' that control so much in our world, there inevitably come times when we need to stand against them – in smaller or greater ways. Then we need to have equipped ourselves for these testing, evil times by having put on 'the whole armour of God'.

This is forged and made our own in those times of sitting with Jesus and with others (some from earlier centuries) who sit with Jesus. That is where the belt of truth is found and fastened, the breastplate of righteousness (Jesus', not ours) is put on, eagerness to share the gospel is inspired, the shield of deep faith is forged, we find the right sized helmet of salvation (some that may fit others are not for us), and we sharpen 'the sword of the Spirit, which is the word of God'.

Daily, as we walk, we practise with all this. The armour is, of course invisible to most eyes, and exercising with it may lead to some odd-seeming behaviour. But when the evil day does come, we are ready to withstand, persevere and give thanks.

COLLECT

Almighty God,
whose Son Jesus Christ is the resurrection and the life:
raise us, who trust in him,
from the death of sin to the life of righteousness,
that we may seek those things which are above,
where he reigns with you
in the unity of the Holy Spirit,
one God, now and for ever.

Reflection by **David Ford**

Easter Season

Monday 26 April
Mark the Evangelist

Psalms 37.23-end, 148
Isaiah 62.6-10
or Ecclesiasticus 51.13-end
Acts 12.25 – 13.13

Acts 12.25 – 13.13

'... straight paths' (13.10)

A friend of mine has learned the whole of Mark's Gospel by heart. He regularly performs the Gospel around the country. I asked him once to name his favourite verse, and straight away he quoted, 'They were on the road, going up to Jerusalem, and Jesus was walking ahead of them' (Mark 10.32). These few words, my friend feels, go to the heart of all the journeys and geography and jeopardy in Mark. There's the rush and spin of a popular, prophetic ministry, but then there's this hub at the centre of the turning wheel, leading the way. The Way, leading.

Every month, Google sends me my location history. The app – I haven't managed to disable it – tracks and traces my itinerary around the parishes I serve. This passage in Acts functions similarly, as a 'location timeline': Jerusalem to Antioch to Seleucia to Cyprus, Salamis and Paphos, before splitting, with Mark heading back to Jerusalem, Paul and Barnabas to Pamphylia.

When plotted on a map, our daily commutes and schedules, like those of the apostles, look like knots or webs, or the spokes of a careering wheel. When Paul castigates Elymas, he accuses him of making complex what is simple, crooked what is straight. We are familiar with Elymas' paths, the world's ways, and our 'groping for someone to lead' us.

But the true Way is always 'ahead of us', straight and true. And leading us.

COLLECT

Almighty God,
who enlightened your holy Church
through the inspired witness of your evangelist Saint Mark:
grant that we, being firmly grounded in the truth of the gospel,
may be faithful to its teaching both in word and deed;
through Jesus Christ our Lord.

Reflection by **Colin Heber-Percy**

Easter Season

Psalms **19**, 147.1-12 *or* **73**
Deuteronomy 17.8-end
1 Peter 1.13-end

Tuesday 27 April

1 Peter 1.13-end
'... obedience to the truth' (v.22)

Surely truth is a value we assign to certain sentences or propositions? Truth means 'in accordance with the facts'; it can be proven by observation or logical deduction. The truth is something we establish; it's not something we *obey*. Or is it?

Jesus comes to testify to the truth. 'Everyone who belongs to the truth,' he says, 'listens to my voice' (John 18.37). The truth is not only something we obey; we belong to it.

So, do we obey and belong to the truth in the way we obey the regulations of a 'members only' club or the law of the land or the rules of a school? No, it's more fundamental. Aristotle opens his *Metaphysics* with the claim: 'By nature, all men long to know.' Our yearning for the truth is innate, and it makes demands of us: that we abandon our conformity 'to the desires [we] formerly had in ignorance'. Our obedience to this truth is a consequence of our purifying ourselves. And it leads to 'genuine mutual love'. The truth is holy.

To those who have come to believe, Jesus says, 'you will know the truth, and the truth will make you free' (John 8.32). This truth cannot be reduced to adequacy or 'correspondence with data'. Nor does it box us into conformity with the ways of the world. Obedience to the truth sets us free.

The truth is a person.

> Almighty God,
> who through your only-begotten Son Jesus Christ
> have overcome death and opened to us
> the gate of everlasting life:
> grant that, as by your grace going before us
> you put into our minds good desires,
> so by your continual help
> we may bring them to good effect;
> through Jesus Christ our risen Lord.

COLLECT

Reflection by **Colin Heber-Percy**

Easter Season

Wednesday 28 April

Psalms **30**, 147.13-end *or* **77**
Deuteronomy 18.9-end
1 Peter 2.1-10

1 Peter 2.1-10

'... a living stone' (v.4)

Raise your eyes and look up at the west front of Girona Cathedral in northern Spain and you will see a mighty statue of Peter – chiselled, muscular –, a rock if ever there was one. Because, of course, Peter – or Cephas in Greek – is a nickname. It means rock or stone. 'You are Peter,' Jesus says, 'and on this rock I will build my church' (Matthew 16.18).

Despite what sculptors and painters down the centuries have tended to suggest, the Peter of the Gospels is not a hero in the epic mould. He's a normal bloke doing a normal job. He's portrayed as vacillating, muddled, weak. And when push comes to shove, he buckles, denying three times that he even knows Jesus. Not so much a rock, more a pebble. Yet Peter is surely one of the most compelling characters in the Gospels. Because we recognize him. Perhaps we recognize ourselves in him.

In this second chapter of the letter that bears his name, Peter takes his own nickname and mirrors it back on Jesus himself. This 'living stone' may be chosen and precious, but to the unbelievers and the disobedient it is a stumbling-block, a 'rock that makes them fall'.

To be 'built into a spiritual house', we must become like Jesus, 'living stones'. Not like the strong men adorning our temples, but as 'God's people', as 'newborn infants', growing into salvation.

COLLECT

Almighty God,
who through your only-begotten Son Jesus Christ
have overcome death and opened to us
    the gate of everlasting life:
grant that, as by your grace going before us
    you put into our minds good desires,
so by your continual help
we may bring them to good effect;
through Jesus Christ our risen Lord.

Reflection by **Colin Heber-Percy**

Easter Season

Psalms **57**, 148 *or* **78.1-39***
Deuteronomy 19
1 Peter 2.11-end

Thursday 29 April

1 Peter 2.11-end

'... with all deference' (v.18)

I know 'Manners maketh man' and all that, but I worry – as we all do, I suspect – when civility is made to mean deference to or tolerance of an unjust dispensation. After all, tolerance is a conditional good; you first have to ask (and answer) the question: tolerance of what? Are slaves really to accept the authority of their harsh masters, *any* masters? According to Peter, yes.

It is easy to criticize Peter, but it is worth remembering the context in which he is writing, and for whom. His brothers and sisters in Christ are being persecuted and martyred for their faith; a counsel of 'keep your head down' and deference is expedient.

But it is more than that. Deference does not imply approval. And in fact, Peter could be seen in this passage as establishing the ground rules for an irresistible insurgency, living 'for righteousness'. Calls to throw off your shackles, rise, take up arms and fight for your rights can all too easily be accommodated in the endless cycles of political powerplay. Jesus understands this when he commands, 'if anyone strikes you on the right cheek, turn the other also' (Matthew 5.39). To behave like this is to place oneself outside of conventional ethics, to break with the world and its ways.

The real difficulty for Christians comes when we are no longer 'aliens and exiles', no longer slaves but masters: the disaster of Christendom.

COLLECT

Risen Christ,
your wounds declare your love for the world
and the wonder of your risen life:
give us compassion and courage
to risk ourselves for those we serve,
to the glory of God the Father.

Reflection by **Colin Heber-Percy**

Easter Season

Friday 30 April

Psalms **138**, 149 *or* **55**
Deuteronomy 21.22 – 22.8
1 Peter 3.1-12

1 Peter 3.1-12

'... all of you' (v.8)

This well-known, or notorious, passage is often read and interpreted as advocating the acceptance of rigid and discriminatory gender roles. And so it is. But to leave our interpretation at that would be to miss Peter's point almost entirely. We may no longer demand or expect (or want) gender-specific conduct and behaviour on the part of husbands and wives; we may no longer even recognize gender as a male/female binary. But we do discriminate, differentiating ourselves from one another in myriad ways. And so we should.

Peter is not simply assigning roles to classes of people for the sake of some conservative social agenda; he's drawing our attention to the differences between us in order to reveal the deeper 'unity of spirit' to which we are all called.

This unity is not threatened by our differences; nor are our differences to be dissolved into a flat equality. Rather, the unity that Peter has in mind depends on or derives from our very differences. As Paul points out to the Corinthians, the sun's glory is different from the moon's glory, 'indeed, star differs from star in glory' (1 Corinthians 15.41).

We differ from one another, and our differences are glorious. The difference could be sex or gender, could be skin colour, could be creed, could be class. Go ahead and discriminate, but discriminate always with 'sympathy, love for one another, a tender heart, and a humble mind'.

COLLECT

Almighty God,
who through your only-begotten Son Jesus Christ
have overcome death and opened to us
    the gate of everlasting life:
grant that, as by your grace going before us
    you put into our minds good desires,
so by your continual help
we may bring them to good effect;
through Jesus Christ our risen Lord.

Reflection by **Colin Heber-Percy**

Easter Season

Psalms 139, 146
Proverbs 4.10-18
James 1.1-12

Saturday 1 May
Philip and James, Apostles

James 1.1-12
'being double-minded' (v.8)

In English, as in many European languages, the word 'doubt' has the same root as the word 'double'. To doubt is to double or to be double. So, when in doubt we say we're in two minds. If something is sure and certain, then there's no shadow of a doubt. Doubts cast shadows, double themselves, proliferate. Doubts creep in. They're plural and pluralizing. In the Gospels, 'Doubting' Thomas is double by nature: he's a twin.

Sometimes we feel assailed by manifold doubts, doubts crashing over us like waves on the shore. But James reverses this way of thinking. When we doubt, it's not the waves pummelling us; we *are* the waves, 'driven and tossed by the wind'. Doubts can be doldrums, or tsunamis.

James talks about the rich in the 'midst of a busy life'. But 'busy' doesn't quite capture his meaning. James chooses a Greek word that describes a life as travelling, passing or criss-crossing. Doubt is associated in his mind with movement, with our being moved. In the tidal currents of our fluid and wavelike lives, we're called to hold fast, to be 'complete, lacking in nothing'. The path to this completeness, simplicity and maturity is endurance.

And it is striking that James does not identify this endurance with strength or resolve, but with love. The 'crown of life' is promised to those who stand the test out of love for God.

COLLECT

Almighty Father,
whom truly to know is eternal life:
teach us to know your Son Jesus Christ
as the way, the truth, and the life;
that we may follow the steps of your holy apostles
Philip and James,
and walk steadfastly in the way that leads to your glory;
through Jesus Christ our Lord.

Reflection by **Colin Heber-Percy**

Easter Season

Monday 3 May

Psalms **65** *or* **80**, 82
Deuteronomy 26
1 Peter 4.1-11

1 Peter 4.1-11

'The end of all things is near' (v.7)

Some may remember the so-called '2012 Phenomenon', a prediction of the end of the world based on 'evidence' in certain ancient Mesoamerican calendars. As the date approached – 21 December was favoured by many – scholars pointed out that the predictions entirely misrepresented Mayan ideas; and astronomers declared themselves unable to detect any worrying cosmic conditions. But some waited, nonetheless, with bated breath. Of course, nothing happened, or nothing cataclysmic.

No doubt Peter means us to understand that the apocalypse is drawing near, that his readers are to prepare for the '*eschaton*', for the end times. Christianity has millenarianism woven through its DNA. But is there an alternative way of understanding eschatology, of reading 'the end of all things is near'?

In Revelation, God describes himself as 'the Alpha and the Omega, the beginning and the end' (Revelation 21.6). What if we're called to wait, not for a specific event on a specific date, but for God, for God *as our end*?

Writing a few hundred years before Peter composed his letter, the Greek philosopher Aristotle described four causes or explanations for anything. Any given thing, he argues, will have a material cause (what it's made of), an efficient cause (what made it), a formal cause (what shape, form or pattern it has), and a final cause (what it's for).

What if God is our final cause, our end, our goal? And he is near.

COLLECT

God our redeemer,
you have delivered us from the power of darkness
and brought us into the kingdom of your Son:
grant, that as by his death he has recalled us to life,
so by his continual presence in us he may raise us
    to eternal joy;
through Jesus Christ our Lord.

Reflection by **Colin Heber-Percy**

Easter Season

Psalms 124, 125, **126**, 127 *or* 87, **89.1-18**
Deuteronomy 28.1-14
1 Peter 4.12-end

Tuesday 4 May

1 Peter 4.12-end

'... something strange' (v.12)

In a foreign city, I always enjoy visiting the churches and cathedrals. But recently, I found myself unsettled. Outside Lisbon, where the Tagus River meets the Atlantic, is the Jerónimos Monastery. In the monastery's refectory is a series of characterful paintings on ceramic tiles, telling the story of Joseph. One scene shows Joseph's brothers selling him into slavery. As Joseph is led away to Egypt, the young men sit around a tree stump, counting out the 20 pieces of silver they've exchanged for their brother.

Although established before Portugal's global empire, this monastery was enriched by the flow of wealth back into the country from its new influence in South America, Africa and the Far East. It's surely no accident that, as ill-gotten colonial wealth poured into the Church's coffers, religious buildings chose to adorn themselves with images of innocence. The transaction depicted on the tiles struck me as an encapsulation of the journey of the Church, from Joseph to his greedy brothers, from 'reviled', 'suffering' and poor to triumphalist, exploitative and rich.

How are we to respond to this radical break with Peter's call 'to obey the gospel' and to 'do good'? Perhaps we could reflect on how Joseph's brothers feel when, years later, Joseph judges them with mercy and forgiveness: 'At this they lost heart and turned trembling to one another, saying, "What is this that God has done to us?"' (Genesis 42.28).

Something strange.

> Risen Christ,
> by the lakeside you renewed your call to your disciples:
> help your Church to obey your command
> and draw the nations to the fire of your love,
> to the glory of God the Father.

COLLECT

Reflection by **Colin Heber-Percy**

Easter Season

Wednesday 5 May Psalms **132**, 133 *or* **119.105-128**
Deuteronomy 28.58-end
1 Peter 5

1 Peter 5

'... clothe yourselves with humility' (v.5)

The close of Peter's first letter echoes the end of John's Gospel. References to flocks and shepherds recall Jesus' commissioning Peter to 'Feed my lambs', 'Tend my sheep', 'Feed my sheep' (John 21.15-17). And Peter urges us to clothe ourselves, just as he clothed himself before jumping out of the boat to greet his Risen Lord on the beach (John 21.7).

But how do we clothe ourselves with humility? In his letter to the Colossians, Paul amplifies Peter's call. He adds compassion, kindness, meekness and patience to the list and concludes 'Above all, clothe yourselves with love' (3.12-14).

Do you put on humility or compassion or love in the way you would a new shirt or coat? If you can put it on, can you take it off again? Are the fruits of the spirit a costume? But Paul continues: 'let the peace of Christ rule in your hearts, to which indeed you were called in the one body' (Colossians 3.15).

You can take off your hat, change your shoes, pull off your sweatshirt, but you can't pull off your *body*. Peter is calling us, not to change our costume, but to change ourselves.

This means recognizing that our true, shared nature is humble, loving. We're good at recognizing our outer garments, good at recognizing what sets us apart from one another, but we're terrible at recognizing what we share – *as one body*.

COLLECT

God our redeemer,
you have delivered us from the power of darkness
and brought us into the kingdom of your Son:
grant, that as by his death he has recalled us to life,
so by his continual presence in us he may raise us
  to eternal joy;
through Jesus Christ our Lord.

Reflection by **Colin Heber-Percy**

Ascension Day

Psalms 110, 150
Isaiah 52.7-end
Hebrews 7. [11-25] 26-end

Thursday 6 May

Ascension Day

Hebrews 7. [11-25] 26-end

'... exalted above the heavens' (v.26)

Depictions of Christ's Ascension tend to be faintly silly: faces craning upwards, the disciples watching Christ disappearing headfirst into a cloud.

The least silly depiction of the Ascension I know is in the thousand year old former church dedicated to the All Blessed Mother of God – the Pammakaristos in Istanbul. In a corner of the building are the remains of a mosaic. It shows three pairs of bare feet. But the pair of feet in the middle are just a hair's breadth off the ground. The artist has chosen to depict not the final awe-inspiring ascent into the sky, like a Marvel superhero, but the first moment of ... lift. There's something natural about its supernaturalness, something intimate.

The writer of the letter to the Hebrews eschews all the special effects and a 'levitationist' reading of the Ascension. In fact, it is neither levitationist nor Levitical because the emphasis here places Christ outside of any human and priestly hierarchy or order. This is a high priest not according to a 'legal requirement concerning physical *descent*' and so this same high priest does not owe their subsequent exaltation to any physical *ascent*.

Exaltation is therefore not measured vertically, but horizontally. We are called to 'approach God *through* him'. For the disciples standing either side of Christ in the Pammakaristos mosaic, it's not a case of looking up for Christ, but of turning to face him. And so it is for us.

COLLECT

Grant, we pray, almighty God,
that as we believe your only-begotten Son
our Lord Jesus Christ
to have ascended into the heavens,
so we in heart and mind may also ascend
and with him continually dwell;
who is alive and reigns with you,
in the unity of the Holy Spirit,
one God, now and for ever.

Reflection by **Colin Heber-Percy**

Ascension until Pentecost

Friday 7 May

Psalms 20, **81** *or* **88** (95)
Exodus 35.30 – 36.1
Galatians 5.13-end

Exodus 35.30 – 36.1

'He has filled them' (35.35)

Imhotep, architect of the pyramid at Saqqara in Egypt, is often referred to as the first artist about whom we know anything at all. But Bezalel and Oholiab must run him a close second.

What I love about this text from Exodus is the way artistic skill is described as given, as filling, as being inspired. Talk to a stonemason or an embroiderer, a poet, a songwriter or a musician, any artist, and their description of their creative practice will often use the same language of givenness and inspiration.

Thomas Aquinas, the great Scholastic theologian, defined a human being as a *capax dei*, a capacity for God. A capacity is an emptiness, a space, a void to be filled; it's a lack. Suitcases have a capacity, and fuel tanks. And so do we.

On 21 December 1817, the poet John Keats wrote a letter to his brothers in which he describes how vital it is for a person to have what he calls a 'Negative Capability, that is, when a person is capable of being in uncertainties, Mysteries, doubts, without any irritable reaching after fact & reason'.

We are called to be uncertain, open to the Mystery (capital M), not busily, fretfully trying to fill the gap with facts and reasons and positivity, but allowing ourselves to be filled by the Holy Spirit. Our emptiness, our brokenness, our need, our *capacity* – is precisely where the Holy Spirit enters.

COLLECT

Grant, we pray, almighty God,
that as we believe your only-begotten Son
    our Lord Jesus Christ
to have ascended into the heavens,
so we in heart and mind may also ascend
and with him continually dwell;
who is alive and reigns with you,
in the unity of the Holy Spirit,
one God, now and for ever.

Reflection by **Colin Heber-Percy**

Ascension until Pentecost

Psalms 21, **47** *or* 96, **97**, 100
Numbers 11.16-17, 24-29
1 Corinthians 2

Saturday 8 May

Numbers 11.16-17, 24-29

'... and the spirit rested on them' (v.26)

There are instructions, elders, officers; there are numbers and a registration process.

And then there's the spirit.

Eldad and Medad appear to fall outside of the designated 'landing zone', and yet the spirit rests on them. Outraged, Joshua wants to ring-fence and guard the spirit, but Moses recognizes the spirit's unruly nature.

Many generations later, Jesus will remind Nicodemus that, 'The wind blows where it chooses' and 'you do not know where it comes from or where it goes' (John 3.8).

Eldad and Medad 'had not gone out to the tent', yet the spirit rests on them all the same. Similarly, Nicodemus chooses to leave the tent of meeting (or the Temple), coming to Jesus secretly and alone, at night, because by day he is numbered among those on the 'inside'. He is a Pharisee, one of the 'elders of the people and officers over them'. In Jesus' day, the elders no longer bear 'the burden of the people'; they *are* the burden of the people.

This passage from Numbers reminds us that there are those who would like to constrain us and force us to comply with the world's rules, to number and classify us, to decide on whom the spirit may rest and on whom it may not. And there are those, like Moses, who wish the spirit might rest on each and every one of us, regardless of the rules. Be like Moses.

COLLECT

Risen Christ,
you have raised our human nature to the throne of heaven:
help us to seek and serve you,
that we may join you at the Father's side,
where you reign with the Spirit in glory,
now and for ever.

Reflection by **Colin Heber-Percy**

Ascension until Pentecost

Monday 10 May Psalms **93**, 96, 97 *or* **98**, 99, 101
Numbers 27.15-end
1 Corinthians 3

Numbers 27.15-end

'... both he and the Israelites with him' (v.21)

I once stood before a room full of theology students, in Spain, speaking in French, and found, to my surprise, that I could not find the words I needed in my mother tongue: French does not have a word for 'leader'. We have different words for different types of leadership in different contexts. Yet the word is ubiquitous in English – and in Church circles too. Scripture gives us many different forms of leadership – none perfect, with many failures (perhaps far more than successes). Leadership is a dangerous enterprise.

More importantly, however, a theme recurs and appears here, as Moses plans for his own successor: that leaders and congregation belong together. Verse 21 makes this very clear: it is not just the new leader who is commissioned, but the new leader *with* the people together. It is a specific shape of relationship that is placed before the Lord. Leaders are shaped by context, and so specific shapes of leadership are context dependent, made possible by the people who choose, or accept, certain leaders. This, in turns, shapes a pattern in Scripture of refusing to simply scapegoat leaders, but instead looking at their joint responsibility and duties.

What shape of leaders do we make possible as communities – locally and nationally? What gaps are there between the leaders we want and the leaders we need? And how do we properly assess the responsibilities of leaders and people each, and the culture we shape together?

COLLECT

O God the King of glory,
you have exalted your only Son Jesus Christ
with great triumph to your kingdom in heaven:
we beseech you, leave us not comfortless,
but send your Holy Spirit to strengthen us
and exalt us to the place where our Saviour Christ
   is gone before,
who is alive and reigns with you,
in the unity of the Holy Spirit,
one God, now and for ever.

Reflection by **Isabelle Hamley**

Ascension until Pentecost

Psalms 98, **99**, 100 or **106*** (*or* 103)
1 Samuel 10.1-10
1 Corinthians 12.1-13

Tuesday 11 May

1 Samuel 10.1-10
'God gave him another heart' (v.9)

I wonder what was going on for Samuel. He had led Israel for decades, and in his waning years, the people asked for a king, rather than Samuel's sons. They wanted to be like everyone else around – even if that meant taking on all the disadvantages of kings and empires, the inequality and oppression that came with them. In the face of their insistence, God makes provision for a king, a provision the people are warned will be disastrous in the end.

What was Samuel thinking as he anointed Saul? There are promises – God will not forget Israel just because they insist on doing things their way. God will not even walk away, but instead, work with Israel in their imperfection and limitations. How hard it must have been for Samuel to see what God's possible future could have been, and yet become an instrument of a negotiated, compromised future – a future nevertheless where God will be present and active, working for the good of God's people.

Saul's kingship will not end well, and the hopefulness and promise of the beginning will collapse, showing that God's previous warnings about kings had been right. Yet, God, Saul and Samuel work together here, because it is a story as all others in Scripture, a story of grace; a story that says, even if you make the wrong choices, God will still work for the good of God's people.

COLLECT

Risen, ascended Lord,
as we rejoice at your triumph,
fill your Church on earth with power and compassion,
that all who are estranged by sin
may find forgiveness and know your peace,
to the glory of God the Father.

Reflection by **Isabelle Hamley**

Ascension until Pentecost

Wednesday 12 May

Psalms 2, **29** or 110, **111**, 112
1 Kings 19.1-18
Matthew 3.13-end

1 Kings 19.1-18

'... a sound of sheer silence' (v.12)

We often talk about the cost of failure. But what about the cost of success? In this extraordinary passage, Elijah triumphs magnificently over the prophets of Baal, showing that God is present and active and will act when summoned – all of which should make him feel on top of the world and secure, knowing that God has responded to him in the face of implacable adversity.

And yet, Elijah is terrified and sinks into a deep depression. He withdraws into himself and flees to the desert. Success has a cost. It has a physical cost (Elijah is told to eat, drink and sleep), an emotional cost (Elijah is fearful of what others will do in the face of his success, and unsure of where he himself stands within it), and a spiritual cost: what do you do when God shows up – and with the fear that God may not show up tomorrow?

God's answer did not come with obvious 'success' – but in an affirmation of God's presence through the ups and downs: in care for Elijah's soul and body, in giving him space in the desert for doubt and exhaustion, and, more than anything, in the revelation of presence in the midst of absence – in a sound of sheer silence, rather than the trappings of outward success. Where do we each look for the presence of God?

COLLECT

O God the King of glory,
you have exalted your only Son Jesus Christ
with great triumph to your kingdom in heaven:
we beseech you, leave us not comfortless,
but send your Holy Spirit to strengthen us
and exalt us to the place where our Saviour Christ
   is gone before,
who is alive and reigns with you,
in the unity of the Holy Spirit,
one God, now and for ever.

Reflection by **Isabelle Hamley**

Ascension until Pentecost

Psalms **24**, 72 *or* 113, **115**
Ezekiel 11.14-20
Matthew 9.35 – 10.20

Thursday 13 May

Ezekiel 11.14-20

'I will give ... them a heart of flesh' (v.19)

Flesh often has bad press in Christian circles. Here, however, 'flesh' is positive. Our bodies are meant to be a place of love, of grace, of the kind of vulnerability that means we treat one another gently and generously.

Ezekiel's vision of a renewed future for Israel is a vision of hearts transformed – from stone to flesh. Hearts of stone are the hearts that lead to increasing inequality and injustice in the nation, of alliance with powerful nations at the expense of trust in God and following God's wisdom on building flourishing communities. Hearts of flesh, in contrast, are bent towards relationship, attentiveness to others and the impact of our actions.

Flesh in the Old Testament is often associated with fragility. To be people of flesh means we do not impose our will on others or act as if we are invulnerable and others do not matter. To recognize that we are flesh is to accept the limitations and fragility of being human, and to construct a world that cares for this reality: a world that gives dignity to one another; that values justice – that cares for the more vulnerable; that shares resources generously and cherishes life. Above all, to be given hearts of flesh is to recognize we are not God – that we are small and in need of God's wisdom, power and strength to be able to build the community that the prophet promises.

COLLECT

Risen, ascended Lord,
as we rejoice at your triumph,
fill your Church on earth with power and compassion,
that all who are estranged by sin
may find forgiveness and know your peace,
to the glory of God the Father.

Reflection by **Isabelle Hamley**

Ascension until Pentecost

Friday 14 May
Matthias the Apostle

Psalms 16, 147.1-12
1 Samuel 2.27-35
Acts 2.37-end

1 Samuel 2.27-35

'... those who despise me shall be treated with contempt' (v.30)

Some messages are best delivered by strangers and neutral, independent parties. Here, an unnamed 'man of God' delivers a message of terrible judgement on Eli and his sons. Eli is a priest, so are his sons – but they are not 'men of God'. They are men who abuse their power and position.

If we read verse 22, a little before today's passage, we find Eli's sons abusing young women who serve at the temple's entrance. In other words – older men abusing vulnerable young women in a religious context. Eli remonstrated feebly with his sons, but took no strong, remedial action. This is a story of abuse, and of the failure of the temple institution to respond well, manipulated by a family out to gain wealth and power rather than serve the people. They have completely perverted the goodness of God's provision.

The man of God's words, harsh as they are, uncover the heart of God for the vulnerable, describing the judgement that rightly comes to those who are meant to enable others to grow in faith, but instead abuse, maim and extinguish life and hope. It is a judgement on someone who knew about the corruption, who had the power to change things and failed to do so.

This text may have been written thousands of years ago, and yet, sadly, its message of judgement for perverted leaders and of God's utter compassion for victims is as needed today as it was then.

COLLECT

Almighty God,
who in the place of the traitor Judas
chose your faithful servant Matthias
to be of the number of the Twelve:
preserve your Church from false apostles
and, by the ministry of faithful pastors and teachers,
keep us steadfast in your truth;
through Jesus Christ our Lord.

Reflection by **Isabelle Hamley**

Ascension until Pentecost

Psalms 42, **43** *or* 120, **121**, 122
Micah 3.1-8
Ephesians 6.10-20

Saturday 15 May

Micah 3.1-8

'Should you not know justice?' (v.1)

Micah does not mince his words. The book is a wholesale upbraiding of the people of God, with a central accusation that they have divorced faith from justice. Prophets can often be described as 'speaking truth to power', whom modern day would-be prophets emulate in impassioned speech, taking issue with all the wrongs of the world. Yet this would only be emulating half of the picture.

The prophets do not simply harangue those who have done wrong; they often weep at the possibility of judgement, ask for mercy and predict God's future compassion and restoration. 'Should you not know justice?' is a question all need to ask: prophetic justice exists in a double solidarity and double compassion: for those who are hurt, and those who sit under judgement (with a significant overlap between the two). Prophetic calls for justice do not assume that the prophet stands over the unjust, in righteous judgement, but instead, they stand as a part of the people who both suffer injustice and will suffer judgement.

Prophetic justice is a call for all to imagine a radically different world, rather than a tweaked version of the present world with different people in charge. It is a call to have our imaginations and actions completely transformed by an economy of radical grace, dignity and generosity. Micah needs to ask the question, because most of us have imaginations too small to comprehend the radical justice of God's kingdom.

COLLECT

O God the King of glory,
you have exalted your only Son Jesus Christ
with great triumph to your kingdom in heaven:
we beseech you, leave us not comfortless,
but send your Holy Spirit to strengthen us
and exalt us to the place where our Saviour Christ
is gone before,
who is alive and reigns with you,
in the unity of the Holy Spirit,
one God, now and for ever.

Reflection by **Isabelle Hamley**

Ordinary Time

Monday 17 May

Psalms 123, 124, 125, **126**
2 Chronicles 17.1-12
Romans 1.1-17

Romans 1.1-17

'For I am not ashamed of the gospel' (v.16)

On the day after Pentecost, we dive into the longest and most complex of the letters of Paul. We have six weeks to mull and reflect on this extraordinary document. Although scholarship is still engaged in active conversation about the Pauline letters, there is pretty firm agreement that this is one of Paul's later compositions, probably written more than 20 years after his conversion (or call). As such, what we find here is Paul's message to the Church at a pretty developed stage of his thinking. It's a big document, both in terms of its relative length compared to Paul's other letters, and in terms of the theology, the message about the gospel, of which he is, in that striking word, unashamed.

We will take it steadily through the first couple of chapters! We might notice two themes as we strike out into this letter: Christ, and community. One day after Whitsun, we read Paul relating the account of the birth, death and resurrection of Jesus Christ, of whom he describes himself as 'a servant'. It is this crucified and risen Christ who forms a community of 'grace and apostleship', and it is that community that Paul addresses in everything that follows, and for whom he prays 'without ceasing'. At the outset of this letter, we might take the opportunity to refocus on the Christ whom we serve, and pray for the community in which we are set.

COLLECT

O Lord, from whom all good things come:
grant to us your humble servants,
that by your holy inspiration
we may think those things that are good,
and by your merciful guiding may perform the same;
through our Lord Jesus Christ.

Reflection by **Tom Clammer**

Ordinary Time

Psalms **132**, 133
2 Chronicles 18.1-27
Romans 1.18-end

Tuesday 18 May

Romans 1.18-end

'Claiming to be wise, they became fools' (v.22)

Having opened the letter with the great vista of the incarnation, death and resurrection of Christ, Paul moves swiftly into a conversation about huge concepts such as 'wrath', 'ungodliness' and the truth. It has often been said that the great theme of the letter to the Romans is the righteousness of God, and even in this opening chapter, we find Paul looking at God, looking at humanity and creation more generally, and noticing that there is a problem. There are aspects of these few verses that some people will struggle with more than others, particularly perhaps those concerning sexuality. Volumes have been written, views expressed, the text parsed, and the conversation continues. So it must, for we must continually wrestle with Scripture, seeking for the living Word: Christ.

In the midst of this message, we find one of the absolutely central challenges of St Paul: humanity has exchanged the *thing* for something *less* than the thing. Idolatry will be a repeated theme, because we commit idolatry each time we worship, prioritize and give power over us to something less than God. Even face to face with the stupendous wonder of the incarnate, crucified and resurrected Christ, and the creation that witnesses to his power and nature, we still reach out our hand and grab something lesser. What is it that we exchange 'the glory of the immortal God' for? What will be the trap, the snare, for us today?

COLLECT

O Lord, from whom all good things come:
grant to us your humble servants,
that by your holy inspiration
we may think those things that are good,
and by your merciful guiding may perform the same;
through our Lord Jesus Christ.

Reflection by **Tom Clammer**

Ordinary Time

Wednesday 19 May

Psalm **119.153-end**
2 Chronicles 18.2 – end of 19
Romans 2.1-16

Romans 2.1-16

'... the riches of his kindness and forbearance and patience' (v.4)

In startling language, Paul continues to unfold important parts of his teaching. Today's reading invites us to reflect on two themes in particular. The first of those concerns the human tendency to pass judgement, and the second has to do with the final judgement.

Taking the first one first: Paul offers a clear challenge to hypocrisy. He accuses his readers of passing judgement on other people while being guilty of doing exactly the same things themselves. This challenge is, of course, not something unique to Paul's writing. We recall Christ's warning to be very careful about picking up on the tiny speck of dust in our neighbour's eye, while we still have a scaffolding plank sticking out of our own. We might take a moment today to notice what particular plank might be bobbing around in front of our face, and take the opportunity for a bit of an honest look at ourselves.

And then there is the final judgement. Paul's language is again vivid. A moment of reckoning, whatever that might actually look like, is a deep part of the Christian tradition. There will come a moment when we and God will have a heart-to-heart. Has our life been lived, as far as possible, as if we really desire 'the riches of his kindness and forbearance'? That's a glorious and positive phrase amid some of the more alarming stuff. How can we live towards that hope today?

COLLECT

O Lord, from whom all good things come:
grant to us your humble servants,
that by your holy inspiration
we may think those things that are good,
and by your merciful guiding may perform the same;
through our Lord Jesus Christ.

Reflection by **Tom Clammer**

Ordinary Time

Psalms 143, 146
2 Chronicles 20.1-23
Romans 2.17-end

Thursday 20 May

Romans 2.17-end

'... it is spiritual and not literal' (v.29)

Today's verses, following immediately on from yesterday, continue to develop the theme of the risks of hypocrisy. Are the people of God those who perform certain actions and undergo certain rituals, or is there something deeper, something inward, that needs to be addressed? Paul is very clear that the nature of our identity as members of God's family has to do with an internal spiritual transformation. It is, in his words, 'a matter of the heart'. And in a long list of virtues and dangers, he contrasts those who live the life of the transformed heart with those who condemn behaviours in others, while at the same time secretly delighting in them in the hidden and secret places of their life.

How will we live the life of the transformed person today? What does that actually look like in our behaviours, our interactions with other people, the decisions we make, the words that we say or choose not to say? In a world where so often it seems that those in leadership, whether secular or religious, seem to have one rule for themselves and one rule for everyone else, there's a call to a radically different way of being here. In those glorious words of Paul, we are invited to accept a transformation that is 'spiritual and not literal'. What might it be like to say yes to that invitation?

COLLECT

O Lord, from whom all good things come:
grant to us your humble servants,
that by your holy inspiration
we may think those things that are good,
and by your merciful guiding may perform the same;
through our Lord Jesus Christ.

Reflection by **Tom Clammer**

Ordinary Time

Friday 21 May

Psalms 142, **144**
2 Chronicles 22.10 – end of 23
Romans 3.1-20

Romans 3.1-20

'Although everyone is a liar, let God be proved true' (v.4)

Three chapters into Romans, it's probably worth restating that Paul is doing something large-scale and reasonably systematic in this letter, which isn't easy to follow in these sorts of bite-sized chunks. Those who want to dig deeper into the structure and complexity of his argument will find any number of commentaries and sermon series to get their teeth into. In this section, Paul wrestles with what the distinct place of the Jewish people might be in God's plan, given what we have explored about circumcision and outward signs of faith in the previous chapter.

A key point to take from this rather complex passage is that we need to be honest about the human condition. Human beings are not God. Paul might be talking specifically about Judaism here, but the point is surely broader. We make a huge mistake when we, whoever we are, forget that God is God and that we are not. His carefully curated quotations, mostly from the Psalms, remind us of that. But the other great reminder here is that no matter how far God's chosen people – and of course at our baptism we are told, 'Christ claims you for his own' – might stray, our inability to answer the call properly can never affect God's 'truthfulness'. Fridays are traditionally days for deeper confession in the Christian tradition. We might spend a moment on that today, while never losing sight of God's unchangeable fidelity.

COLLECT

O Lord, from whom all good things come:
grant to us your humble servants,
that by your holy inspiration
we may think those things that are good,
and by your merciful guiding may perform the same;
through our Lord Jesus Christ.

Reflection by **Tom Clammer**

Ordinary Time

Psalm 147
2 Chronicles 24.1-22
Romans 3.21-end

Saturday 22 May

Romans 3.21-end

'... he justifies the one who has faith in Jesus' (v.26)

The church that I attended as a teenager was keen on 'memory verses'. We were encouraged to write down scriptural texts and carry them around in our pocket, for several weeks, taking them out and reading them at opportune moments. Two of those memory verses came from this chapter. For weeks as a teenager, I carried around 'all have sinned and fall short of the glory of God', as well as 'a person is justified by faith apart from works prescribed by the law'. Excellent texts, certainly, opening up all sorts of important things about being honest about our sins, and about how we are saved.

I wish we had memorized other verses in this section. Into this chapter, the striking name of Jesus Christ appears like a lightning bolt. Suddenly rather than wrestling with theological concepts we are looking at a man. In six verses, Paul mentions Jesus by name three times, and we are reminded of the absolute centrality of the relationship with a *person*, not a set of doctrinal precepts, that is at the heart of Paul's faith. The Damascus Road was an encounter with a man: 'I am Jesus, whom you are persecuting' (Acts 9.5).

It is at once extraordinarily profound and beautifully simple to remember that when we try to respond in faith to our God, we are reaching out for a person. For a best friend. Someone in whose grace we find our justification.

> O Lord, from whom all good things come:
> grant to us your humble servants,
> that by your holy inspiration
> we may think those things that are good,
> and by your merciful guiding may perform the same;
> through our Lord Jesus Christ.

COLLECT

Reflection by **Tom Clammer**

Ordinary Time

Monday 24 May

Psalms 1, 2, 3
2 Chronicles 26.1-21
Romans 4.1-12

Romans 4.1-12

'... such faith is reckoned as righteousness' (v.5)

Hot on the heels of wrestling with the doctrine of the Trinity yesterday, we return to Romans and more wrestling: this time about the relationship between how we are saved and what we might do as an expression of that salvation. Again, Paul is thinking aloud about the relationship between Jews and Gentiles because his ministry has primarily been among the latter, and he's trying to work out where the ancient and important mark of circumcision fits into salvation history. Among other things, we have an extraordinary image of the history of the Abrahamic faith today, summarized in that description of Abraham receiving circumcision, ultimately, as the ancestor of 'all who believe without being circumcised'.

The heart of this passage is about getting straight in our heads that the things that we do (whether that be rituals, particular prayers, giving of our time or money, paid or charitable work, or whatever) are all responses to grace freely received, and not means of purchasing or convincing God into giving them to us. The word that Paul uses is 'seal', which is a word that is very much associated with the operation of the Holy Spirit, and with the way in which God's promises are mediated to us. We might think over our particular ministries, our offerings to God, and pray into them today. We might also remind ourselves that all of them are an enormous 'thank you'.

COLLECT

Almighty and everlasting God,
you have given us your servants grace,
by the confession of a true faith,
to acknowledge the glory of the eternal Trinity
and in the power of the divine majesty to worship the Unity:
keep us steadfast in this faith,
that we may evermore be defended from all adversities;
through Jesus Christ our Lord.

Reflection by **Tom Clammer**

Ordinary Time

Psalms **5**, 6 (8)
2 Chronicles 28
Romans 4.13-end

Tuesday 25 May

Romans 4.13-end

'Hoping against hope, he believed' (v.18)

Striking in today's reading is the introduction of the word 'hope'. It is an important word for Paul, and perhaps most famously appears in his great assertion that 'faith, hope, and love abide, these three' (1 Corinthians 13.13). Hope would seem to be baked into the Christian experience, the Christian journey. We are to hope even in apparently hopeless circumstances. Christians are those who, despite all evidence to the contrary, are convinced that things will get better rather than worse.

Abraham appears again today in Paul's working out of exactly what justification and righteousness might be like, and he is held up as an example of faithful hoping. Though ancient himself, and married to someone seemingly unable to bear a child at this stage in life, hope allows him to stare into the sky and imagine descendants as numerous as the starry lights above him.

What do we hope for? Where does hope fit into our daily life of prayer, and perhaps our active life as Christians as well? Are there seemingly insurmountable challenges, intractable problems? Do we sometimes feel walled in? Trapped? How big do we allow our hope to be? We could do worse things than return to the 'faith, hope, love' model of that which is eternal, and use it as a touchstone, daily, of how our lives of faith are progressing.

COLLECT

Holy God,
faithful and unchanging:
enlarge our minds with the knowledge of your truth,
and draw us more deeply into the mystery of your love,
that we may truly worship you,
Father, Son and Holy Spirit,
one God, now and for ever.

Reflection by **Tom Clammer**

Ordinary Time

Wednesday 26 May

Psalm 119.1-32
2 Chronicles 29.1-19
Romans 5.1-11

Romans 5.1-11

'... we have peace with God through our Lord Jesus Christ' (v.1)

Having spent the last four chapters in a detailed and complex working through of concepts of justification, righteousness, faith, works, and the way in which Jews and Gentiles alike have access to God's grace, chapter 5 feels like a set of summary conclusions. This is reinforced in the English translation by the chapter beginning with the word 'Therefore ...'. Three sections of this chapter actually begin like that, though we won't notice that as profoundly this year because of tomorrow's feast. Do take the time to read the whole chapter at some point though and feel the emphasis of those 'Therefores ...'.

Another important word is striking today: 'peace'. What our justification means is that we have 'peace with God'. That's another extraordinary and wonderful statement, and one that it might be worth just holding in our minds today. What does it mean to have peace with God? Think about the most peaceful, the most harmonious, human relationship that you can imagine, and extrapolate that. And then maybe just play with the list of really important words in verses 3-6. Endurance, character and hope are wonderful, deep, words in which we can explore some of what it might be like to have the Holy Spirit entering into our hearts as the very presence of God's love.

Is there something you need to endure today? How might your Christian character and your Christian hope resource and ready you for that?

COLLECT

Almighty and everlasting God,
you have given us your servants grace,
by the confession of a true faith,
to acknowledge the glory of the eternal Trinity
and in the power of the divine majesty to worship the Unity:
keep us steadfast in this faith,
that we may evermore be defended from all adversities;
through Jesus Christ our Lord.

Reflection by **Tom Clammer**

Ordinary Time

Psalm 147
Deuteronomy 8.2-16
1 Corinthians 10.1-17

Thursday 27 May
Day of Thanksgiving for the Institution of Holy Communion (Corpus Christi)

Deuteronomy 8.2-16

'You shall eat your fill and bless the Lord' (v.10)

Our adventure through the opening chapters of Romans is broken today by the lovely feast of Corpus Christi: an opportunity outside Holy Week to give thanks for the institution of the Holy Communion. At first glance, it might seem peculiar that the compilers of this resource have given us the Deuteronomy reading to reflect on, rather than that from 1 Corinthians, which explicitly refers to the sharing of bread and wine. Further reflection, however, helps us to see that the themes in both readings today are to do with faithfulness and nourishment. We are to remember God's faithfulness to us, and to believe that God will nourish us in the future.

'Remember', we are commanded in verse 2, and that word is of course absolutely inseparable from the communion service: 'Do this in remembrance of me.' God's faithfulness is such that, metaphorically at least, no matter what it is that we are carrying, no matter what our burdens might be, and no matter how long or difficult our Christian journey might feel at times, our clothes don't wear out and our feet don't swell. In other words, we are nourished to sufficiency. And as the reading progresses, we are asked to remember and recognize that source of nourishment, and accord God the glory, rather than congratulating ourselves and swiftly forgetting the reality of our journey, which can so easily be the trap into which we fall.

COLLECT

Lord Jesus Christ,
we thank you that in this wonderful sacrament
you have given us the memorial of your passion:
grant us so to reverence the sacred mysteries
of your body and blood
that we may know within ourselves
and show forth in our lives
the fruits of your redemption;
for you are alive and reign with the Father
in the unity of the Holy Spirit,
one God, now and for ever.

Reflection by **Tom Clammer**

Ordinary Time

Friday 28 May

Psalms 17, 19
2 Chronicles 30
Romans 6.1-14

Romans 6.1-14

'... we have been buried with him by baptism into death' (v.4)

Easter joy crackles through the opening section of chapter 6. This reminds us, apart from anything else, that we are never far away from the door of the empty tomb. Many of Paul's words from this chapter will have been read, reflected and preached on over the recent weeks of Eastertide, and those words are trying to express the mysterious and wonderful truth of the relationship between Christ's death and our Christian life.

I remember a preacher at a baptism once saying that when we get baptized, God connects one end of a great metaphorical elastic band to the font and connects the other end to us, so that no matter how far we might stray away, it is always possible to spring back to the place where our life was indelibly changed. Today's section of this chapter is Paul's attempt to explain why that is so, and the final three verses remind us that if we really have died and risen with Christ, if we are attached by an unbreakable cord to the font, then we ought to act like it.

Today is a day for thanksgiving for the extraordinary gift that Easter bestows upon us, but also, like every Friday in the Christian tradition, an opportunity to do a mini stocktake of the way in which we have responded to that gift. What one thing might we address today, and be a little better at doing tomorrow?

COLLECT

Almighty and everlasting God,
you have given us your servants grace,
by the confession of a true faith,
to acknowledge the glory of the eternal Trinity
and in the power of the divine majesty to worship the Unity:
keep us steadfast in this faith,
that we may evermore be defended from all adversities;
through Jesus Christ our Lord.

Reflection by **Tom Clammer**

Ordinary Time

Psalms 20, 21, **23**
2 Chronicles 32.1-22
Romans 6.15-end

Saturday 29 May

Romans 6.15-end

'You are slaves of the one whom you obey' (v.16)

The themes today are straightforward, but no less awesome for that. We are presented with another of Paul's great juxtapositions, and it has to do with where we fix our allegiance. To use the analogy of the age of sea battles, Paul is saying something like this: we need to be really careful which mast we choose to nail our colours to, because it's quite hard to get the nails out again afterwards. Committing to something has consequences. So, we have these great juxtapositions between being slaves to sin and slaves of righteousness, or 'presenting our members' either in the service of impurity or righteousness.

Philosophers, preachers and self-help gurus have been reminding humanity for generations that choices have consequences. One of my formative memories is being challenged by my parents: 'Do you really want to spend all of your pocket money on *that*? It's your choice, but think about it?' At its heart, this is all about what we were thinking about last Tuesday: do we want the *thing*, or do we want something *less* than the thing? Our 'yes' to God, our yes to the tomb, the font and the morning of resurrection presents us with, in Paul's glorious words, 'sanctification' and 'eternal life'. And even more wonderfully, unlike the more tawdry but seductive options, we don't even need to spend our pocket money on them. They are pure free gift.

> Holy God,
> faithful and unchanging:
> enlarge our minds with the knowledge of your truth,
> and draw us more deeply into the mystery of your love,
> that we may truly worship you,
> Father, Son and Holy Spirit,
> one God, now and for ever.

COLLECT

Reflection by **Tom Clammer**

Ordinary Time

Monday 31 May
Visit of the Blessed Virgin Mary
to Elizabeth

Psalms 85, 150
1 Samuel 2.1-10
Mark 3.31-end

1 Samuel 2.1-10

'Hannah prayed and said ...' (v.1)

One winter's evening I found myself chastizing some snowball-throwers for targeting elderly pedestrians from behind our church wall. The next morning I discovered a broken window in my living room and a golf ball on the carpet as evidence of an act of retribution. A flood of emotions washed over me, and I found myself compelled to sit at the piano, untouched by the shards of glass, and loudly praise God. The broken window became an opportunity to raise the sound of joy and hope in the face of someone's desire to raise fear.

Hannah's prayer is a mighty song that is heard through other broken windows. Whereas her previous prayer is silent (1 Samuel 1.13), here it finds voice as she praises the holy God. Arising from an act of creation (her son's birth) rather than vandalism, her song remembers those still found behind broken windows, fingering the ash of grief or the dust of death. Her song of joy could have been all about her beautiful boy; instead, she remembers those still lamenting and uses her voice to sing of God's vindication through the windows broken by those greedy for war and wealth.

True rejoicing is that which remembers the broken windows and loudly sings through them to reveal God's victory. Perhaps today, when we also remember Mary's song of praise (Luke 1.46-55), we can join these fearless women in loudly singing of God's victory through every crack and gaping hole.

COLLECT

Mighty God,
by whose grace Elizabeth rejoiced with Mary
and greeted her as the mother of the Lord:
look with favour on your lowly servants
that, with Mary, we may magnify your holy name
and rejoice to acclaim her Son our Saviour,
who is alive and reigns with you,
in the unity of the Holy Spirit,
one God, now and for ever.

Reflection by **Emma Parker**

Ordinary Time

Psalms 32, **36**
2 Chronicles 34.1-18
Romans 7.7-end

Tuesday 1 June

Romans 7.7-end

'... when I want to do what is good' (v.21)

Looking out of the window on a gloomy, overcast day is very different from looking out of it when the sun is shining. It is only when the sun casts its light onto the window that you see all the dust, sticky handprints, wet doggy noseprints, muddy water splashes, greasy streaks and other curious marks. In the same way, the closer we draw to God, the more the light of his holiness shines upon us and reveals the dust and dirt in our lives. We can suddenly become more aware of our sins and inability to do simple acts of goodness. We hear afresh the voice in our head that judges others, that is racist, that blames the other sex, that condemns the elderly or undermines children. The closer we are to God, the more clearly we see what goodness and holiness look like, and how sin has marked the window of our soul.

This passage is very complex and commentators disagree over how to understand it clearly. For our own prayerful reflection, it might be worth simply pondering upon Paul's depiction of the inner struggle between good and evil. Paul rejoices that Jesus will rescue us from this struggle, and yet he laments the way it is so easy to bend to the whims of evil. Perhaps today we need to intentionally come closer to the light of God's holiness, asking Christ to cleanse and renew us.

COLLECT

O God,
the strength of all those who put their trust in you,
mercifully accept our prayers
and, because through the weakness of our mortal nature
we can do no good thing without you,
grant us the help of your grace,
that in the keeping of your commandments
we may please you both in will and deed;
through Jesus Christ our Lord.

Reflection by **Emma Parker**

Ordinary Time

Wednesday 2 June

Psalm **34**
2 Chronicles 34.19-end
Romans 8.1-11

Romans 8.1-11

'... to set the mind on the Spirit is life' (v.6)

As I first explored the ministry of preaching, my mentor would always tell me to pay attention to anything that itches in the passage (the puzzling part) and not be afraid to scratch it, but he would also ask with delight and sincerity, 'What's the good news?' Our passage today is part of a wider argument where Paul is wrestling with understanding huge concepts of sin and law, death and life, goodness and evil, flesh and spirit, freedom and slavery, to name a few. Although we might want to scratch at every verse, it is impossible not to see the good news in today's passage: we have been given God's Spirit, and God's Spirit always brings life and is life.

And thus, Paul tells us to set our mind on the Spirit. We should intentionally do this as we awake each day. It should be as much a part of our daily routine as brushing our teeth or making a cup of tea. But how much more important!

Setting our mind on the Spirit will transform all life around us as our words and actions seek to edify and bring life, as we witness to hope rather than fear. Fixing our mind to the Spirit helps us to reach for miracles in hope and to find goodness through the shadowy valleys. Death and life teeter together along the thin veil between heaven and earth, but the Spirit will always anchor us to life. What good news indeed!

COLLECT

O God,
the strength of all those who put their trust in you,
mercifully accept our prayers
and, because through the weakness of our mortal nature
we can do no good thing without you,
grant us the help of your grace,
that in the keeping of your commandments
we may please you both in will and deed;
through Jesus Christ our Lord.

Reflection by **Emma Parker**

Ordinary Time

Psalm **37***
2 Chronicles 35.1-19
Romans 8.12-17

Thursday 3 June

Romans 8.12-17

'... all who are led by the Spirit ... are children of God' (v.14)

'He's your child, you deal with him!' said a fellow student, as she looked up to heaven and addressed our Father God about a mutual friend who was not making wise decisions. It made me smile at first, but I have found myself praying this on many occasions since!

At church, we may often hear that we are God's children in the liturgy, in our hymns and worship songs, through sermons and intercessions. It is a chorus that should be on repeat in our minds, and yet I wonder if we fully live as children of God, realizing the grace, the power, the wonder of this fact and letting it direct our daily walk with God and shape all our relationships.

In the same way that the Spirit anchors us to life, rather than to death, the Spirit anchors us to God, revealing us as his children. God's Spirit dwelling in us fastens us to God so that we belong to him, not as slaves or possessions, but as his children. You have been adopted by God. God saw you. God chose you. God wanted you. God rescued you. God loved you. God said, 'My child,' and you said, 'Father'.

You are a child of God. Ponder this afresh today; let it bring you joy and relief, as you hold ever more tightly that eternal, beautiful anchor joining you to God.

COLLECT

God of truth,
help us to keep your law of love
and to walk in ways of wisdom,
that we may find true life
in Jesus Christ your Son.

Reflection by **Emma Parker**

Ordinary Time

Friday 4 June

Psalm 31
2 Chronicles 35.20 – 36.10
Romans 8.18-30

Romans 8.18-30

'... that very Spirit intercedes with sighs too deep for words' (v.26)

When I was a child, the party game 'pass the parcel' had just one present at the centre; nowadays there are small presents each time a layer of paper is ripped off, thus increasing the chances of everyone winning something. As we read through these chapters and verses, every time Paul mentions the Spirit, it is as if the music stops and yet another gift is revealed between the layers of rich theology. The Spirit not only anchors us to life and to God, revealing our adoption as his children, but now we discover that the Spirit intercedes for us and helps us in our weakness. The Spirit truly is the gift that keeps on giving. As we unwrap yet another layer, Paul reassures us that when we do not know how to pray, God's Spirit prays for us.

I find this almost too wonderful to understand. God's Spirit dwelling in us is actively praying for us. In the face of tragedy, confusion, grief, illness or exhaustion, when our lips are unmoving and our hearts at a loss as to know how and what to pray, our silence is replaced by a sighing that reaches the heavens. The Spirit turns our painful silence into a powerful sound of sighs. Be reassured: hand over your helpless silences and let the Spirit turn them into holy sounds of hope. Listen carefully: for the whole of creation is caught in a mighty chorus of prayer.

COLLECT

O God,
the strength of all those who put their trust in you,
mercifully accept our prayers
and, because through the weakness of our mortal nature
we can do no good thing without you,
grant us the help of your grace,
that in the keeping of your commandments
we may please you both in will and deed;
through Jesus Christ our Lord.

Reflection by **Emma Parker**

Ordinary Time

Psalms 41, **42**, 43
2 Chronicles 36.11-end
Romans 8.31-end

Saturday 5 June

Romans 8.31-end

'... we are more than conquerors through him who loved us' (v.37)

For a time, I lived in Zambia, where I loved listening to the local radio station. One day, I heard the presenter say about God: 'He never promised an easy journey, only a safe arrival.' Paul certainly didn't have an easy journey, and he knew of the trials that other disciples encountered. The early Christians, including those in Rome, faced opposition and persecution, suffering and loss. Christians around the world today still face persecution, and even without this form of suffering, life can throw unimaginable pain in our path, and we can cry out like the psalmist, 'How long, O Lord?' (Psalm 13). A natural reaction to suffering can be, 'Why? Why me?'

Paul's response is to point us to that which cannot be taken away from us: the love of God in Christ Jesus our Lord. Like everyone, we too will face difficult times and challenges. But we have just read verse upon verse telling us that we are not alone, that God's Spirit helps us, that in and through all things we will find life. And now, Paul says that we will always find love: the holy, powerful, wonderful love of God in Christ.

Evil, sin, injustice and confusion may provoke and harm us, but they cannot steal us from the eternal and almighty arm of Christ that steadfastly holds us in love. Keep your eyes on Jesus, keep hold of love: it is this that makes us conquerors.

COLLECT

God of truth,
help us to keep your law of love
and to walk in ways of wisdom,
that we may find true life
in Jesus Christ your Son.

Reflection by **Emma Parker**

Ordinary Time

Monday 7 June

Psalm **44**
Ezra 1
Romans 9.1-18

Romans 9.1-18

'... and from them ... comes the Messiah, who is over all' (v.5)

In most cultures, there is an understanding of group boundaries that identify 'insiders' and 'outsiders'. Becoming members of social groups might involve the transfer of gifts or the making of promises, and once an 'insider' – whether it be the Scouts, Mother's Union or Slimming World – there is an acceptance of a code of behaviour or values that helps to unify the group. In this chapter, Paul is trying to discern where the boundaries are found for the group of people held together by the Messiah, and hence who is 'in' and who is 'out'. He is specifically concerned about the Israelites and how the covenant promises link with the gospel of Christ.

In the midst of this passage, we find four words that we must return to whenever we are reflecting on boundaries and insiders and outsiders, whether this is to do with Jews and gentiles, Christians and people of other faiths or no faith, church denominations and factions within a wider group. These are: 'who is over all'. Jesus, as the Saviour and Lord of all, is *over all*. He is the head of the Body, the foundation of the Church, but he is also the Messiah who reigns over, looks over, loves over, sees over all people – insiders and outsiders.

In our eagerness to define boundaries and determine who is in and who is out, let us remember that Christ cannot be contained by boundaries: he is over all. Thanks be to God.

COLLECT

Lord, you have taught us
that all our doings without love are nothing worth:
send your Holy Spirit
and pour into our hearts that most excellent gift of love,
the true bond of peace and of all virtues,
without which whoever lives is counted dead before you.
Grant this for your only Son Jesus Christ's sake.

Reflection by **Emma Parker**

Ordinary Time

Tuesday 8 June

Psalms **48**, 52
Ezra 3
Romans 9.19-end

Romans 9.19-end

'... but as if it were based on works' (v.32)

'But what can I do now?' is a question I am asked by church members who have experienced life-changing illnesses that mean they are no longer able to serve in their usual way. It is a question charged with fear and grief, rooted in a sense that they have lost something of their identity and worth.

Physical acts of service are important in how we attain a sense of belonging, identity and purpose, and in how we express our love for God; but sometimes we cling to these acts so much that they become our everything, and without them we feel we are nothing. We can almost idolize our works and forget Paul's argument that everything we gain in Christ is because of faith, not works.

This pastoral problem is not exactly what Paul is talking about here in this passage, in which he is trying to explore and understand God's plan of salvation for Jews and gentiles, but the heart of Paul's argument is that Christ is at the heart of salvation, rather than ourselves. Works, service, ministry, roles, vocations, obeying God's commands – they are all important, but they are not at the centre of salvation. Rather, it is faith in Christ that enables us to find our place in God's plan of redemption, which means that all people, from all corners of the world, regardless of what they can or cannot do, can find a place in God's salvation story.

COLLECT

Faithful Creator,
whose mercy never fails:
deepen our faithfulness to you
and to your living Word,
Jesus Christ our Lord.

Reflection by **Emma Parker**

Ordinary Time

Wednesday 9 June

Psalm **119.57-80**
Ezra 4.1-5
Romans 10.1-10

Romans 10.1-10

'Jesus is Lord ... raised ... from the dead' (v.9)

At the heart of our faith is our affirmation that Jesus is divine and has conquered death: Jesus is Lord! It is a sigh of relief and a cry of victory that Jesus, as our Lord, has supreme authority over everything in creation, and therefore that in him, we find our sanctuary.

Proclaiming 'Jesus is Lord' can be done with joy and dancing; but it can be uttered in pain through clenched jaws or whispered through tears. For proclaiming 'Jesus is Lord' is the song of both praise and of lament. When we can taste the first fruits of God's kingdom, we can declare that Jesus is indeed Lord. But when we rub shoulders with injustice and death and the things of the old order, then our cry may be more of *'maranatha'* – a cry for Christ to come, for the day when everything in creation will finally bow to Christ as Lord. It is a prayer of persistent faith.

Whether shouted from the rooftops or softly muttered under breath, it is a definitive cry telling everyone that no one and nothing else is lord. For Paul, it therefore means that lips and heart must be linked. It is not just a phrase: it is powerful, it is transformative, it is active, it ripples through the whole of the cosmos bringing salvation and hope. Today, let us align the whole of our lives to the greatest cry of all: Jesus is Lord!

COLLECT

Lord, you have taught us
that all our doings without love are nothing worth:
send your Holy Spirit
and pour into our hearts that most excellent gift of love,
the true bond of peace and of all virtues,
without which whoever lives is counted dead before you.
Grant this for your only Son Jesus Christ's sake.

Reflection by **Emma Parker**

Ordinary Time

Psalms 56, **57** (63*)
Ezra 4.7-end
Romans 10.11-end

Thursday 10 June

Romans 10.11-end

'... how are they to hear without someone to proclaim him?' (v.14)

One evening, our Bible study group reflected on the difficult messages the Old Testament prophets had to proclaim, including messages of rejection or condemnation, and those warning of impending disaster. As we prayed, one member of the group sensed God reminding us that the message we need to proclaim today is good. We are called to speak of the good news of Jesus: our message is of invitation, not rejection; of mercy, not condemnation; of salvation, not disaster. And yet, we can shy away from proclaiming this wonderful message of Christ.

Paul reminds us that if all people from all nations can now call upon the Lord and be saved, they must first hear about him. And who is going to proclaim Jesus Christ? Paul invites us to respond by becoming those beautiful feet prophesied by Isaiah of those delivering the message of God's coming salvation and peace. The time of defeat and disaster is over. Ours are the feet that take us to those waiting for good news, those who have hunkered down in the darkness who are longing for light. Ours are the feet that take us to those who long for words of love instead of harshness and for promises of companionship.

Salvation is God's work, but proclamation is now ours. Pray for opportunities to do this today, and for courage, sensitivity and joy as you deliver the greatest news the world could ever hear.

> Faithful Creator,
> whose mercy never fails:
> deepen our faithfulness to you
> and to your living Word,
> Jesus Christ our Lord.

COLLECT

Reflection by **Emma Parker**

Ordinary Time

Friday 11 June
Barnabas the Apostle

Psalms 100, 101, 117
Jeremiah 9.23-24
Acts 4.32-end

Acts 4.32-end

'... Joseph, to whom the apostles gave the name Barnabas' (v.36)

When we encounter the act of naming or renaming in biblical narrative, it is not merely to add detail to the story; it points to a deeper level of meaning within the narrative that regularly sends ripples of significance into the continuing story of God's people. Naming and renaming is often a divine act and can be linked to a character trait, to a specific calling or to a promise of redemption. In our passage today, the apostles rename Joseph as Barnabas, which points both to his identity as an encourager, but also his mission to encourage others in their faith and ministry.

As we read more of Barnabas in the book of Acts, we see that his generosity sparks his ability to encourage: whether this is generosity with his possessions, generosity to believe in others, generosity in courageously preaching the gospel or generosity in forgiving colleagues. Such generosity leads to others being encouraged to turn to Christ and to use their gifts to serve God.

The purpose of the name change in the narrative thus points beyond Barnabas to the importance of all disciples inhabiting an attitude of encouragement for the continuous revealing of God's redemption in all generations. Encouragement is the fuel that spurs on conversion, persistence in evangelism, generosity in supporting, forgiveness in collaboration, and courage in serving. Encouragement always leads to growth; may God release a spirit of encouragement in his Church today!

COLLECT

Bountiful God, giver of all gifts,
who poured your Spirit upon your servant Barnabas
and gave him grace to encourage others:
help us, by his example,
to be generous in our judgements
and unselfish in our service;
through Jesus Christ our Lord.

Reflection by **Emma Parker**

Ordinary Time

Psalm **68**
Ezra 6
Romans 11.13-24

Saturday 12 June

Romans 11.13-24

'So do not become proud, but stand in awe' (v.20)

Paul now specifically addresses the gentiles, as he is worried that they might boast in their salvation over and against their Jewish neighbours who are struggling or refusing to believe in Jesus as the Messiah. Although Paul, as an apostle to the gentiles, rejoices in their salvation, he nevertheless still laments those who have fallen away from God. He therefore warns the gentiles not to become proud, but to stand in awe.

Awe should always be the response to God's mercy and invitation. As we gaze upon the beauty of God's salvation, realizing its unfathomable complexity and yet its stark simplicity of the King on a cross, we should be brought to a place of awe. Our salvation is neither something to be taken for granted nor a reason to show apathy towards others or judge them, especially broken branches. Rather, belonging to God's majestic salvation story should fill us with awe as we gratefully look to God, and with compassion as we pray for those who have not yet grasped hold of the invitation to belong.

A few years ago, I met Gerty in a care home. One day she told me of how she longed to see Christ, but she was afraid that in her delight she would forget to bow down. She said, 'I always tell myself, "Eh Gerty, don't forget to curtsey!"' What a wonderful picture of awe!

How might we too come before God in awe today?

COLLECT

Lord, you have taught us
that all our doings without love are nothing worth:
send your Holy Spirit
and pour into our hearts that most excellent gift of love,
the true bond of peace and of all virtues,
without which whoever lives is counted dead before you.
Grant this for your only Son Jesus Christ's sake.

Reflection by **Emma Parker**

Ordinary Time

Monday 14 June

Psalm **71**
Ezra 7
Romans 11.25-end

Romans 11.25-end

'For who has known the mind of the Lord?' (v.34)

There is a scene in Kevin Smith's film about fallen angels, *Dogma*, where God makes an appearance on earth in the form of Alanis Morissette. When she speaks, something remarkable happens: rather than words issuing forth, she utters overwhelming white noise. It is not that *Dogma's* God speaks nonsense; rather God's pure, exquisite mind is simply too much for humans to comprehend. While I imagine many people will be shocked or even repelled by Smith's representation of God, I admire his appreciation for the way in which God exceeds our understanding.

Paul, of course, knew this too, but he goes further. Paul reminds the church in Rome that it is tempting to claim that we are wiser than we actually are, taking the path where we rush to judgement, not least about who will be saved by the living God. We, too, can make fools of ourselves by pretending we have more wisdom and judgement than is actually the case. Just when we think we have a grip on the ways of God, he humbles us with the riches of his wisdom and knowledge. We cannot puzzle out the mysteries of his ways.

We may think we can translate God's word into plain speak. It would be wiser, however, to be silent and attend, in awe, to the pure music of God that exceeds all understanding.

COLLECT

Almighty God,
you have broken the tyranny of sin
and have sent the Spirit of your Son into our hearts
    whereby we call you Father:
give us grace to dedicate our freedom to your service,
that we and all creation may be brought
    to the glorious liberty of the children of God;
through Jesus Christ our Lord.

Reflection by **Rachel Mann**

Ordinary Time

Psalm **73**
Ezra 8.15-end
Romans 12.1-8

Tuesday 15 June

Romans 12.1-8

'... present your bodies as a living sacrifice' (v.1)

For all his wonderful rhetorical gifts and theological vision, it is St Paul's startlingly embodied understanding of the Church that I find gripping. If his picture of the Church as the Body of Christ is most definitively explored in the First Letter to the Corinthians, in Romans too he reminds us of the theological power of the body and how we are beautifully entangled in creation and in one another. Not only does this make Paul, to use that modern phrase, 'relatable', but it also challenges us never to reduce our faith to a set of beliefs or ideas or values. Rather, Paul's focus on the body is a call to embody our faith in the world. Salvation is not simply words or a formula we can repeat; it must be lived out. Paul exhorts us to present our bodies – not our minds or souls – as a living sacrifice.

For his early audiences, surrounded by the sights, sounds and smells of sacrifices in Rome and across the Empire, this would have been a pungent image. The idea of a 'living' sacrifice might even have been frightening, certainly disconcerting. Nonetheless, as Paul reminds us, our bodies are not made to be sites of mere pleasure or self-indulgence, but offerings of love made across our whole lives to the God of all creation.

God our saviour,
look on this wounded world
in pity and in power;
hold us fast to your promises of peace
won for us by your Son,
our Saviour Jesus Christ.

COLLECT

Reflection by **Rachel Mann**

Ordinary Time

Wednesday 16 June

Psalm **77**
Ezra 9
Romans 12.9-end

Romans 12.9-end

'Bless those who persecute you; bless and do not curse them' (v.14)

Few people in a comfortable, liberal democracy such as the UK can seriously claim to have been persecuted for their faith. Those who have experienced such persecution may have escaped the violence and negative targeting found in countries where Christianity is a minority faith treated as a dangerous challenge to the prevailing regime. Those who have that experience will, I suspect, read St Paul's letter to the Romans with a very different slant from most of us.

If I have any insight, however slight, into the vile dynamics of persecution, it is gleaned from my experience of being a trans woman in a UK culture that, progressively, has indulged those who say people like me are a danger and a problem. In recent years, I have received death threats, been publicly demeaned, and targeted on social media simply for being transgender. I have sought to pay close attention to my reaction to that experience. I am ashamed to admit that, instinctively, I have wanted revenge for the deep hurts I have received. As a result of my own modest experience of 'persecution', I have found it so difficult to forgive and to bless. Nonetheless, God invites me into the ways of blessing. Not because it is easy, but because it is holy. And where God is, there is the fullness of life.

COLLECT

Almighty God,
you have broken the tyranny of sin
and have sent the Spirit of your Son into our hearts
    whereby we call you Father:
give us grace to dedicate our freedom to your service,
that we and all creation may be brought
    to the glorious liberty of the children of God;
through Jesus Christ our Lord.

Reflection by **Rachel Mann**

Ordinary Time

Psalms **78.1-39***
Ezra 10.1-17
Romans 13.1-7

Thursday 17 June

Romans 13.1-7

'Let every person be subject to the governing authorities' (v.1)

When I came to faith in my twenties, a priest told me that the Christian life is a call to obedience. I did not like the sound of that. It made discipleship sound like something suitable for dogs. I rail against any conception of faith that involves losing hard-won freedoms or personal judgement. However, I have also come to a richer appreciation of being obedient, obedient to the call of Christ, which is perfect freedom. Nonetheless, we all must negotiate the rules and limits imposed by the society in which we live.

When Paul says 'let every person be subject to the governing authorities', he reminds the people of God that faith is a worldly matter that requires practical wisdom. Christians may be called to be citizens of heaven, but that does not permit fantasies about what it means to be citizens on earth. I do not mind admitting that I find Paul's blanket suggestion that we be subject to the governing authorities a challenge, and not only because of the instinctive rebel in me. What should we do when a government, society or political leader allows their nation to become a persecuting community or wilfully destructive? I suspect Paul, like Jesus, would remind us to give to Caesar what is his due, but that is as nothing compared to giving God his due.

COLLECT

God our saviour,
look on this wounded world
in pity and in power;
hold us fast to your promises of peace
won for us by your Son,
our Saviour Jesus Christ.

Reflection by **Rachel Mann**

Ordinary Time

Friday 18 June

Psalm **55**
Nehemiah 1
Romans 13.8-end

Romans 13.8-end

'... the night is far gone, the day is near' (v.12)

The Bible is replete with poetry. I suspect, however, that few of us go to Paul to find it. He is a writer who typically uses a beguiling mix of high-flown rhetoric, sharp theological phrasing, and exhortation to make his point ... and then he arrests his reader with a phrase, sweet with poetic resonance. 'The night is far gone, the day is near' is, for me, precisely such a moment. Paul uses it to remind the Roman church to be ready for the arrival of the day of the Lord, echoing Jesus' reminder that the people of God should be like virgins trimming the wicks of their candles, ready for the day when salvation draws near.

Paul casts a vision where not only is the night ending, but it is 'far gone'. It is as if the night has grown old and fragile and totters on the edge. The day – full of promise and possibility and new things – beckons. This age – which is full of the menaces of night and where wicked things can happen without challenge – is far gone, and God's glorious day is dawning. Excitement and hope should grip us, but sadly so often we fail to live like that.

Paul's poetic phrase not only makes God's call to live in hope memorable, but brings its promise alive, inviting us into Christ's new day.

COLLECT

Almighty God,
you have broken the tyranny of sin
and have sent the Spirit of your Son into our hearts
   whereby we call you Father:
give us grace to dedicate our freedom to your service,
that we and all creation may be brought
   to the glorious liberty of the children of God;
through Jesus Christ our Lord.

Reflection by **Rachel Mann**

Ordinary Time

Psalms **76**, 79
Nehemiah 2
Romans 14.1-12

Saturday 19 June

Romans 14.1-12

'Why do you pass judgement on your brother or sister?' (v.10)

Romans is a great feast of theological insight, the kind of writing on which whole intellectual careers have been based. However, no one should underestimate its grip on the basic psychology of being human. The question, 'Why do you pass judgement on your brother or sister?' is as pressing now as it was in first-century Rome. I cannot be alone in struggling to stop myself from judging others, especially my co-religionists, rather than seeking the ways of humility and graciousness, heeding Jesus' call to love my neighbour as myself.

Someone once quipped that an English person only needs to open their mouth for them to be judged by another. Anglican clergy only need to catch sight of another's shoes, colour of clerical shirt or style of prayer to pass judgement on a colleague. There is as much, if not more, snobbery and pretentiousness in the Church as outside of it. As Paul reminds us, each of us – from the humblest to the highest – will, ultimately, come before the judgement seat of Christ, and none of us can claim we are worthy of his presence. All shall be called to account.

In my imagination, Christ will invite us to speak of how we demonstrated and dwelled in love. It is a question that will expose how we see our siblings in Christ.

> **COLLECT**
>
> God our saviour,
> look on this wounded world
> in pity and in power;
> hold us fast to your promises of peace
> won for us by your Son,
> our Saviour Jesus Christ.

Reflection by **Rachel Mann**

Ordinary Time

Monday 21 June

Psalms **80**, 82
Nehemiah 4
Romans 14.13-end

Romans 14.13-end

'Let us then pursue what makes for peace ...' (v.19)

Food matters. Without food and water, a human body begins to fade very quickly. As someone who lives with intestinal failure, I know only too well the impact of food deprivation or of being unable to get enough calories or electrolytes from foodstuffs.

Food is freighted with theological and political significance too. Think only of the magisterial meanings of the Eucharist. Food also tells others who we think we are. It is never simply 'fuel for life'. Thus, Paul writes about pursuing 'what makes for peace and mutual edification': there is a fracture between the Christians in Rome, between those whom Paul calls the weak and the strong; between those who claim Jewish and those who claim Gentile heritage. Food is being used as a weapon in a disagreement, a power move to assert righteousness, and both the 'weak' and the 'strong' have a case, as far as Paul is concerned, to answer.

Paul reminds us that the precious markers of our identity – whether that be sacred ideas about food or our freedoms around food as well as countless others – are not to be used as devices to separate us. Such behaviours grieve God. The vocation of those who follow the Way is to pursue all that which makes for peace and mutual edification. It is a call to conversion, both to God and to one another.

COLLECT

O God, the protector of all who trust in you,
without whom nothing is strong, nothing is holy:
increase and multiply upon us your mercy;
that with you as our ruler and guide
we may so pass through things temporal
that we lose not our hold on things eternal;
grant this, heavenly Father,
for our Lord Jesus Christ's sake.

Reflection by **Rachel Mann**

Ordinary Time

Psalms 87, **89.1-18**
Nehemiah 5
Romans 15.1-13

Tuesday 22 June

Romans 15.1-13

'For Christ did not please himself' (v.3)

Imagine if Christ had simply 'pleased himself'. Would he have, thereby, simply acted like many young men of his day or ours – doing those things that at least some people have always done, focusing on their own self-centred priorities. While that might be interesting, imagine if Christ, the Son of God, the one without sin, had simply 'pleased himself'. That is, imagine he had acted in such a way that merely fulfilled his own desires, expectations and ambitions, without consideration for those of others. For me, such a Christ would be no Christ at all. He would be more like a Greek or Roman god: exceptionally powerful, remarkable even, but capricious and selfish. Like Dionysus, to whom Christ has sometimes been compared, perhaps he would be quite fun, but also dangerous and a little monstrous.

That kind of divine being would have been very familiar to those who lived not only in the eastern Mediterranean but in the Rome of St Paul's day. Such a god expected compliance and, typically, required tribute. This is not a picture of the God who saves. In reality, as Paul reminds us, Christ did not please himself but took onto himself the insults and suffering that should fall on us. Jesus takes the sin of the world onto himself and, in his loving sacrifice, offers the promise of new life.

COLLECT

Gracious Father,
by the obedience of Jesus
you brought salvation to our wayward world:
draw us into harmony with your will,
that we may find all things restored in him,
our Saviour Jesus Christ.

Reflection by **Rachel Mann**

Ordinary Time

Wednesday 23 June

Psalm 119.105-128
Nehemiah 6.1 – 7.4
Romans 15.14-21

Romans 15.14-21

'I have reason to boast of my work for God' (v.17)

In the modern world, boasting is equivalent to bragging. Bragging itself is, straightforwardly, a kind of showing-off, a display of one's achievements or connections. While it is supposed to prove one's superiority over others, ironically it often only reveals a person's deep insecurities.

Boasting has, by contrast, a literary history, displayed in characters such as Beowulf, Falstaff and Italian Comedy's Scaramouche. It can be read positively, as with Beowulf, where he uses a ritual boast to pump himself up to go into combat against Grendel's terrifying mother. More often, as with Falstaff and Scaramouche, boasting only exposes the foolishness of the boaster.

Paul has a tendency towards boasting, primarily by reminding his readers of his credentials and accomplishments. He is confident in his evangelistic ministry, and he is not afraid to remind others of it. However, if in doing so, he risks becoming absurd or appearing pompous, I do not think we can accuse him of self-aggrandisement. His focus is always on Christ and his ambition is to proclaim God's good news. He embodies that phrase attributed to Dolly Parton: 'Figure out who you are and do it on purpose.' God does not want us to hold back on being our true selves in Jesus Christ. Like Paul, let us have reasons to boast of our work for him.

COLLECT

O God, the protector of all who trust in you,
without whom nothing is strong, nothing is holy:
increase and multiply upon us your mercy;
that with you as our ruler and guide
we may so pass through things temporal
that we lose not our hold on things eternal;
grant this, heavenly Father,
for our Lord Jesus Christ's sake.

Reflection by **Rachel Mann**

Ordinary Time

Psalms 50, 149
Ecclesiasticus 48.1-10
or Malachi 3.1-6
Luke 3.1-17

Thursday 24 June
Birth of John the Baptist

Luke 3.1-17
'Bear fruits worthy of repentance' (v.8)

Perhaps it is a token of my neurodivergent brain, but I often misunderstand the intention of a spoken or written phrase. 'Bear fruits worthy of repentance' is one such phrase. In my head, John is saying that our vocation – indeed the very best thing to do – is to act in such a way that we produce things (or 'fruits') of which we need to repent. In essence, that the naughtier we are the better, because then we will have something good about which to repent. When I give this idea a moment's thought, I realize such a reading is not only wrong, but absurd. John is challenging his audience to bear good fruit, the fruit worthy of those who have had that profound change of heart that leads them back towards God.

What could that fruit look like? Well, since it flows from a profound change of heart, the fruits would surely be full of passion richness and love. They would be enough to terrify those whom John calls in this passage a 'brood of vipers'. I suspect if I had been there to hear John's words, I would have been more than a little alarmed. Not because, with my neurodivergent brain, I misunderstood the implications of John's words. Rather, because I would have understood them only too clearly and was challenged to commit to the difficult rather than the easy path.

COLLECT

Almighty God,
by whose providence your servant John the Baptist
was wonderfully born,
and sent to prepare the way of your Son our Saviour
by the preaching of repentance:
lead us to repent according to his preaching
and, after his example,
constantly to speak the truth, boldly to rebuke vice,
and patiently to suffer for the truth's sake;
through Jesus Christ our Lord.

Reflection by **Rachel Mann**

Ordinary Time

Friday 25 June

Psalms **88** (95)
Nehemiah 9.1-23
Romans 16.1-16

Romans 16.1-16

'Greet Andronicus and Junia ... who were in prison with me' (v.7)

Paul loves to close a letter with a list of commendations, greetings and salutations to old friends. This list in the Letter to the Romans is next level, however. It is almost a stream of consciousness, a flow of names that reminds me of the way in which some neurodivergent people like me cannot stop once we start on a subject.

Amid Paul's 'shout-out', there is one name that, for me, always stands out: Junia. Though one third of the people mentioned are women, a testimony to their importance in the early Church, Junia is fascinating precisely because she has a disputed history. Since at least the thirteenth century, there have been those who contend that Junia was 'Junias', a man. Between 1927 and 1997, the *Nestle–Aland Greek New Testament* suggested that 'Junias' was the best reading of the word. There has also been a long dispute over whether Junia was or was not an apostle, with various scholarly takes on that suggestion.

Junia appears precisely once in the Bible, in this list of greetings, yet controversy has circled her. Paul remembers her as a friend and relative. I always remember her when I see her name because I think she represents all those who, through no fault of their own, have had their lives and stories erased or disputed by the Church. Let's remember them in our prayers today.

COLLECT

O God, the protector of all who trust in you,
without whom nothing is strong, nothing is holy:
increase and multiply upon us your mercy;
that with you as our ruler and guide
we may so pass through things temporal
that we lose not our hold on things eternal;
grant this, heavenly Father,
for our Lord Jesus Christ's sake.

Reflection by **Rachel Mann**

Ordinary Time

Psalms 96, **97**, 100
Nehemiah 9.24-end
Romans 16.17-end

Saturday 26 June

Romans 16.17-end

'... by smooth talk and flattery they deceive' (v.18)

We live in an age of scammers. Some scams are easy to spot, like the completely made-up 'Nigerian Prince' – a royal in need of help who promised big rewards for upfront donations. Others less so. Using the gift of the gab, some scammers deploy their unpleasant skills to trick the smartest people out of their money, dignity and possessions. There would have been plenty who did that in Paul's day too. He would also have been aware of other ways in which 'smooth talkers' can exploit others. He reminds the Roman church to be alert to those who would divide and damage the community for their own ends; such people do not serve our Lord Christ, but their own appetites.

When I read Paul's words, I am drawn up short. I see how readily they could apply to the modern Church and our serial failures around safeguarding. Paul grasps that the Church – perhaps *especially* the Church – is fertile ground for those who exploit others for their own selfish and sometimes grim ends. He suggests that in response we should seek to be wise in what is good, and guileless in what is evil. Of course, it is very far from an adequate substitute for modern policies, practices and processes to keep people safe. But I do wonder what the Church might look like if only we attended to Paul's words with great commitment and seriousness.

COLLECT

Gracious Father,
by the obedience of Jesus
you brought salvation to our wayward world:
draw us into harmony with your will,
that we may find all things restored in him,
our Saviour Jesus Christ.

Reflection by **Rachel Mann**

Ordinary Time

Monday 28 June

Psalms **98**, 99, 101
Nehemiah 12.27-47
2 Corinthians 1.1-14

2 Corinthians 1.1-14

'If we are being afflicted, it is for your consolation ...' (v.6)

When we face times of affliction, it can be difficult to orientate ourselves towards God, to turn the map of our inner lives the right way up and to navigate a new and turbulent spiritual landscape. Sometimes it can feel as if God is absent in our suffering; sometimes we cry out to God in lament, longing for things to change; sometimes we wonder why God has given us such a challenging set of circumstances, especially when other peoples' lives seem to contain no such difficulties!

Although it often doesn't feel this way at the time, our times of struggle present opportunities for us to enter into deeper relationship with God, as much as our times of enjoyment and plain sailing. Paul opens this letter to the Corinthians with thanksgiving for God's consolation in suffering, which draws him into an intimate sharing of Jesus' suffering and the comfort he received from his Father. Through his suffering, Paul not only receives consolation for himself but also shares this with those who are afflicted.

Likewise, in our times of struggle, we may experience not only God's deliverance but also God's consoling presence in and through our sufferings, which we are often drawn to share with those around us. In this way, the most painful moments in our lives can also become sources of God's blessing that extend beyond us to soothe and heal the wounds of others, as they enable us to listen more attentively and respond with greater sympathy and compassion.

COLLECT

Almighty and everlasting God,
by whose Spirit the whole body of the Church
    is governed and sanctified:
hear our prayer which we offer for all your faithful people,
that in their vocation and ministry
they may serve you in holiness and truth
to the glory of your name;
through our Lord and Saviour Jesus Christ.

Reflection by **Angela Sheard**

Ordinary Time

Psalms 71, 113
Isaiah 49.1-6
Acts 11.1-18

Tuesday 29 June
Peter the Apostle

Acts 11.1-18
'... not to make a distinction between them and us' (v.12)

In our communities, there is often a blurred and dynamic boundary between 'inside' and 'outside'. For example, who is (or isn't) part of our family? Sometimes people become part of our family only for a time; sometimes families expand or contract as relationships change; sometimes we have friends or families of choice who are closer than our families of origin. If we don't pay attention to such nuances, we can make assumptions about who our family is, assumptions that are too narrow and overlook the true diversity of our close relationships.

Today the church remembers the apostle Peter. His name, given by Jesus, means 'rock', and Peter is in many ways a foundation stone of the church. In this reading, his words lay down an important foundational principle: that God has incorporated gentiles into God's people. As a person of significant reputation, he explains to the believers in Judea how he has come to this understanding and convinces them. His justification is that God has made the Jews and gentiles into one people, in which there is no 'distinction between them and us'.

This radical new perspective expanded enormously the family of the early Church, and it still challenges us today. Our diversity of faith, ethnicity, culture, gender, sexuality, disability, neurodiversity and so much else must be celebrated, but must never lead us to assume the existence of divisions between us. Instead, if we pay attention, we will discern God's call for us to reimagine our relationships with one another.

> COLLECT
>
> Almighty God,
> who inspired your apostle Saint Peter
> to confess Jesus as Christ and Son of the living God:
> build up your Church upon this rock,
> that in unity and peace it may proclaim one truth
> and follow one Lord, your Son our Saviour Christ,
> who is alive and reigns with you,
> in the unity of the Holy Spirit,
> one God, now and for ever.

Reflection by **Angela Sheard**

Ordinary Time

Wednesday 30 June

Psalms 110, **111**, 112
Nehemiah 13.15-end
2 Corinthians 2.5-end

2 Corinthians 2.5-end

'So I urge you to reaffirm your love for him' (v.8)

I once received some wise advice regarding a real and very present danger: the sending of angry emails. 'When you receive an email that makes you feel angry, frustrated or otherwise upset,' said my guide, 'and you dash off a response in haste, pause before pressing "Send". Sleep on it and return to your draft the next day. With a calmer heart and mind, you'll be able to shape your words to avoid saying anything that you may regret later.'

Responding thoughtfully to situations of conflict or injustice is always important, especially when our response impacts the lives of others for whom we are responsible. In this reading, Paul advises how the Corinthians should respond to a person who has offended the community. The Corinthians feel that Paul should have visited them to exact his discipline personally; but Paul responds that he avoided this in order not to behave harshly towards them and inflict sorrow unnecessarily. Instead, he wrote them a letter, which the community used to discipline the offender. The offender has now repented, and so in a further act of mercy Paul urges them to forgive him and welcome him back into the community.

In our communities, wrongdoing should be named and justice restored – but to avoid adding further wrongdoing to the situation, we should seek to respond in ways which hold God's truth together with God's mercy.

COLLECT

Almighty and everlasting God,
by whose Spirit the whole body of the Church
   is governed and sanctified:
hear our prayer which we offer for all your faithful people,
that in their vocation and ministry
they may serve you in holiness and truth
to the glory of your name;
through our Lord and Saviour Jesus Christ.

Reflection by **Angela Sheard**

Ordinary Time

Psalms 113, 115
Esther 1
2 Corinthians 3

Thursday 1 July

2 Corinthians 3

'... from one degree of glory to another' (v.18)

Prayer is an essential part of the Christian life: it can express our gratitude for the blessings of our lives, our confession of how we have wronged others, our lament at the injustice of our world, our plea for God's help and so much besides. But what difference does all this make? What does God do in and through our prayer?

In a radio broadcast, Rowan Williams compared prayer to sunbathing: 'When you're lying on the beach something is happening, something that has nothing to do with how you feel or how hard you're trying ... All you have to do is turn up. And then things change, at their own pace. You simply have to be there where the light can get at you.'

Prayer opens us up to God's transforming grace, which changes us over a lifetime – one degree at a time – so that we become more and more like God. Paul reminds the Corinthians of this journey of transformation, which is at the heart of our discipleship.

There are so many other ways that we encounter God's grace: reading Scripture, challenging injustice, seeking reconciliation, receiving a gift from a stranger. What are the practices and situations in your life that allow God to transform you from one degree of glory to another?

> Almighty God,
> send down upon your Church
> the riches of your Spirit,
> and kindle in all who minister the gospel
> your countless gifts of grace;
> through Jesus Christ our Lord.

COLLECT

Reflection by **Angela Sheard**

Friday 2 July

Psalm 139
Esther 2
2 Corinthians 4

2 Corinthians 4

'...so that the life of Jesus may be made visible' (v.11)

Although they seem like opposites, life and death are often inextricably bound together. In our families, friendship groups or church communities, we sometimes grieve the loss of loved ones even as we celebrate new life or new hope for the future. A christening, birthday or wedding might include photographs and stories of loved ones who have died, but who are still very much alive in the memories of the living.

At baptism, we enter into this mysterious relationship between life and death in a new way: we are buried with Christ in order that we might share in Christ's resurrection. This can give us a new perspective on the times in our lives that are marked by suffering, loss, fragmentation and death. For Paul, it is the power of the resurrection that sustains him through afflictions, persecutions, times of bewilderment and forces that threaten to destroy him. Resurrection is a source of hope for the future, but it also nurtures and sustains his life in the present.

Resurrection is also at work in our own lives, even in situations of seemingly insurmountable or irredeemable suffering. It is revealed through something as simple as a shared meal, a gesture of tenderness or the voice of a marginalized person being heard for the first time. Resurrection promises us that even in the midst of suffering, we can know the healing and justice-seeking power of God.

COLLECT

Almighty and everlasting God,
by whose Spirit the whole body of the Church
    is governed and sanctified:
hear our prayer which we offer for all your faithful people,
that in their vocation and ministry
they may serve you in holiness and truth
to the glory of your name;
through our Lord and Saviour Jesus Christ.

Reflection by **Angela Sheard**

Ordinary Time

Psalms 92, 146
2 Samuel 15.17-21
or Ecclesiasticus 2
John 11.1-16

Saturday 3 July
Thomas the Apostle

John 11.1-16

'Let us also go, that we may die with him' (v.16)

The saying 'actions speak louder than words' reminds us of the enormous power of what we do over what we say to communicate what we really think. Words are, of course, powerful – but in difficult or challenging situations, it is often easier to speak without acting accordingly. Sometimes, even if we want to act, our courage fails us and we retreat into paying lip service to the problem.

Today, the Church remembers Thomas, apostle and martyr. Thomas ultimately gave his life for his faith, and yet his words in this reading are not borne out in his later actions. Thomas urges the others to travel with Jesus to Bethany, despite the risk of being stoned along the way. His words show a willingness to stay with Jesus even unto death. And yet, along with most of the other disciples, Thomas abandoned Jesus, first at Gethsemane and again during his trial and passion. Despite all his promises, ultimately he did not stand at the foot of the cross. Against this backdrop, his words stand empty, paying lip service to the cost of discipleship.

In our own discipleship, we are not likely to be asked to risk our lives, but when invited to move beyond our comfort zones, perhaps we might recall those who went before us. Do we recognize those times when we, like Thomas, made promises that we failed to act on? Each such threshold is an opportunity for us to gather afresh the moral courage we need to stand in solidarity with our crucified world.

COLLECT

Almighty and eternal God,
who, for the firmer foundation of our faith,
allowed your holy apostle Thomas
to doubt the resurrection of your Son
till word and sight convinced him:
grant to us, who have not seen, that we also may believe
and so confess Christ as our Lord and our God;
who is alive and reigns with you,
in the unity of the Holy Spirit,
one God, now and for ever.

Reflection by **Angela Sheard**

Ordinary Time

Monday 5 July

Psalms 123, 124, 125, **126**
Esther 4
2 Corinthians 6.1 – 7.1

2 Corinthians 6.1 – 7.1

'What agreement has the temple of God with idols?' (6.16)

On my daily commute, I used to scroll through various social media feeds. It was a habit that developed so slowly that I barely noticed it. I scrolled for various reasons – to pass the time, to keep up to date, to feel like I was doing something. Ultimately, I was looking for a distraction from being with myself. On a silent retreat, I became more sensitive to my inner landscape – and when I resumed scrolling afterwards, I felt a deadening of my spirit. I knew that I had to change my relationship with social media, because it was preventing me from being present to myself, and to God.

In today's reading, Paul gives the Corinthians a stark choice: they must either be reconciled with him (and therefore with God) or with his rivals. There is no possibility of them embracing both: this would be like trying to create agreement between the temple of God and idols. When we hear the word 'idol', we may think of physical objects like the golden calf – but an idol is anything that draws us away from God, that distracts us from our calling.

Some of the most powerful idols can creep up on us in subtle ways – like social media scrolling – or masquerade as virtues – like overworking. Whatever our idols may be, our task is first to notice their presence in our lives and then to let them go as we turn back towards God.

COLLECT

Merciful God,
you have prepared for those who love you
such good things as pass our understanding:
pour into our hearts such love toward you
that we, loving you in all things and above all things,
may obtain your promises,
which exceed all that we can desire;
through Jesus Christ our Lord.

Reflection by **Angela Sheard**

Ordinary Time

Psalms **132**, 133
Esther 5
2 Corinthians 7.2-end

Tuesday 6 July

2 Corinthians 7.2-end

'I rejoice, because I have complete confidence in you' (v.16)

Years ago, I found myself in conflict with a friend around our student accommodation. The matter was resolved and our lives moved on peaceably, but with some distance between us. A few months later I received a birthday card from this friend expressing a desire for our relationship to 'start again' and hopefully return to something like what it was. The occasions when we've run into each other since then have felt like a new beginning.

In today's reading, Paul resumes his reflection on a previous letter in which he advised the Corinthians to deal with an offender. Although the matter was now resolved, Paul was concerned that the letter was not favourably received by all, and so the community may not honour its promise to give money to the poor Jerusalem church. So, he reframes the whole incident as a revelation of the Corinthians' faithfulness to God, evident not only in their obedience to his teaching but also in their hospitality towards his messenger, Titus.

We might view Paul's relationship building here as 'buttering up' the Corinthians so that they might give generously. But regardless of Paul's motivations, releasing the Corinthians from any lingering judgement seeks to clear the way for deepening their relationship. In our own lives, the ongoing work of reconciliation is important even after conflict is resolved. It requires attentiveness both to the particular gift of the other, and to the subtle dynamics within ourselves that prevent us from fully embracing them.

COLLECT

Creator God,
you made us all in your image:
may we discern you in all that we see,
and serve you in all that we do;
through Jesus Christ our Lord.

Reflection by **Angela Sheard**

Ordinary Time

Wednesday 7 July

Psalm 119.153-end
Esther 6.1-13
2 Corinthians 8.1-15

2 Corinthians 8.1-15

'... a fair balance between your present abundance and their need'
(vv.13-14)

Friendship often involves sharing food and drink, whether that be coffee with work colleagues, a church bring-and-share lunch or a large family Christmas dinner. At their best, these expressions of friendship seek true equity through mutual generosity. But where do the boundaries of our generosity lie? How far are we prepared to extend a hand of friendship?

In today's reading, Paul seeks to persuade the Corinthians to give to the poor church in Jerusalem, which was in a time of crisis. He appeals to the Greek notion of equality as a mark of friendship, with the collection becoming a measure of the Corinthians' love for their sister church. In the Greek tradition, equality was also an important principle of justice, and Paul connects this with the Israelites gathering manna in the wilderness (Exodus 16): when God provided for the people directly, everyone had no more or less than they needed.

Paul's plea might prompt us to consider our relationship to this 'fair balance' that he seeks. It is important to respond to local needs in our churches and the communities they serve; however, we cannot ignore the manifold crises of our wider world, especially the suffering of our fellow Christians. As we long for a just economy, we are invited to notice whether there are limits to our own friendship and generosity, and day by day find ways to go beyond them.

COLLECT

Merciful God,
you have prepared for those who love you
such good things as pass our understanding:
pour into our hearts such love toward you
that we, loving you in all things and above all things,
may obtain your promises,
which exceed all that we can desire;
through Jesus Christ our Lord.

Reflection by **Angela Sheard**

Ordinary Time

Psalms 143, 146
Esther 6.14 – end of 7
2 Corinthians 8.16 – 9.5

Thursday 8 July

2 Corinthians 8.16 – 9.5
'... I am sending the brothers' (9.3)

Many of us have individuals or communities in our lives that have inspired and encouraged us on our journeys of discipleship. My earliest and deepest inspiration is my mother, who directs the choir at my local church. Her role is as much a pastoral one as a musical one. Growing up, I saw how she listened in a faithful and costly way to the stories of those in the choir. She made space for their gifts and empowered those who lacked confidence. Thanks to her wise leadership, the choir is a place where people flourish and make music together that enriches the wider church.

Paul informs the Corinthians about a delegation he is sending to collect money that they have promised for the poor church in Jerusalem. This will include Titus, two others known for their proclamation of the gospel and their eagerness despite being tested, and possibly some from the Macedonian church, who have heard of the Corinthians' generous pledge and been inspired by it. Encouraged by the eagerness and generosity of this delegation, Paul hopes the gifts collected will be given not begrudgingly but willingly.

In situations where we are conflicted, fearful or simply reluctant to do what is right, we too can draw upon God's grace poured into our lives by holy people, seeking to learn from their example and to hear afresh God's challenge to us to do likewise.

COLLECT

Creator God,
you made us all in your image:
may we discern you in all that we see,
and serve you in all that we do;
through Jesus Christ our Lord.

Reflection by **Angela Sheard**

Ordinary Time

Friday 9 July

Psalms 142, **144**
Esther 8
2 Corinthians 9.6-end

2 Corinthians 9.6-end

'… you glorify God … by the generosity of your sharing' (v.13)

In my church, when the bread, wine and collection are brought to the altar during the offertory, we say a prayer over the gifts. I particularly appreciate the line, 'All things come from you, and of your own do we give you'. It reminds me that before we can give, we must acknowledge that all we have comes from God.

A central act of our discipleship is then to give back to God what was always God's to begin with. Then our offering is an act of refocusing our lives, placing God back at the centre, and it is something we do not only in church, but throughout our lives. Everything in our lives is a gift that can deepen our response to God. But if we place these gifts at the centre, they displace God and so hinder our movement towards God's love.

Paul reminds the Corinthians of the fundamental relationship between giver, gift and God. Their giving will have multiple effects. It will provide for the needs of the saints in Jerusalem; it will be a witness to the gospel; it will inspire others in prayer; but most importantly, it will glorify God and re-orientate them towards God's love. This is the ultimate gift that they will receive as a result of their generosity; one that cannot be measured because it is the source from which all other gifts flow.

COLLECT

Merciful God,
you have prepared for those who love you
such good things as pass our understanding:
pour into our hearts such love toward you
that we, loving you in all things and above all things,
may obtain your promises,
which exceed all that we can desire;
through Jesus Christ our Lord.

Reflection by **Angela Sheard**

Ordinary Time

Psalm 147
Esther 9.20-28
2 Corinthians 10

Saturday 10 July

2 Corinthians 10

'... our authority, which the Lord gave for building you up' (v.8)

When we think of strength, we might think first of physical strength – like that of a weightlifter, or an endurance athlete. We might think of strength of personality – those who have a loud voice, who command the attention of a room, whose judgement is widely respected. But strength can manifest itself in other seemingly contradictory ways.

The Corinthians object to a mismatch between Paul's words and actions: although he writes bold letters to them from a safe distance, he does not speak with the same boldness when physically present. The Corinthians feel that Paul is avoiding being frank with them – but Paul responds that his gentleness is deliberate and is a quality of Christ himself. While he is prepared to destroy any obstacles to the Corinthians' relationship with Christ, he seeks not to tear them down but to build them up.

Elsewhere, Paul would write that Christ's power is made perfect in weakness, recalling that in his life Jesus showed immense strength in and through his vulnerability. This same strength – which the Corinthians disregarded – is evident in our world, often in those whom society tends to overlook, belittle and marginalize. It is made known in non-violent resistance to forces of domination and control, in flourishing despite hostility and in survival against all odds. In our discipleship, may we also seek the gentleness that builds us up in love – the gentleness that is true strength.

> Creator God,
> you made us all in your image:
> may we discern you in all that we see,
> and serve you in all that we do;
> through Jesus Christ our Lord.

COLLECT

Reflection by **Angela Sheard**

Ordinary Time

Monday 12 July

Psalms 1, 2, 3
Jeremiah 26
2 Corinthians 11.1-15

2 Corinthians 11.1-15

'God knows I do!' (v. 11)

'Trust me,' says Paul. If there is a tone of exasperation here, it is because the stakes are high. The Corinthians are in mortal danger. Paul pleads with them to bear with him a little. He seeks to establish a sound basis on which to win their trust. He might have plenty of theological arguments at the ready, but he does not use those here. Rather, he wants to underline why this community should listen to him at all. He admits to a fierce divine jealousy; he wants to protect these easily influenced Christians from deception. This jealousy is rooted in his deep love for a community he has invested in, who seem not to understand the peril they are in.

Paul's love is one reason why they should trust him. Another is his knowledge and training; he is every bit as good as the 'super-apostles', even if he does not have their refinement of speech. How easily people can be swayed by smooth, apparently educated words. Be more discerning, Paul is saying. He then appeals to the practical evidence of his love, his generosity in placing no burdens on them for his support, which has come from Macedonian friends. Perhaps the mention of the Macedonians is a hint that he has friends who evidently trust him enough to support him.

How might vulnerable Christians be discerning? By asking where is the love, generosity and personal investment behind the persuasive words?

COLLECT

Lord of all power and might,
the author and giver of all good things:
graft in our hearts the love of your name,
increase in us true religion,
nourish us with all goodness,
and of your great mercy keep us in the same;
through Jesus Christ our Lord.

Reflection by **Julia Mourant**

Ordinary Time

Psalms **5**, 6 (8)
Jeremiah 28
2 Corinthians 11.16-end

Tuesday 13 July

2 Corinthians 11.16-end

'I will boast of the things that show my weakness' (v.30)

Warming to his theme, Paul widens his argument. While fully aware of the danger of being foolish, he risks speaking boldly. Paul even suggests that as the Corinthians already listen to fools, if they think him one, that should not stop them paying attention. He is not concerned about whether he is considered a fool or a hero, but his credentials speak for themselves. He can not only level with these false teachers, but outdo them, though that is not the point. After his breathless recitation of the things he does not really want to dwell on, he turns to his real credential: weakness.

It is Paul's humanity and vulnerability that he holds as his greatest badge of honour. He invites the Corinthians to pay more attention to his weakness than his track record of exploits, persecution and suffering. His weakness is a reminder that he is a vessel, a servant, a means by which others may flourish. This is the hallmark of a true teacher.

When we state our credentials, will they include weakness as well as experience? What is at the centre? Is it reputation, self-preservation or the flourishing of all? In the end, Paul desires that the Corinthians will have the wisdom to judge teachers for themselves. He invites the Corinthians to look for authenticity, love and humility. Vulnerability, weakness and humanity may say more about a leader than their CV.

COLLECT

Generous God,
you give us gifts and make them grow:
though our faith is small as mustard seed,
make it grow to your glory
and the flourishing of your kingdom;
through Jesus Christ our Lord.

Reflection by **Julia Mourant**

Ordinary Time

Wednesday 14 July

Psalm 119.1-32
Jeremiah 29.1-14
2 Corinthians 12

2 Corinthians 12

'My grace is sufficient for you' (v.9)

Paul moves from his experience of suffering to highlighting his spiritual experience. He is unwilling to boast of visions and voices, and still insists that these are not really relevant. If spiritual experience gives him authority, he can lay claim to it, but he would rather talk about weakness.

There have been many theories as to the nature of Paul's 'thorn in the flesh', from mental health to migraine or eye problems. Some believe it refers to his opponents. We cannot know, but there is a spiritual lesson here with wide application. Paul values his weakness above all his knowledge, suffering and spiritual experience. This is no pious statement, born of superficial over-spiritualization. Paul speaks not of some mere inconvenience or passing discomfort. The metaphor suggests something intractable, sharp and debilitating. We have a brief insight into a deep spiritual struggle. Paul prayed three times for the resolution of this difficulty, perhaps in desperation and agony of body and soul.

At such times, we are in spiritual agony, the desolation of unanswered prayer. We could serve God so much better, we might think. There comes a point of letting go of our agendas, but it does not always happen without a struggle. Paul has found contentment in weakness, but there is no shortcut to this peace. First, he had to have at least three robust conversations with God. What conversations with God do you need to have?

COLLECT

Lord of all power and might,
the author and giver of all good things:
graft in our hearts the love of your name,
increase in us true religion,
nourish us with all goodness,
and of your great mercy keep us in the same;
through Jesus Christ our Lord.

Reflection by **Julia Mourant**

Ordinary Time

Psalms 14, **15**, 16
Jeremiah 30.1-11
2 Corinthians 13

Thursday 15 July

2 Corinthians 13

'Examine yourselves ...' (v.5)

Paul's tone becomes more severe as he closes his letter. He has said more than enough about his credentials, while at the same time refusing to compete with the 'super-apostles'. The focus changes from which leaders will hold sway to whether the Corinthians are prepared to look in the mirror and examine themselves. It is all too easy to give leaders and preachers marks out of ten and yet fail to apply their message. There comes a point of reflection when we must ask if we are really flourishing. Paul is called to build up, encourage and support rather than exercise judgement and discipline.

There is some risk in exhorting the Corinthians to discern for themselves whether they 'pass the test'. We all take refuge in self-justification and denial at times. Paul knows when he has said all he can. He has not held back, but now it is up to these Christians to discern. Only they can commit to the life of purity Paul longs for in them. He speaks to a community, not merely a group of individuals. The community will discern whom they trust, whom they listen to.

Are we prepared to move from assessing the teacher to looking within and discerning what transformation might be life-giving? Paul ends with a note saying that he hopes to find agreement and peace among them. Surely this is what every teacher longs for.

> COLLECT
>
> Generous God,
> you give us gifts and make them grow:
> though our faith is small as mustard seed,
> make it grow to your glory
> and the flourishing of your kingdom;
> through Jesus Christ our Lord.

Reflection by **Julia Mourant**

Ordinary Time

Friday 16 July

Psalms 17, **19**
Jeremiah 30.12-22
James 1.1-11

James 1.1-11

'... consider it nothing but joy' (v.2)

James may be thinking of trials, which are a consequence of faith, but even so, considering everything a joy sounds challenging. Some things are definitely not a cause for joy. It is hard to be thankful for circumstances that are difficult, even if in endurance we are maturing. Perhaps one perspective is to ask if there may be a hidden gift alongside difficulty. There is no need to over-spiritualize our circumstances and deny the pain and distress we experience. Sometimes it is necessary to rage at God before we can ask whether there is anything else in the mix alongside the heartache. A mature faith has thankfulness as a bass note in all things. This does not make difficulty go away, but it is a way of holding it.

A 'strong' faith is not necessarily one that insists on a series of doctrinal assertions. Rather, it is the faith that flows from a deeply thankful encounter with God in the soul. There can be more maturity, joy and liberation in saying 'I do not know' than in hanging on to a dissonant framework of concepts and beliefs that aren't 'working' or making sense. There is a time to hold fast to what we have learnt and continue to believe. There is also a time to ponder what grounds our faith in experience and encounter in the soul, to rest in God and wait for the storm to pass.

COLLECT

Lord of all power and might,
the author and giver of all good things:
graft in our hearts the love of your name,
increase in us true religion,
nourish us with all goodness,
and of your great mercy keep us in the same;
through Jesus Christ our Lord.

Reflection by **Julia Mourant**

Ordinary Time

Psalms 20, 21, **23**
Jeremiah 31.1-22
James 1.12-end

Saturday 17 July

James 1.12-end

'Blessed is anyone who endures temptation' (v.12)

Temptations are yet another kind of soul difficulty, stemming from our needy desires, so easily lured. Enticement makes promises that will never be fulfilled because they are lies. Temptation does not come from God. We are called to take responsibility for our choices and actions. James has a lovely image of double rooting – we are rooted in the word, which is rooted in us. From this grounded perspective, we find a measured perspective. We remember who God is.

Any idea that God might somehow lure us into evil is a human projection. Whatever our struggles, there is a constancy in God. Our best course may be to take our focus off the temptations we face and engage with the practicalities of life. Perhaps this is why James then invites us to listen and be slow to anger. He does not say don't be angry, just be slow about it. This requires self-awareness, and the mirror is a good metaphor. When we see ourselves getting angry, we might notice what is going on. We can become angry for many reasons, some of them undoubtedly righteous. But anger in itself achieves little; it disrupts the soul and may misdirect our focus. Look in the mirror, says James. Outward directed anger may in due course have a place, but first see who you are, and whatever you have to say, say it from a place of self-knowledge.

COLLECT

Generous God,
you give us gifts and make them grow:
though our faith is small as mustard seed,
make it grow to your glory
and the flourishing of your kingdom;
through Jesus Christ our Lord.

Reflection by **Julia Mourant**

Ordinary Time

Monday 19 July

Psalms 27, **30**
Jeremiah 31.23-25, 27-37
James 2.1-13

James 2.1-13

'... if you show partiality, you commit sin' (v.9)

James goes to the heart of what happens when we lose sight of the big picture and live from our own petty perspectives and prejudices. Assumptions about others creep in, resulting in a failure to see others as they are. We are also unable to see ourselves with any clarity, and so we are in delusion and denial.

James has an eye for irony here and almost makes fun of his readers. The very people we favour in our naivety may well be the ones who will take advantage of us. This is surely as true now, as evidenced by scandals and accusations of every kind. Everything we do has some influence on how the world works. If we desire to live in a world where the poor are not despised and overlooked, then we must acknowledge all people as worthy of respect. James calls attention to the kingdom, and it is the life of the kingdom that is sometimes more readily understood by those who are not rich.

James invites us to be the same all the way through, to be consistent. He also reminds us there is no balance sheet for our choices and behaviours. We cannot offset our selfish and privileged choices against other good behaviours and end up with a 'pass' overall. The centre of gravity is mercy. Where there is mercy, we will find the kingdom of God.

COLLECT

Almighty Lord and everlasting God,
we beseech you to direct, sanctify and govern
    both our hearts and bodies
in the ways of your laws
    and the works of your commandments;
that through your most mighty protection, both here and ever,
we may be preserved in body and soul;
through our Lord and Saviour Jesus Christ.

Reflection by **Julia Mourant**

Ordinary Time

Psalms 32, **36**
Jeremiah 32.1-15
James 2.14-end

Tuesday 20 July

James 2.14-end

'... was not Rahab the prostitute justified by works ...?' (v.25)

James argues for consistency and integrity. Doing and believing are one and the same. Belief that is not matched by action is no belief at all, since it has no roots in the heart. What we really believe in, we act on without overthinking. 'It's obvious,' says the person living from mercy, free from prejudice and concern with status.

James suggests it is 'works' rather than beliefs that are non-negotiable. What would he make of our concerns about whether a person's beliefs pass the test? Teaching and theology are undoubtedly important, but 'works' spring from our lives as people deeply connected both to the world and to the kingdom of God.

Spirituality is really about knowing that we are not able to live on this earth at the centre of a self-defined world. Rahab did what she thought was right. In the life that she had, in the context of all that had led her to that place and time, she made a choice. She did a good thing, and in some way, she was saved by it.

Where do your actions or omissions challenge the things you want to believe in? Where in your life do you act from grace, without overthinking? This need not be a cause for self-condemnation; we are all a work in progress. Look in the mirror and pray for grace.

COLLECT

Lord God,
your Son left the riches of heaven
and became poor for our sake:
when we prosper save us from pride,
when we are needy save us from despair,
that we may trust in you alone;
through Jesus Christ our Lord.

Reflection by **Julia Mourant**

Ordinary Time

Wednesday 21 July

Psalm **34**
Jeremiah 33.1-13
James 3

James 3

'... all of us make many mistakes' (v.2)

James offers both warning and comfort for teachers. They will be held to high standards, and yet they will make mistakes. The invitation is to keep both perspectives in view. High standards are a reminder not to be complacent or lazy. Teaching is a vocation, a humble response to a call, undertaken in frailty and in dependence on grace. Mistakes can be acknowledged, learnt from and noted as reminders not to be too harsh with other teachers. Teachers and preachers can easily become isolated and out of touch, even though theirs is a very visible ministry. There will always be praise and criticism, which need to be received with discernment and in the context of wisdom from others.

James moves on immediately to speak about the tongue. Perhaps teaching is the context he has in mind. Preachers can encourage, but may wound or mislead. The teacher cannot always know who is listening, their story and context. There is another invitation here not to make assumptions or be influenced by prejudice. Our words may have more impact than we know. James employs the metaphor of fruit on a tree: words can only be consistent with the source they spring from. The words we use to teach the faith are worthless without a life marked by gentleness and wisdom. Every talk, sermon or study might be grown and watered in the fresh water of a heart ready to bless rather than judge.

COLLECT

Almighty Lord and everlasting God,
we beseech you to direct, sanctify and govern
    both our hearts and bodies
in the ways of your laws
    and the works of your commandments;
that through your most mighty protection, both here and ever,
we may be preserved in body and soul;
through our Lord and Saviour Jesus Christ.

Reflection by **Julia Mourant**

Ordinary Time

Psalms 30, 32, 150
1 Samuel 16.14-end
Luke 8.1-3

Thursday 22 July
Mary Magdalene

Luke 8.1-3

'Mary ... Joanna ... and Susanna ... and many others' (vv.2-3)

We know very little about Mary Magdalene. Her name probably indicates where she was from. She had a life-changing encounter with Jesus, although there is no narrative that explains the 'seven demons' driven from her. There is no evidence to support the popular idea that she was a prostitute. Perhaps it makes no difference; Jesus loved and welcomed her, but it is not right to build a story around an invented background. Mary stayed with Jesus as part of a group of women who supported him from their own means. We know very few names other than Mary, the mother of James, and Joanna. Salome is mentioned at the tomb. Mary of Bethany and her sister Martha are also named.

Mary Magdalene and other women, including Jesus' own mother, were there as Jesus died. Some accompanied Mary Magdalene to take spices to the tomb (Luke 24), becoming the first witnesses to the resurrection. Mary was courageous enough to proclaim this news, knowing she would be disbelieved. The twelve disciples are carefully named in the Gospels, yet the women are mostly nameless.

Next time you sit with an imaginative contemplation on a Gospel narrative, picture these women, not as shadowy figures who were tolerated, but alongside the disciples as equal members of this community, future teachers, preachers and prophets. Give them names and faces. Thank them for their ministry.

COLLECT

Almighty God,
whose Son restored Mary Magdalene to health of mind and body
and called her to be a witness to his resurrection:
forgive our sins and heal us by your grace,
that we may serve you in the power of his risen life;
who is alive and reigns with you,
in the unity of the Holy Spirit,
one God, now and for ever.

Reflection by **Julia Mourant**

Ordinary Time

Friday 23 July

Psalm 31
Jeremiah 35
James 4.13 – 5.6

James 4.13 – 5.6
'What is your life? (4.14)

The message is timeless. It is easier to have plans and fantasies than to acknowledge we only ever have today. James rebukes the fantasy of self-sufficiency, the delusion that we can secure our destiny on our own terms. How quickly life can change, in unforeseen and dramatic – sometimes traumatic – ways. James invites us to consider what we invest in. Today we have resources, energy and love to spend. These are more valuable than having more money in the bank than we really need. We can choose to invest our love, gifts and experience in ways that make a difference. James invites and challenges us not to withhold our soul investment.

The mis-invested life is wasted. James paints a picture of rotting riches and moth-eaten clothes. Supposedly valuable items lie unused, tarnished and rusted, vulnerable to silent decay. Spring cleaning can be uncomfortable when we unearth unused things we forgot we owned, some still in their boxes. It happens with 'stuff', but it is also true of spiritual resources.

James invites his readers to look in the mirror again. The illusions of self-sufficiency are ridiculous, because the treasure and finery turn to dust, as you will too. Such a life is not just pathetic; it also reveals a deep unrighteousness. Worse than the useless goods is the fact that gaining them involved exploiting others. Where are you invested today?

COLLECT

Almighty Lord and everlasting God,
we beseech you to direct, sanctify and govern
   both our hearts and bodies
in the ways of your laws
   and the works of your commandments;
that through your most mighty protection, both here and ever,
we may be preserved in body and soul;
through our Lord and Saviour Jesus Christ.

Reflection by **Julia Mourant**

Ordinary Time

Psalms 41, **42**, 43
Jeremiah 36.1-18
James 5.7-end

Saturday 24 July

James 5.7-end

'... the earth ... receives the early and the late rains' (v.7)

James offers a vision of a radical change of values. Rather than focusing on achievement and illusory security, life is marked by patience, endurance and truthful plain speaking. A rhythm of prayer, singing and ministry to the sick shapes a community with humility and humanity, where wanderers are brought home.

The metaphor of the farmer waiting for rain underlines the need for patience. One shower, or even one season, of rain is not sufficient. The early rains come; there is a season of growth, perhaps slow, perhaps underground. In due course, the longed-for later rains arrive. Then we might begin to see the possibility of harvest. In times when little seems to be happening, impatience can undermine unity, and grumbling sets in.

As a community, we take courage and comfort from those who went before us. Some pray to the saints; their lives and witness hold gifts for us still. James brings the theme of rain and the prophets together by pointing to Elijah, whose prayers were answered. James stresses that Elijah had no more power than any other human being, but he prayed, and rain came.

James ends his letter on an intriguing note. In our life together, what matters is whether we are truly a community in which the wanderers find their way home. Against this perspective, many other faults, failings, frailties and inadequacies may be forgiven.

COLLECT

Lord God,
your Son left the riches of heaven
and became poor for our sake:
when we prosper save us from pride,
when we are needy save us from despair,
that we may trust in you alone;
through Jesus Christ our Lord.

Reflection by **Julia Mourant**

Ordinary Time

Monday 26 July

Psalm **44**
Jeremiah 36.19-end
Mark 1.1-13

Mark 1.1-13

'... the good news of Jesus Christ, the Son of God' (v.1)

There's a breathless quality to the opening of St Mark's Gospel. In just 13 verses, the reader is introduced to Jesus, to John the baptizer, to the people of Judea and Jerusalem, to the river, to the wilderness, to the wild beasts and to the angels. Quite the rollercoaster!

But Mark can afford to be succinct, fast paced and direct. He can, because with his very first words he has disclosed to his readers his entire purpose. There's no plot twist or hidden denouement: 'The beginning of the good news of Jesus Christ, the Son of God' – thirteen words that tell us everything we need to know. Jesus is the anointed one, the Christ: he is the fulfilment of God's historic promise and of his people's hopes. Jesus is the Son of God: he is in a unique relationship with the Creator of all that is, and embodies the Creator for the creation.

And Jesus is good news: for those with whom he meets in person, and for those who meet him through Mark's writing. Hence John acclaims him; hence the Spirit descends on him; hence the angels wait on him. There's only one outcome to the story that Mark is beginning.

COLLECT

Almighty God,
who sent your Holy Spirit
to be the life and light of your Church:
open our hearts to the riches of your grace,
that we may bring forth the fruit of the Spirit
in love and joy and peace;
through Jesus Christ our Lord.

Reflection by **Nicholas Papadopulos**

Ordinary Time

Psalms **48**, 52
Jeremiah 37
Mark 1.14-20

Tuesday 27 July

Mark 1.14-20

'Follow me' (v.17)

Our smartphones allow us to move between different worlds at the tap of a screen. Inside one minute, we can check work emails, read a foreign newspaper's headlines and follow up on the stories of old school friends through our social media. And all without leaving the comfort of a favourite armchair!

Such luxury was not available to the fishermen of Galilee. Their sea-borne trade, the nets and boats that enabled them to fish the landlocked Sea of Galilee; their homes and their families: these were their world. No other was open to them – and certainly not at the tap of a screen. Until Jesus passed along the shore with his invitation, 'Follow me'. In that instant, their world was turned upside down. They abandoned their boats, their nets, their trade, the sea's familiar horizon, their homes and their families. They left it all behind and stepped into the unknown.

Frankly, it makes me shiver. I love the freedom that my apps give me to inhabit very different spaces ... but to make a switch in the *real* world, not the virtual world, a switch that is irretrievably life-changing ... that's very different. Am I ready to do that? And for what – or for whom?

> Gracious Father,
> revive your Church in our day,
> and make her holy, strong and faithful,
> for your glory's sake
> in Jesus Christ our Lord.

COLLECT

Reflection by **Nicholas Papadopulos**

Ordinary Time

Wednesday 28 July

Psalm 119.57-80
Jeremiah 38.1-13
Mark 1.21-28

Mark 1.21-28

'A new teaching – with authority!' (v.27)

I'm a sucker for a clever advert. I really am. I'm almost ashamed to admit it. And the genius (or curse) of the algorithms with which we all live is that the adverts that flash up on our PCs and phones are tailored to our interests and tastes. I find myself clicking them and following them up far more often than I should. It's the appeal of the unexplored, of the unimagined, of the unsought. It's the allure of the new.

Jesus flashes up at the synagogue in Capernaum. He teaches, and what he teaches is new. The congregation have never heard anything like it. But it's not just new; it's authoritative. Which is what the algorithm-driven adverts rarely are. Eye-catching, they appear to respond to individual need or personal fascination. But invariably what they offer is a product, potentially a product repackaged, possibly a product upgraded, probably a product we really can manage without. That's manifestly not what Jesus offers.

In his mastery of the spirit world and in the words he utters, Jesus is not pushing snake-oil or rehashing last year's offer wrapped up in glittery ribbon. This is ground-breaking, unprecedented. It's *new*. Those who hear him acknowledge the power of his presence. So does Mark. It's what he wants us to hear – what he wants us to know.

COLLECT

Almighty God,
who sent your Holy Spirit
to be the life and light of your Church:
open our hearts to the riches of your grace,
that we may bring forth the fruit of the Spirit
in love and joy and peace;
through Jesus Christ our Lord.

Reflection by **Nicholas Papadopulos**

Ordinary Time

Psalms 56, **57** (63*)
Jeremiah 38.14-end
Mark 1.29-end

Thursday 29 July

Mark 1.29-end

'If you choose ...' (v.40)

The number of choices I make every day is quite bewildering. What I drink: latte or cappuccino. How I exercise: the gym or a walk. What I listen to: a podcast or music. These are three that I make without thinking – and they are all about my own comfort and enjoyment. How often do I make a choice that places my stake in society – even, perhaps, my life – in jeopardy? Rarely, thankfully.

Yet that is the sort of choice that Jesus makes as he goes through Galilee, proclaiming the message and casting out the demons. He chooses to heal the man with leprosy. He does so explicitly and demonstrably. He reaches out his hand to touch him. This is an act that (according to the understanding of the time) puts him at risk of contracting the disease and that renders him unclean. Jesus chooses personal danger and social ignominy. Jesus chooses healing and life.

The journey through Galilee is fuelled by solitary prayer before daybreak; its work is deliverance and proclamation; its fruit is the drawing together of great crowds. Time and again, Jesus chooses to heal; time and again, Jesus chooses to forget his own comfort and enjoyment.

The number of choices I make every day is quite bewildering ...

COLLECT

Gracious Father,
revive your Church in our day,
and make her holy, strong and faithful,
for your glory's sake
in Jesus Christ our Lord.

Reflection by **Nicholas Papadopulos**

Ordinary Time

Friday 30 July

Psalms **51**, 54
Jeremiah 39
Mark 2.1-12

Mark 2.1-12

'When Jesus saw their faith ...' (v.5)

'Jesus and the Four Kind Friends' is one of the earliest miracle stories that I ever came across. I read it again and again in my Children's Bible. I remember beautiful illustrations of a flat-roofed house with a conveniently placed staircase, of squares of turf being carefully removed, and of the four lowering their paralyzed companion down into Jesus' presence. It was artfully pitched. Children know what friends are long before they have any idea about faith, sin or forgiveness. And the four friends are at the heart of this story.

It's said that you can judge a person by their friends. The most remarkable feature of this story is that it's the friends' faith that Jesus acts upon. He sees it and immediately tells the paralyzed man that his sins are forgiven. The friends have struggled up that conveniently placed staircase; they have cut out the squares of turf; they have lowered their friend. Their faith in Jesus' power to heal is evident. And that seems to be enough. Their faith. His forgiveness.

The 'Four Kind Friends' set the bar very high for us and for our relationships. They can never be all about our convenience and our satisfaction. Who we are, how we are, who we trust and how we believe: all these have a colossal impact on those with whom we share our lives. It's not a bad lesson for friends of any age.

COLLECT

Almighty God,
who sent your Holy Spirit
to be the life and light of your Church:
open our hearts to the riches of your grace,
that we may bring forth the fruit of the Spirit
in love and joy and peace;
through Jesus Christ our Lord.

Reflection by **Nicholas Papadopulos**

Ordinary Time

Psalm **68**
Jeremiah 40
Mark 2.13-22

Saturday 31 July

Mark 2.13-22

'... the new from the old' (v.21)

The discipline of fasting has enjoyed a comeback. Fitness gurus commend its health-giving properties. Campaign groups practise it as an expression of solidarity with the oppressed. And people of faith have rediscovered it as a spiritual exercise not just for Lent but throughout the year.

Fasting necessarily involves a degree of self-denial and hence a degree of suffering (even if it's just a fast from chocolate, crisps or Chianti). Naturally, commitment to self-denial and personal suffering is the hallmark of a certain sort of religion. Which is why the disciples of Jesus scandalize the Pharisees when they refuse to fast – when they refuse to subscribe to this accepted sign of a devout life.

Fasting is unthinkable to the disciples. For they are in the presence of Jesus, and to be in the presence of Jesus is to step inside the gates of eternity. Every day that they spend with him, the abundance of heaven stands open before them. We stand with them.

Fasting represents the old order, and the old order has no place in the new, inaugurated by Jesus: the order of joy, of life eternal. Here, at least, the disciples have found the courage to embrace the new order – to live with hope. Have we?

> Gracious Father,
> revive your Church in our day,
> and make her holy, strong and faithful,
> for your glory's sake
> in Jesus Christ our Lord.

COLLECT

Reflection by **Nicholas Papadopulos**

Ordinary Time

Monday 2 August

Psalm 71
Jeremiah 41
Mark 2.23 – 3.6

Mark 2.23 – 3.6

'Is it lawful …?' (3.4)

Mark offers us two stories in succession – a double bill, focusing on Jesus' relationship with the sabbath, and on the divine commandment to abstain from work (and instead to rest). In both stories, Jesus' interpretation of the commandment causes controversy.

The Pharisees rebuke him for allowing his disciples to pluck heads of grain on the sabbath – and by the end of the passage, they are conspiring 'to destroy him'. But it's not that Jesus has no regard for tradition. And it's not that Jesus is disrespectful of the inheritance of faith in which he has been raised. It's just that he refuses to overlook the author of the tradition – the one from whom the inheritance is received. So, in the cornfield, Jesus reminds the Pharisees that the sabbath 'was made'. It was God's institution – God's gift.

In the synagogue, Jesus reminds them that for God's gift to be received and enjoyed by all God's people – including the man with the withered hand – then he and, by implication, the Pharisees have work to do. 'Is it lawful to do good … on the sabbath?' It's not for us to presume to harness God's purposes to our own religious ambitions. God's purposes always make demands of us – greater demands than we can imagine.

COLLECT

Let your merciful ears, O Lord,
be open to the prayers of your humble servants;
and that they may obtain their petitions
make them to ask such things as shall please you;
through Jesus Christ our Lord.

Reflection by **Nicholas Papadopulos**

Ordinary Time

Psalm **73**
Jeremiah 42
Mark 3.7-19a

Tuesday 3 August

Mark 3.7-19a

'... to be sent out' (v.14)

Would Jesus survive a modern HR process, or be selected for ministry in today's Church? It's worth asking because he appears very directive. That is somewhat at odds with contemporary expectations. He calls 'those whom he wanted'. Presumably, there were disappointed candidates – but we hear nothing of them. He appoints twelve – there does not appear to have been a long-list, a short-list, or an interview process. He renames some of them. Did they mind? And he sends them out. They may have had ageing parents or young children or thriving businesses – but off they go.

Simon, James, John and the rest do not agonize about what is being asked of them. They do not ask – in anguished earnestness – 'but is this the ministry to which I am called?' No. Jesus calls, appoints, renames and sends. They follow, and they go.

We may use our imaginations to fill in the Biblical narrative, creating answers to questions about disappointed candidates or abandoned families. We may allow that Jesus speaks with unique power and authority. But we are still left with an account that clashes with our proper sense of 'best practice' and that agitates our sensibilities. These twelve men are ready to be sent. They do not question. They do not challenge. They just ... go.

> Lord of heaven and earth,
> as Jesus taught his disciples to be persistent in prayer,
> give us patience and courage never to lose hope,
> but always to bring our prayers before you;
> through Jesus Christ our Lord.

COLLECT

Reflection by **Nicholas Papadopulos**

Ordinary Time

Wednesday 4 August

Psalm **77**
Jeremiah 43
Mark 3.19*b*-end

Mark 3.19*b*-end

'... whoever blasphemes against the Holy Spirit' (v.28)

I find this one very tough. Eternal sin? I would much rather believe there's no such thing – no such thing as something that cannot be forgiven by the all-loving God in whom I place my absolute trust. Mark's Jesus is ready to command, of course: we saw him in directive mode as he summoned the Twelve yesterday. Yet here his words go far beyond that: they are stark, uncompromising, and they compel us to listen.

So, what does it mean to blaspheme against the Holy Spirit? The illustration we are given is that the scribes had accused Jesus of having an unclean spirit – of allying himself with the prince of the demons. This goes beyond a careless slur or an ill-chosen remark. This is to invert the reality of creation. It is, in effect, to call what is one thing, another. It is to call what is supremely and eternally good, supremely and eternally evil. It's this that cannot be forgiven.

Among the very first words that Mark records as coming from the mouth of Jesus is 'repent'. It means nothing more and nothing less than 'change'. It's to this command that the teaching on blasphemy sends us. We are at liberty to turn God's creation upside down and curse what he calls good and beautiful. But in so doing, we place ourselves in grave peril. We must change.

COLLECT

Let your merciful ears, O Lord,
be open to the prayers of your humble servants;
and that they may obtain their petitions
make them to ask such things as shall please you;
through Jesus Christ our Lord.

Reflection by **Nicholas Papadopulos**

Ordinary Time

Psalm **78.1-39***
Jeremiah 44.1-14
Mark 4.1-20

Thursday 5 August

Mark 4.1-20

'And as he sowed ...' (v.4)

During the Covid lockdowns, I cultivated a vegetable garden for the first time and found great pleasure in it. Being new to horticulture, I bought a 'how to' book and followed its advice diligently. I took care over the depth of my drills; measured their distance one from another; and spaced out my seed potatoes, onion sets and pea plants perfectly (the peas never grew, but that's a different matter).

It's made me read this parable very differently and, if I'm honest, it's led me to take a very dim view of the sower. What on earth was he doing? Seed on the path, seed on the rocks, seed among the thorns. Really? How about a nice, neat trench and some thought-through positioning of the future crop?

But that's not the sower's style – and in the lives of our churches perhaps it shouldn't be ours, either. The sower sows recklessly. He's not too fussed about where the seed lands. I wonder if he even knows where the good soil is? He's content just to fling the seed wherever. And sometimes it falls into good soil. And then it produces. Big time.

As a strategy for mission, it will be risky. Perhaps one-quarter of the 'seed' will fail to land. But when it does ...

> COLLECT
>
> Lord of heaven and earth,
> as Jesus taught his disciples to be persistent in prayer,
> give us patience and courage never to lose hope,
> but always to bring our prayers before you;
> through Jesus Christ our Lord.

Reflection by **Nicholas Papadopulos**

Ordinary Time

Friday 6 August
Transfiguration of Our Lord

Psalms 27, 150
Ecclesiasticus 48.1-10
or 1 Kings 19.1-16
1 John 3.1-3

1 John 3.1-3

'We will see him as he is ...' (v.2)

Harry Potter's first class at Hogwarts is Transfiguration, taught by Professor Minerva McGonagall (played memorably in the film adaptations by the late and very great Dame Maggie Smith). With a flick of her wand, McGonagall turns her desk into a pig – and back again. Harry and his friends spend the rest of the lesson trying to turn matchsticks into pins ...

Transfiguration, Hogwarts-style, means turning something into something else. Who wouldn't want that superpower? Just think of the transformations we could effect on our possessions, our surroundings, our lifestyles and (let's face it) ourselves. All at the flick of a wand!

But Transfiguration, Jesus-style, means something rather different. On the mountain top, Jesus does not become someone else. Peter, James and John see him and know him. It's just that he's changed. Heaven's light streams from him. They see their friend, and they see God's anointed one, and they see that these are the same.

It's not God's plan to turn us into what we're not; God's plan is that what we most truly are will ultimately be seen. And what we most truly are is what God knows us to be. Not desks into pigs or matchsticks into pins, but his beloved creation, known and cherished from the very depths of eternity.

COLLECT

Father in heaven,
whose Son Jesus Christ was wonderfully transfigured
before chosen witnesses upon the holy mountain,
and spoke of the exodus he would accomplish at Jerusalem:
give us strength so to hear his voice and bear our cross
that in the world to come we may see him as he is;
who is alive and reigns with you,
in the unity of the Holy Spirit,
one God, now and for ever.

Reflection by **Nicholas Papadopulos**

Psalms **76**, 79
Jeremiah 45
Mark 4.35-end

Saturday 7 August

Mark 4.35-end

'Other boats were with him' (v.36)

When I think of the night the barbeque wouldn't light, I break out in a cold sweat. My guests were about to arrive, and there was no one to whom I could turn. So – inexplicably and inexcusably – I blamed my parents. They had given me the charcoal, and it was obviously of terrible quality. When the pressure mounts, an immediate human response is to locate a scapegoat. Who is doing this to us? Why don't they care? Why don't they stop?

I'd love to know what the response of the occupants of the other boats was when the great storm arose. They couldn't shake Jesus awake and pour out all their panic. Perhaps they blamed one another. Perhaps they screamed across the water. Perhaps they were silent, unable to speak, rigid with fright.

We cannot know. But the rebuke that Jesus addresses to his own shipmates applies equally to them. He has launched this flotilla. He is in their midst. And therefore – however fierce the tempest – there is nothing to fear.

You and I are in one of those other boats. Jesus is not recumbent at our feet, sleeping on a cushion. Yet our journey is his journey, and he is with us. Looking for someone to blame is a waste of energy. Better by far to remember that – whatever – he is with us.

> Let your merciful ears, O Lord,
> be open to the prayers of your humble servants;
> and that they may obtain their petitions
> make them to ask such things as shall please you;
> through Jesus Christ our Lord.

COLLECT

Reflection by **Nicholas Papadopulos**

Ordinary Time

Monday 9 August

Psalms **80**, 82
Micah 1.1-9
Mark 5.1-20

Micah 1.1-9

'… lo, the Lord is coming' (v.3)

Martin Luther moaned that the Old Testament prophets 'have a queer way of talking … instead of proceeding in an orderly manner, they ramble from one thing to the next so that you cannot make head nor tail of them or see what they are getting at'. Hello Micah!

Micah's book is not a single logical argument, but his 'greatest hits' selected from 30 years of pronouncements in Judah seven centuries before Jesus walked there. He is addressing a society that is comfortable and prosperous. The northern part of the country (here given the name Samaria) has grown wealthy by unjust and corrupt practices – the inhabitants might just as well be prostitutes. The southern part (represented as Jerusalem) has so compromised its worship of the true God that the inhabitants might as well be idol-worshippers.

It's OK though, isn't it? God is impossibly distant in heaven, from where he looks down dependably on his covenant people. But what if God leaves his heaven and crashes down on the mountains, which then melt as he wreaks terrible destruction in response to the people's sin? At the moment, one man dares to suggest this – a forlorn, humble lament. Nobody wants to hear a warning so discordant that it might as well belong to a jackal or an ostrich. Surely Micah's unpopular portents of doom will never come true. Reader, I am sorry to inform you that they did!

COLLECT

O God, you declare your almighty power
most chiefly in showing mercy and pity:
mercifully grant to us such a measure of your grace,
that we, running the way of your commandments,
may receive your gracious promises,
and be made partakers of your heavenly treasure;
through Jesus Christ our Lord.

Reflection by **Peter Graystone**

Ordinary Time

Psalms 87, **89.1-18**
Micah 2
Mark 5.21-34

Tuesday 10 August

Micah 2

'Is the Lord's patience exhausted?' (v.7)

Micah's home town was Moresheth-Gath, 25 miles south-west of Jerusalem. It was an agricultural region that was being militarized in anticipation of the threat from Assyria. That may have made Micah an eyewitness to the appropriation of land, which he denounces in the first section of this chapter. Or maybe unscrupulous merchants were using oppression and bribery to amass their own wealth – dreaming up schemes at night and enacting them by day. It was (and still is) a terrible injustice. But Micah warns the powerful that there is a Landowner who is altogether righteous and can ruin them when, in time or out of it, he redistributes their wealth in 'the assembly of the Lord'.

In the second section, Micah rounds on those trying to silence him because people don't want to hear bad news about what their future holds if they don't change their ways. 'Do not preach!' Every scientist, politician or prophet who has tried to explain the threat to our environment from human irresponsibility understands Micah's dilemma – a tax reduction on alcohol is more of a vote-winner than a ban on fossil fuels.

The last two verses of the chapter foresee a later time. The catastrophe that the prophets warned of has happened: Israel has been overrun and its inhabitants scattered abroad. Micah offers a vision of hope. Restoration is possible. Refuge is possible. A new and godly king is possible. Never despair!

COLLECT

God of glory,
the end of our searching,
help us to lay aside
all that prevents us from seeking your kingdom,
and to give all that we have
to gain the pearl beyond all price,
through our Saviour Jesus Christ.

Reflection by **Peter Graystone**

Ordinary Time

Wednesday 11 August

Psalm 119.105-128
Micah 3
Mark 5.35-end

Micah 3

'... filled with power, with the Spirit of the Lord' (v.8)

When Netflix commissions *Micah, the Movie*, the cannibalism sequence will earn it an 18 certificate. Maybe Micah found it hard to attract attention with a soberly reasoned plea to Israel's rulers, so he resorted to sensationalism. God gave those leaders the responsibility to create a thriving nation, but instead they exploited the citizens for their own gain. When they call on God in the hour of need that is inevitably coming, their prayers will be met with silence.

Micah sets himself apart from other prophets, as Amos had done a generation previously (Amos 7.14). There were perhaps seers who, in return for money, would use means similar to a clairvoyant today to divine the future. To people who made sure they were paid and fed, the fortune tellers would deliver good news – a peaceful future. It was a far cry from the integrity of Micah's message, which was fearless in its condemnation of injustice and corruption even if it antagonized priests, rulers or fraudulent prophets. The difference was that the Holy Spirit of God had given Micah an insight into what should be regarded as sin and what its consequence would be – the collapse of the nation into 'a heap of ruins'.

Anyone who suggests that God's blessing needs to be purchased is abusing you. That hasn't changed during the 27 centuries between us and Micah. The Holy Spirit is yours free of charge and will always incline you towards justice.

COLLECT

O God, you declare your almighty power
most chiefly in showing mercy and pity:
mercifully grant to us such a measure of your grace,
that we, running the way of your commandments,
may receive your gracious promises,
and be made partakers of your heavenly treasure;
through Jesus Christ our Lord.

Reflection by **Peter Graystone**

Ordinary Time

Psalms 90, **92**
Micah 4.1 – 5.1
Mark 6.1-13

Thursday 12 August

Micah 4.1 – 5.1

'... the Lord will redeem you' (4.10)

The patchwork quilt that comprises this book has three sections here. They refer to distinct ages – one timeless, one in Micah's future, one in Micah's present.

In the first five verses of chapter 4, Micah defies the sorrow of his beleaguered country and anticipates a time in the future when the temple where God is worshipped will be the most exalted setting known to humankind. But it will be a spiritual temple, built from recognition of God's supreme goodness. People the world over will be so attracted by his justice that they will flood towards him, knowing that under his leadership they will find peace, purpose and security.

Verses 6 to 8 address people who are the survivors of a terrible future onslaught. Wounded and forsaken Jews have been scattered or driven into exile. God is a God who does not abandon the weakest, and he will gather them and rehabilitate them. They will return reinvigorated to the lands surrounding Jerusalem, and Mount Zion will be like a shepherd's watchtower from which God oversees the safety of his sheep.

The final six verses then leap back in time and address the Jews in the heart of battle, as the military might of the enemy sweeps in. It's a desperate time. But even when the suffering is most intense, God has a plan. The adversaries have no concept that the Lord is a redeeming God. This is not the end of the story.

> God of glory,
> the end of our searching,
> help us to lay aside
> all that prevents us from seeking your kingdom,
> and to give all that we have
> to gain the pearl beyond all price,
> through our Saviour Jesus Christ.

COLLECT

Reflection by **Peter Graystone**

Ordinary Time

Friday 13 August

Psalms **88** (95)
Micah 5.2-end
Mark 6.14-29

Micah 5.2-end

'He shall be the one of peace' (v.5)

Assyria was an ever-present threat during Micah's lifetime. In 722 BC, King Shalmaneser V invaded the northern kingdom of Israel. Two years later, his son Sargon II completed the conquest and deported the population. In the southern kingdom of Judah, King Hezekiah, whose health was precarious, watched power changing hands in neighbouring countries. When Sargon's son Sennacherib succeeded his father, Hezekiah calculated that the best prospect of security was to curry favour with Babylon instead, so he stopped paying tribute to Assyria. Both Micah and Isaiah warned him that this was folly. It was.

In 701 BC, Sennacherib's army swept horrifically through Judah and laid siege to Jerusalem trapping Hezekiah 'like a bird in a cage', as the Assyrian account puts it. But the siege failed. Isaiah 37.36–38 relates that an angel of the Lord miraculously intervened. Other historians refer to a mouse-borne plague decimating the Assyrian camp. Overwhelmed, Sennacherib withdrew.

In that tumultuous context, Micah looked forward to a new ruler who would come from the home of the venerated King David. His defining characteristic would be the pursuit of peace. He would be completely unlike Sennacherib and completely unlike Hezekiah. All the warmongering kings tried to outdo each other in horses and chariots, strongholds and sorcerers, idols and images. But as Christians know, 'God chose what is weak in the world to shame the strong' (1 Corinthians 1.27). Out of tiny little Bethlehem came a Saviour.

COLLECT

O God, you declare your almighty power
most chiefly in showing mercy and pity:
mercifully grant to us such a measure of your grace,
that we, running the way of your commandments,
may receive your gracious promises,
and be made partakers of your heavenly treasure;
through Jesus Christ our Lord.

Reflection by **Peter Graystone**

Ordinary Time

Psalms 96, **97**, 100
Micah 6
Mark 6.30-44

Saturday 14 August

Micah 6
'... what does the Lord require of you ...?' (v.8)

We are in court. It is an immense, outdoor court and the mountains surrounding it are the judges. God is arguing his case. He has been utterly faithful and does not deserve the disdain with which he is treated. He summons character witnesses – Moses, Aaron, Miriam. He cites evidence – he overturned the intentions of the seer Balaam so that instead of cursing the Israelites, he blessed them (Numbers 22-24).

In verses 9-12, God rounds on the people and accuses them. Their lives are characterized by violence, lying, deceit and cheating (a merchant who hollowed out the weights on his scales gave his customer less grain than they paid for). The court's sentence is pronounced in verses 13-16. The guilty nation will be punished.

Between God's indictments, we hear from Micah, speaking in the witness box on behalf of the community. He knows what is needed in order to give God what he longs for. It's not the rituals of religion. Not even thousands of sacrifices or millions of prayers. Rather it is to do justice (so that those who have enough change the circumstances of the poor), to love mercy (so that vulnerable people live without fear), and to walk humbly with God (so that we know his ways and experience his love). Today, which is the day when the Orthodox Church commemorates Micah, is a good day to recognize that this appears to cost nothing but actually requires everything.

COLLECT

God of glory,
the end of our searching,
help us to lay aside
all that prevents us from seeking your kingdom,
and to give all that we have
to gain the pearl beyond all price,
through our Saviour Jesus Christ.

Reflection by **Peter Graystone**

Ordinary Time

Monday 16 August

Psalms **98**, 99, 101
Micah 7.1-7
Mark 6.45-end

Micah 7.1-7

'... as for me, I will look to the Lord' (v.7)

Theologians disagree over whether Micah is the work of a single author, writing in the eighth century BC, or whether we hear several voices. The book is so prescient about the experience of the Jews two centuries later in exile in Babylon that perhaps it was there that Micah's original prophecies were expanded into the book we are now reading. Either way, there is something poignant about Chapter 7 being narrated in the first person. Whether Micah is speaking for himself or for the whole of Israel, it feels personal.

The tone is initially sad. Micah sets out to look for pockets of hope where people are faithful to God, like a farmer seeking out tasty early figs as a first sign of a later harvest. But there is nothing. In fact, things are worse than he feared. There isn't even a vine anymore, just the thorns of wickedness. The day of reckoning is imminent – the one the prophets (sentinels and watchmen) warned of. It's about to turn nasty. Trust no one in the battle for survival, not even the person you're in bed with.

Then apparently from nowhere comes a tiny voice, whispering an alternative. There is another future, and it involves putting your trust in God. If there is only one person doing it, so be it. It is the way of salvation, and it is a cause for hope. God, as always, is listening.

COLLECT

Almighty and everlasting God,
you are always more ready to hear than we to pray
and to give more than either we desire or deserve:
pour down upon us the abundance of your mercy,
forgiving us those things of which our conscience is afraid
and giving us those good things which we are not worthy to ask
but through the merits and mediation
of Jesus Christ our Lord.

Reflection by **Peter Graystone**

Ordinary Time

Psalms **106*** (*or* 103)
Micah 7.8-end
Mark 7.1-13

Tuesday 17 August

Micah 7.8-end

'Who is a God like you …?' (v.18)

We are in darkness. But look up, because the sky is dotted with explosions of brightness. Dawn is on its way, and it heralds light for the whole world. This is Vincent van Gogh's sensational painting *The Starry Night*. It is also the beginning of this final hymn of Micah's book – a repentant recognition that Jerusalem's destruction is a result of its own wrongdoing, a prophecy of its restoration, a prayer that the future will not be like the past, and finally a hymn of praise that God's forgiveness is incomparable. But Micah did something that van Gogh didn't – he signed his work. The painter only placed his name Vincent on a picture if he thought it was absolutely perfect. Micah's name means, 'Who is like God?' And there it is at the foot of his book in verse 18. Perfect!

God did 'marvellous things' for the Israelites escaping Egypt when he hurled their enemies into the Red Sea, and now he will 'cast all our sins into the depths of the sea'. From now on they (and we) experience him not as a God of anger but as a God of mercy. It is undeserved. It is worldwide. It is awe-inspiring. As van Gogh wrote in a letter to his brother in November 1878: 'What lies beyond this is a great mystery that only God knows, but has revealed absolutely through his word, that there is a resurrection of the dead.'

COLLECT

God of constant mercy,
who sent your Son to save us:
remind us of your goodness,
increase your grace within us,
that our thankfulness may grow,
through Jesus Christ our Lord.

Reflection by **Peter Graystone**

Ordinary Time

Wednesday 18 August

Psalms 110, 111, 112
Habakkuk 1.1-11
Mark 7.14-23

Habakkuk 1.1-11

'Be astonished! Be astounded!' (v.5)

Time has passed since Micah delivered his prophecies. Habakkuk belongs to a century later, but it is difficult to tell because his book does not introduce him. Clues in the prophecies themselves suggest that it is no longer Assyria that is the main threat to Jerusalem and its surroundings. It is the Babylonians (or Chaldeans, depending on which translation you read) who are to be feared, which places Habakkuk in the last few years of the seventh century BC. Whatever the date, the questions that begin the book are timeless. Why is the world mired in violence and injustice? Why has God, who holds absolute power and could change things in a heartbeat, done nothing? How long will it be until the promised end to suffering comes?

Unusually, this comes in the form of a dialogue. The first four verses are Habakkuk's yearning cry to God. The rest of the passage is God's reply: 'I am about to take action and it is going to be astounding. But that doesn't mean you're going to like it. Terrifying, all-conquering Babylon is not just a human army; it is the embodiment of my intention to fulfil my purpose in history.'

'Why is there suffering?' is the correct question to ask. But as we shall see over the coming days, the answer won't fit inside a fortune cookie. God is God, and God will do what God will do.

COLLECT

Almighty and everlasting God,
you are always more ready to hear than we to pray
and to give more than either we desire or deserve:
pour down upon us the abundance of your mercy,
forgiving us those things of which our conscience is afraid
and giving us those good things which we are not worthy to ask
but through the merits and mediation
of Jesus Christ our Lord.

Reflection by **Peter Graystone**

Ordinary Time

Psalms 113, **115**
Habakkuk 1.12 – 2.5
Mark 7.24-30

Thursday 19 August

Habakkuk 1.12 – 2.5

'If it seems to tarry, wait for it' (2.3)

How can God possibly be helping the situation when his chosen way to end the rule of one oppressor is to send a different oppressor? That's the question Habakkuk asks in this new exchange of dialogue. He's fully aware that God is holy, pure and eternal. However, he cannot reconcile that with what he sees. Wicked enemies are treating people ruthlessly, just as fish are swept indiscriminately into a dragnet behind a trawler. The fishermen are oblivious to what the Lord thinks of them because the only god they seek to satisfy is their net.

At the beginning of Chapter 2, Habakkuk refuses to give up on God and sets us an example to follow. He commits himself to do whatever it takes to listen, learn and understand. Nobody, not even a prophet, can compel God to speak. But Habakkuk will not budge until God is ready to respond.

God's message to Habakkuk and to us is that he has a plan to end suffering and he will be completely dependable in fulfilling it. But we will need to wait with patience and trust. For those with eyes to see, the first indications that good will overcome evil are visible. Are proud people fully alive? No, they are disturbed inside. Are avaricious and arrogant people living their best life? No, they are agonizingly insatiable for wealth or wine or whatever cannot last. But faith gives righteous people a living hope.

COLLECT

God of constant mercy,
who sent your Son to save us:
remind us of your goodness,
increase your grace within us,
that our thankfulness may grow,
through Jesus Christ our Lord.

Reflection by **Peter Graystone**

Ordinary Time

Friday 20 August

Psalm 139
Habakkuk 2.6-end
Mark 7.31-end

Habakkuk 2.6-end

'... let all the earth keep silence' (v.20)

How are we to behave during the long wait for God to respond to the world's injustice? In five negative ways and two positive ways.

The five negative ways involve taunting contemptuously those who defy the way of God. Scorn the aggressors – the message to those who have plundered is that the tables will be turned on them. Scorn those who think their power has made them unassailable – if humans can't shame them, the very bricks of their houses will. Scorn the violent – whatever they procure will eventually go up in smoke. Scorn the sexual abusers – they will be utterly disgraced by the Lord. Scorn the idol-worshippers – whatever treasure they depend on that shimmers with silver and gold (or bleeps or speeds or plays music or connects with the internet) will gather lifeless dust.

The two positive ways sing with poetry. First, cling to the fact that a future day will come when God reveals himself fully and there will be worldwide understanding of why he has done what he has done. Just as there is not one millilitre of sea that is not full of water, so there will not be one millimetre of earth where God's glory is unrecognized.

Second, acknowledge here and now how absolutely holy God is. Bring yourself to a place where the taunting has finished, all the words are exhausted, the questions can wait, and the only thing that matters is silent adoration.

COLLECT

Almighty and everlasting God,
you are always more ready to hear than we to pray
and to give more than either we desire or deserve:
pour down upon us the abundance of your mercy,
forgiving us those things of which our conscience is afraid
and giving us those good things which we are not worthy to ask
but through the merits and mediation
of Jesus Christ our Lord.

Reflection by **Peter Graystone**

Ordinary Time

Psalms 120, **121**, 122
Habakkuk 3.2-19*a*
Mark 8.1-10

Saturday 21 August

Habakkuk 3.2-19*a*

'I stand in awe, O Lord' (v.2)

A Force 12 God is about to hurtle through this chapter, and it could easily end in devastation. In a surprising turn of emotions, it doesn't.

Habakkuk's extraordinary psalm begins with him doing three vital things. He looks back at mighty acts God has brought about in the past; he marvels awestruck at what the Lord can do; and he prays for God to have mercy as he did in ancient days on a nation about to be engulfed in wrath.

Then comes the vision of divine intervention, and it is difficult to decide whether it is glorious or terrifying. The people of God are saved and their enemies destroyed, but that is brought about by horror and destruction. When Habakkuk realizes that the future God has revealed to him is dreadful, he is filled with dismay. He knows that calamity will finally come upon the aggressors, but a lot of bad things will happen first. He resigns himself to waiting patiently for them to pass.

How can he survive? By choosing to rejoice in God even in the worst of the trouble that lies ahead. He will actively seek joy, and he can only do that because he knows that God is his Saviour. In that he will find strength – not the strength of a dinosaur whose power tramples everything, but the strength of a deer whose feet are nimble, secure and can find a way on difficult terrain.

> God of constant mercy,
> who sent your Son to save us:
> remind us of your goodness,
> increase your grace within us,
> that our thankfulness may grow,
> through Jesus Christ our Lord.

COLLECT

Reflection by **Peter Graystone**

Ordinary Time

Monday 23 August

Psalms 123, 124, 125, **126**
Haggai 1.1-11
Mark 8.11-21

Haggai 1.1-11

'... while this house lies in ruins?' (v.4)

It must have been hard to resettle in a ruined city post-exile, where each house needed desperate repair. But the step beyond repair criticized here by Haggai is of a lavish outfitting of houses, while the temple, the place of their worship, still lay in ruins. Think house extensions and attic conversions while temple walls crumbled in the wind. Sometimes a good thing can become a bad thing when it becomes the ultimate thing, because it displaces the most important thing – worship of God.

Amid life's complexities, finding a well-ordered life, where priorities take a right hierarchy, can be hard to achieve. But here, at least, there is clarity – worship of God takes first place. God is the one we are made by and for, to whom worship is due, and whom we will perpetually worship in heaven's eternity. We are made to worship, destined to worship and called to worship him as a priority in the present.

Haggai's words challenge us to ask whether there are things that we might be prioritizing above God, even if they are good things in themselves. If there are, that is where our worship lies – and it is wrongly located. Rebuilding true worship in our lives means attending to the temple in our hearts, repairing the altar of worship within, where Jesus is found, worshipped and glorified.

COLLECT

Almighty God,
who called your Church to bear witness
that you were in Christ reconciling the world to yourself:
help us to proclaim the good news of your love,
that all who hear it may be drawn to you;
through him who was lifted up on the cross,
and reigns with you in the unity of the Holy Spirit,
one God, now and for ever.

Reflection by **Jitesh Patel**

Ordinary Time

Psalms 86, 117
Genesis 28.10-17
John 1.43-end

Tuesday 24 August

Bartholomew the Apostle

Genesis 28.10-17

'This is none other than the house of God' (v.17)

St Bartholomew, whose feast day is today, was one of the chosen twelve apostles of Jesus, sent out by the Great Commission, empowered by the events of Pentecost, to take the gospel to the world. The early Church historian Eusebius suggests that he went as far as India, which – if true – as an Indian myself, means I am a particularly big fan of his!

Wherever he did end up, no doubt the strength that he lived by was the same that God gave to Jacob in today's reading. On the run from his brother, scared and alone, God visits him in a night vision and reveals that he is with him and will always be so; that every place he goes is holy ground, because the Holy One is present with him. He thought he was alone, yet surprisingly encountered God in great power and glory.

Loneliness is an epidemic in our modern world. Mother Teresa once went as far as to say that loneliness is 'the leprosy of the Western world', and evidence suggests it is increasingly not just confined to the West. Yet there is a powerful ointment that brings healing and relief to this condition: the knowledge of a God who, through Jesus, is continually with us and will never leave us or forsake us (Hebrews 13.5). What good news we can live by and, like St Bartholomew, share with the world around us!

Almighty and everlasting God,
who gave to your apostle Bartholomew grace
truly to believe and to preach your word:
grant that your Church
may love that word which he believed
and may faithfully preach and receive the same;
through Jesus Christ our Lord.

COLLECT

Reflection by **Jitesh Patel**

Ordinary Time

Wednesday 25 August

Psalm 119.153-end
Haggai 2.10-end
Mark 8.27 – 9.1

Haggai 2.10-end

'From this day on I will bless you' (v.19)

Our God is a blessing God. From the blessing he speaks over creation's beautiful diversity, endowing its living creatures with a purpose to 'be fruitful and multiply and fill' (Genesis 1.22), through to the climax of his blessings found in Christ, through whom we have been blessed 'with every spiritual blessing in the heavenly places' (Ephesians 1.3). For Israel in today's reading, God's blessing nature is set against the backdrop of the people's unfaithfulness to him and the ensuing calamity. Yet despite this, God promises to turn the hourglass of their misfortune around in a single day and bless them beyond expectation.

For us, as for them, God's favour is completely unmerited and unearned. Something that gives us confidence to approach God, whose hands hold blessing ready to be poured out upon us. The testimony of his abundant generosity in both creation and salvation shows that he is no miser, and Israel's example here shows how we can approach him regardless of our worthiness to receive it.

Of course, God's blessings are often mediated through people. In today's reading, blessing is mediated by the prophet who makes it known. And the ultimate expression of God's blessing nature came through the humanly incarnated person of Christ. Therefore, we should expect that God both blesses us through others and calls us to be his means of blessing to others: communities of blessing reflecting a blessing, blessed, God.

COLLECT

Almighty God,
who called your Church to bear witness
that you were in Christ reconciling the world to yourself:
help us to proclaim the good news of your love,
that all who hear it may be drawn to you;
through him who was lifted up on the cross,
and reigns with you in the unity of the Holy Spirit,
one God, now and for ever.

Reflection by **Jitesh Patel**

Ordinary Time

Psalms 143, 146
Zechariah 1.1-17
Mark 9.2-13

Thursday 26 August

Zechariah 1.1-17
'Return to me ... and I will return to you' (v.3)

Sometimes we feel we have to make the first step with God, and it seems like this for God's people in these words. They are called to return to God after their return from exile, where they have been disciplined for turning away from him. Only then would God return to them.

However, the bigger picture was that God had never left them. He had been with them in exile, protecting and refining them, and had instigated their miraculous return from it. For them, and us, God often calls us to re-turn our face towards him, so that we can see his face, which has never turned away – appearing like his return to us. It is all about relative perspective: like when the sun can suddenly 'appear' from behind clouds, while never having gone anywhere at all.

The philosopher Søren Kierkegaard famously prayed: 'You have loved us first many times and every day and our whole life through. When we wake up in the morning and turn our soul toward You – You are the first – You have loved us first.' Before we turn our gaze to him in love, he has already turned his to us first; we will never get there before him. When we turn back to him in repentance, he is already there waiting to embrace us – the Father who waits and runs towards the returning prodigal, continually inviting us to return to him.

> Almighty God,
> you search us and know us:
> may we rely on you in strength
> and rest on you in weakness,
> now and in all our days;
> through Jesus Christ our Lord.

COLLECT

Reflection by **Jitesh Patel**

Ordinary Time

Friday 27 August

Psalms 142, **144**
Zechariah 1.18 – end of 2
Mark 9.14-29

Zechariah 1.18 – end of 2

'... one who touches you touches the apple of my eye' (2.8)

Eyes are amazing. Largely gelatinous balls of fluid moving in unison, like many body parts, they are much more than what they are made of. They enable us to see everything around us, from the faces of precious loved ones to the wider beauty of God's creation, all in glorious three-dimensional omni-colour, better than any camera can imitate. They are also delicate and vulnerable. They are not encased in protective bone or tissue, but out of necessity are exposed to the world they see. Because of their importance and vulnerability, we seek to protect them from damage. Many of us would not dare touch our naked eyes, let alone allow anything else to touch them.

In today's passage, God says that his people are as important and precious to him as the apple of his eye, the iris, its most sensitive, vulnerable part. This is why he rescues and redeems Israel from Babylon's power, and why he rescues and redeems us from evils we may face.

God's promise is not that we will never experience evil in this fallen broken world. Rather, he promises that when it touches our lives, he acts and reacts because something precious and important to him has been touched. Though we may have questions about how he is acting when evil befalls us, we can be assured that he always is in some way, because we're precious to him – indeed, precious enough to die for.

COLLECT

Almighty God,
who called your Church to bear witness
that you were in Christ reconciling the world to yourself:
help us to proclaim the good news of your love,
that all who hear it may be drawn to you;
through him who was lifted up on the cross,
and reigns with you in the unity of the Holy Spirit,
one God, now and for ever.

Reflection by **Jitesh Patel**

Ordinary Time

Psalm 147
Zechariah 3
Mark 9.30-37

Saturday 28 August

Zechariah 3

'I have taken your guilt away from you' (v.4)

In this vision, Joshua, representing as high priest the whole people of God, suffers Satan's accusation that they are unclean, clothed in the filthy rags of their sin, unfit to stand in God's presence and be his chosen people. And yet, while not denying the fact that they had got themselves dirty in idolatrous sin, God assures them that he has dealt with it, removing filthy rags and redressing them in clean festal clothing of true worship. Their exile has dealt with their sin; God has taken guilt away from them.

This vision was given to assure Israel of this, countering the temptation to ascribe some of their present harsh conditions as ongoing 'payment' for their sin. Yet, it was not; God had removed their guilt and they had a fresh new start.

For us, the finished work of the cross brings the same assurance that God has dealt with our sin and removed our guilt. To say different is to say the cross was not enough. Though we may be tempted to link some of our tough life circumstances to personal sin, Jesus' cross is where God has taken our guilt away from us – past tense – before we were born or ever sinned. Sometimes we need to come back to the cross to see this afresh; often we need to ignore accusing voices to the contrary, hearing instead God's peace-speaking voice of assurance and hope.

> Almighty God,
> you search us and know us:
> may we rely on you in strength
> and rest on you in weakness,
> now and in all our days;
> through Jesus Christ our Lord.

COLLECT

Reflection by **Jitesh Patel**

Ordinary Time

Monday 30 August

Psalms 1, 2, 3
Zechariah 4
Mark 9.38-end

Zechariah 4

'Not by might, nor by power, but by my spirit' (v.6)

The third of five visions Zechariah is given in quick succession is of olive trees feeding oil to the burning lamps of the lampstand that was meant to stand in the Jerusalem temple – a promise of restored temple worship that must have felt impossible given the devastation of Jerusalem and the rebuilding work needed to restore the temple. However, the oil in the picture represents more than fuel for the temple's lamp; it is the anointing-oil of the Spirit, by whom the impossible would be made possible. The same Spirit who anointed Jesus, the Messiah, the anointed one, for the miraculous, would anoint the exiles for the same. The same Spirit who anoints us to see impossibilities made miraculously possible.

The point is that when God calls us to a task, he gives us the means to complete it. Often it is not by some external resource or expertise sent to our aid, but his Spirit's anointing power, empowering us for sometimes seemingly impossible tasks. As the ancient prayer, *Veni Creator Spiritus*, petitions: 'Come with Thy grace and heavenly aid, and fill the hearts which Thou hast made.'

For what tasks – perhaps those that especially feel beyond you – do you need to ask for a fresh anointing of the Spirit? Jesus promises that God gives the Spirit to those who ask him (Luke 11.13), meaning we can ask with assurance and expectation.

COLLECT

Almighty God,
whose only Son has opened for us
a new and living way into your presence:
give us pure hearts and steadfast wills
to worship you in spirit and in truth;
through Jesus Christ our Lord.

Reflection by **Jitesh Patel**

Ordinary Time

Psalms **5**, 6 (8)
Zechariah 6.9-end
Mark 10.1-16

Tuesday 31 August

Zechariah 6.9-end

'Here is a man whose name is Branch' (v.12)

Both pre- and post-exilic prophets prophesied of one to come called 'the Branch'. For Isaiah and Jeremiah, he would be the perfect king, ruling with wisdom and righteousness. Here, however, this figure has a specific task – to build the temple of the Lord. Is this Joshua the high priest, given that a crown is placed on his head? No – as the crown is to be kept in the temple as a memorial – pointing forward towards a high priest who would also be king, two roles normally mutually exclusive. We, of course, should be strongly pointed towards the coming of Jesus, the king who powerfully rules over the universe, yet also the high priest who 'lives to make intercession for us' (Hebrews 7.25) – the one who rules and is to be obeyed, yet vouches for us when we fail.

This is both a comfort and a challenge to us. The challenge is to see Jesus as not just the priest who sympathizes in our weaknesses, knowing what it is to be human with all that afflicts us, but also as the king to be respected and obeyed. Yet we can be comforted that, as this king, he is not unapproachably tyrannical or terrifying, but is the priest who invites us to call to him and intervenes for us when we do – with a crown on his head, and us in his heart.

COLLECT

Merciful God,
your Son came to save us
and bore our sins on the cross:
may we trust in your mercy
and know your love,
rejoicing in the righteousness
that is ours through Jesus Christ our Lord.

Reflection by **Jitesh Patel**

Ordinary Time

Wednesday 1 September

Psalm 119.1-32
Zechariah 7
Mark 10.17-31

Zechariah 7

'... show kindness and mercy to one another' (v.9)

Religious hypocrisy is a subtle danger: it means worshipping God upwards in 'spiritual' acts, such as Israel does here in fasting and prayer, while all the time missing what true worship looks like. True worship also looks outwards with God's compassionate heart towards the marginalized, calling us to be agents of his kindness and mercy toward them, or at least not to exacerbate their plight through either active or passive oppression. This is, as Zechariah's fellow prophet Isaiah puts it, the true fast that God delights in (Isaiah 58.6).

This type of hypocrisy, condemned by Jesus in his teaching, is an ever-present danger. It is the self-deception of busy spiritual activity masking an awareness of some very unspiritual attitudes in our hearts towards those in need – at worst shunning them as 'trouble' or 'needy', or perhaps more commonly suffering an easing of interest when it comes to alleviating their plight.

The one who says that whatever we do to the least we do unto him (Matthew 25.40) asks us not to ignore the needy. Today, hear God's invitation to seek out the person in need – you probably will not have to search far. Receive the challenge to think about your lifestyle, and who might be being downtrodden to enable it. Choose the harder path that alleviates the suffering of others at cost to self. Doing this for God as an act of worship brings him joy, perhaps more than anything else we could do.

COLLECT

Almighty God,
whose only Son has opened for us
a new and living way into your presence:
give us pure hearts and steadfast wills
to worship you in spirit and in truth;
through Jesus Christ our Lord.

Reflection by **Jitesh Patel**

Ordinary Time

Psalms 14, **15**, 16
Zechariah 8.1-8
Mark 10.32-34

Thursday 2 September

Zechariah 8.1-8

'Even though it seems impossible' (v.6)

It was the White Queen in Lewis Carroll's *Through the Looking Glass* who claimed to have believed as many as six impossible things before breakfast. In today's reading, Israel was asked to believe not six impossible things, but just one: Jerusalem would be restored to its former glory. Yet, for Zechariah's post-exilic returnees to a broken-down, burnt-to-the-ground city, this would have felt overwhelmingly impossible to believe – at any time of day!

However, God delights in doing things we think are impossible, which are not for him. Just as (despite what she thinks!) driving a car is impossible for my two-year-old daughter, yet not for me, God can do things that are simply impossible for us, his children. And therefore, if he has said he will do something, he will, however impossible it may seem.

Many of these seemingly impossible things are contained in the promises of Scripture. For example, do you really believe that God will raise your body from death to life? Do you really believe that he will one day wipe away all suffering in this world? Or that he really does work all things together for the good of those who love him, including you? Some of these promises feel as impossible as the promise he makes here in Zechariah to restore Jerusalem. Yet, just as he kept that promise, he will keep all his promises to us, however seemingly impossible.

COLLECT

Merciful God,
your Son came to save us
and bore our sins on the cross:
may we trust in your mercy
and know your love,
rejoicing in the righteousness
that is ours through Jesus Christ our Lord.

Reflection by **Jitesh Patel**

Ordinary Time

Friday 3 September

Psalms 17, 19
Zechariah 8.9-end
Mark 10.35-45

Zechariah 8.9-end

'… we have heard that God is with you' (v.23)

With these words, we are reminded that what was promised to be true for the Israelites in Zechariah's generation is true for us today. God is with us. We do not have a God who set the universe spinning and then retreated. Neither do we have a God indistinguishable from creation, as some Eastern philosophies teach. Rather, we have a God who decisively steps into his creation in the person of his Son by the power of his Spirit.

God is with us. Not just next to us, or in front of or behind us, but *with* us. He lives intimately within us by his Spirit, promising that this is a permanent dwelling, not a temporary lodging. This unity with divinity is what we were made for, then lost, and now have been given again through Jesus. And it is what the world around us often unknowingly aches for.

The seventeenth-century French philosopher Blaise Pascal, extending St Augustine's ideas, spoke of the 'hole in the soul' that only God can fill, and the more we seek to fill this 'hole' with the God who is with us, rather than other hopes, the more a longing world around us will say, as in today's passage, 'Let us go with you …'. Let us go with you to Jesus and his cross, to his promise of 'life to the full' with him, forever. In other words, this truth is a call. God is with us; let us be with God.

COLLECT

Almighty God,
whose only Son has opened for us
a new and living way into your presence:
give us pure hearts and steadfast wills
to worship you in spirit and in truth;
through Jesus Christ our Lord.

Reflection by **Jitesh Patel**

Ordinary Time

Psalms 20, 21, **23**
Zechariah 9.1-12
Mark 10.46-end

Saturday 4 September

Zechariah 9.1-12

'... humble and riding on a donkey' (v.9)

Cue Palm Sunday celebrations with donkeys – or at least people in costumes pretending to be. Cue Palm crosses and shouts of 'Hosanna!' Cue the start of Holy Week and then Easter festivities.

It is easy when we come across Old Testament prophecies later described as fulfilled by Jesus to miss their original importance. Here, we should not miss that for Zechariah's generation, devoid of the Davidic line of kings they thought had been promised forever, these words would have elicited a joyful gasp of relief. We are not going to be kingless forever! In an age of kings who embodied national hope and identity, this meant they could lift their heads up high again. They longed for a king who would vanquish enemies and rule from coast to coast. This is what Zechariah's generation longed for and what the crowds on Palm Sunday were hoping for in Jesus.

However, contained in this prophecy is a surprising truth: this ultimate king is the humble king who rides not on a royal steed but on a donkey; into a city not for coronation but crucifixion; defeating not imperial overlords but darker enemies of sin, death and evil; establishing not a global empire of domination but an eternal kingdom of peace. This is why we are to rejoice living under the rule of this king, so different and more powerful than any other – the only king worthy to be king of our lives and of the nations.

COLLECT

Merciful God,
your Son came to save us
and bore our sins on the cross:
may we trust in your mercy
and know your love,
rejoicing in the righteousness
that is ours through Jesus Christ our Lord.

Reflection by **Jitesh Patel**

Ordinary Time

Monday 6 September

Psalms 27, **30**
Zechariah 10
Mark 11.1-11

Zechariah 10

'I am the Lord their God and I will answer them' (v.6)

There are three different descriptions of the people of God in this chapter, each with very different mood music, highlighting different aspects of the Lord's interaction with them.

To begin with, the people are like sheep, straying helplessly around, so confused that they cannot even correctly discern the seasons. Their supposed shepherds consult every kind of authority, except the Lord, the creator of all that the sheep depend upon. The contrast here is between the faithfulness of God and the faithlessness of other authorities.

Secondly, in anger at the betrayal by the leaders of the people, God dismisses the 'shepherds' and turns the sheep into warhorses, able, in God's strength, to find unity of purpose and fight for themselves. God's faithfulness here is energizing, filling the people with courage and joy.

And finally, God, the faithful watchman, calls the scattered and bereft people home. Far away, even believing they are forgotten, still the people have taught their children about the Lord, and their trust is rewarded. As they journey home, God simply removes all dangers and obstacles. The Lord's name is their safe pathway.

In all three 'moods', God's faithfulness is key; sometimes full of compassion, sometimes strong and spirited, sometimes far-sighted as an eagle, but always faithful, always mindful of the people, chosen, beloved, never abandoned. The people may feel lost, afraid, abandoned, but only when they forget the God who never forgets them.

COLLECT
> God, who in generous mercy sent the Holy Spirit
>   upon your Church in the burning fire of your love:
> grant that your people may be fervent
> in the fellowship of the gospel
> that, always abiding in you,
> they may be found steadfast in faith and active in service;
> through Jesus Christ our Lord.

Reflection by **Jane Williams**

Ordinary Time

Psalms 32, **36**
Zechariah 11.4-end
Mark 11.12-26

Tuesday 7 September

Zechariah 11.4-end

'Oh, my worthless shepherd, who deserts the flock!' (v.17)

Today, we encounter a bitter and angry prophet. Others speak about the culpable failure of Israel's shepherds (Jeremiah 23.1-4 and Ezekiel 34), who seek only their own comfort and wealth and care nothing for the sheep. But in Ezekiel and Jeremiah, God sacks the bad shepherds and takes their place, as Jesus does (John 10.11-14). The sheep belong to God, not to the hired and faithless shepherds. Zechariah offers no such consolation.

Instead, he enacts a prophetic sign, breaking the two shepherd's crooks with which he should be guarding and guiding the favoured and united flock. He abandons the sheep to their fate: some will die, some will be destroyed, some will turn carnivore – a truly horrible picture of peaceful grass-eating sheep becoming ravening wolves. The prophet walks away from his flock, like a hired hand, demanding his wages and then flinging the price of his labours away, with contempt.

In Ezekiel (37.15-23), the two shepherd's sticks become a symbol of the reunited land, the reaffirmation of God's promise to the people. But in Zechariah, at least in this chapter, there is no happy ending.

The prophet's calling is painful and humiliating, endlessly focusing on the venality and waywardness of the people, their endless ability to ignore and despise the ways of God that the prophet shows to them, preferring their own stupid choices that lead, repeatedly, to destruction. Who would be a prophet?

> Lord God,
> defend your Church from all false teaching
> and give to your people knowledge of your truth,
> that we may enjoy eternal life
> in Jesus Christ our Lord.

COLLECT

Reflection by **Jane Williams**

Ordinary Time

Wednesday 8 September

Psalm **34**
Zechariah 12.1-10
Mark 11.27-end

Zechariah 12.1-10

'I will pour out a spirit of compassion and supplication on the house of David' (v.10)

It is not clear what, if any, historical setting this oracle has. What is described is more than a return of the peoples of Judah and Jerusalem, which the Persian Emperor Darius seems to have permitted. This is a triumphant victory, vividly described in fiery images. Yet, despite the overwhelming victories that Judah and Jerusalem win, they do not for one moment deceive themselves into thinking this is due to their own strength. It is the Lord, the one who brought creation into existence in the beginning, who has re-created the people and filled them again with life. God shields the people of Jerusalem, who would be weak without this protection, and yet, with it, they have the strength of the great King David.

A striking mark of the fact that it is God's victory is the way in which the people respond, with 'compassion and supplication'. There is no self-congratulatory triumphing over the fallen, but an acknowledgement of pain and loss. God is reforming the people from within as well as restoring their outward fortunes.

It is impossible to tell who the one 'pierced' is in Zechariah's oracle, and why this death provokes such mourning. John 19.37 picks it up and applies it to Jesus, whose death at our hands reforms us from within, offering us, as we weep, the costly victory that God alone can win.

COLLECT

God, who in generous mercy sent the Holy Spirit
    upon your Church in the burning fire of your love:
grant that your people may be fervent
in the fellowship of the gospel
that, always abiding in you,
they may be found steadfast in faith and active in service;
through Jesus Christ our Lord.

Reflection by **Jane Williams**

Ordinary Time

Psalm **37***
Zechariah 13
Mark 12.1-12

Thursday 9 September

Zechariah 13

'They will call on my name, and I will answer them' (v.9)

At the end of chapter 12, we leave the people of Judah and Jerusalem full of pity and calling on the Lord, as they weep over the one 'whom they have pierced'. That confessional theme extends into the beginning of chapter 13 as these same people are cleansed from their sin by a fountain of grace.

But that inner cleansing will not be enough. The 'spirit of compassion and supplication' must now meet, head on, the 'unclean spirit' that still endangers the land, in the form of idolatry and prophecy. Now the ones to be 'pierced' will be viewed not with pity but with ruthless determination; even their mothers will not defend them. Zechariah does not distinguish between true and false prophets. It is as though the whole prophetic calling has been so debased that it must be rooted out completely. It is such a mark of shame to prophesy and have visions that any remaining prophets lie about their calling and hide the wounds of their prophetic frenzies.

With bitter sarcasm, the Lord breaks into poetry to condemn the 'shepherd', who claimed to be God's friend. The drastic sifting that is described is in terrible contrast to the gentle fountain of clear water in verse 1. There can be no more compromise or excuse; only a radical cleansing will enable the people again to know that they are God's people and the Lord is their God.

COLLECT

Lord God,
defend your Church from all false teaching
and give to your people knowledge of your truth,
that we may enjoy eternal life
in Jesus Christ our Lord.

Reflection by **Jane Williams**

Ordinary Time

Friday 10 September

Psalm 31
Zechariah 14.1-11
Mark 12.13-17

Zechariah 14.1-11

'... the Lord will become king over all the earth' (v.9)

Zechariah is a perplexing book, almost certainly not written as a whole, or even all by the same person. It reflects a period of anguished soul-searching by the people, bitter anger against their leaders, and a passionate commitment to discerning the nature and will of God, who seems sometimes wrathful and sometimes compassionate, but who always fills the writer's horizons.

The first part of chapter 14 is clearly written by someone who has witnessed the devastation of war, and who longs to see what is described: the warrior God, defending Jerusalem. At last, the Lord will be the true king, the fitting leader, not only for his people, but for all the peoples of the earth. The lands all around will be levelled, so that all will be able to look up and see Jerusalem, the holy city, with its king at its heart.

'Jerusalem shall abide in security' breathes such longing and hope, and resonates down the ages to today. Zechariah's consistent message is that no human leader can bring about this golden time: only the Lord. God's people and all the peoples of the earth are driven about by every passing storm, but the Lord stands forever, holding in his mighty hands summer and winter, day and night, living water and eternal hope.

COLLECT

God, who in generous mercy sent the Holy Spirit
    upon your Church in the burning fire of your love:
grant that your people may be fervent
in the fellowship of the gospel
that, always abiding in you,
they may be found steadfast in faith and active in service;
through Jesus Christ our Lord.

Reflection by **Jane Williams**

Ordinary Time

Psalms 41, **42**, 43
Zechariah 14.12-end
Mark 12.18-27

Saturday 11 September

Zechariah 14.12-end

*'... there shall be inscribed on the bells of the horses,
"Holy to the Lord"' (v. 20)*

Like the earlier part of chapter 14, this second half is also divided into devastation and restoration. Just as the people of Jerusalem were sifted, with some being taken into exile, so, now, the peoples who have been waging war against Jerusalem will suffer a similar fate. Some will die of terrible plagues, losing everything they own, including their vital animals.

But those who survive will become God's people, free to come and worship the Lord in the holy city of Jerusalem. This is a vision of the end-times, when all will know the Lord. There will be no further need for a temple to offer sacrifices: every domestic hearth and saucepan will become a sacred vessel; there will be no need for priests or prophets or even for other rulers, for the Lord will be close, at home with the people as they are with him. There will be no division between things set aside for the Lord and things that are common or profane; everything will be 'Holy to the Lord'.

We see and hear the horses going about their everyday business, ringing out the praise of the Lord. No one will have to pay to make sacrifices and prayers because the whole of life will be filled with the presence and joy of the Lord.

COLLECT

Lord God,
defend your Church from all false teaching
and give to your people knowledge of your truth,
that we may enjoy eternal life
in Jesus Christ our Lord.

Reflection by **Jane Williams**

Ordinary Time

Monday 13 September

Psalm **44**
Ecclesiasticus 1.1-10
or Ezekiel 1.1-14
Mark 12.28-34

Ezekiel 1.1-14

'... the heavens were opened, and I saw visions of God' (v.1)

The themes of the book of Ezekiel are front and centre of this first chapter. The Lord is God of the whole world, and is gloriously, transcendently holy.

Very briefly, Ezekiel introduces himself and his call. He comes from a priestly family, and his message comes to him in exile, one of the Judeans taken into captivity by the Babylonians in the turbulent last days of Judah and Jerusalem. Both of these facts are apparent in the writing: Ezekiel often mentions the worshipping life of the people of Israel, and their betrayal of God's calling, seeing the destruction of his homeland as the inevitable result of unfaithfulness.

Before Ezekiel begins his prophetic ministry, he is taken into the presence of the Holy One of Israel, whose power is emphasized by storms, burning coals, lightning and extraordinary, indescribable forms of life. Despite the detailed description of the living creatures, they are almost impossible to picture. They do not belong in the everyday world at all. They are the protectors of the ark in the holy of holies at the heart of the temple, their touching wings shielding the precious covenant between God and God's people. Yet they come to Ezekiel on the banks of the River Chebar, in Babylon, far away from Jerusalem. God is not confined to any human place, however sanctified; God is the Lord of all the earth, and the clouds may open to reveal God's sanctuary anywhere.

COLLECT

O Lord, we beseech you mercifully to hear the prayers
    of your people who call upon you;
and grant that they may both perceive and know
    what things they ought to do,
and also may have grace and power faithfully to fulfil them;
through Jesus Christ our Lord.

Reflection by **Jane Williams**

Ordinary Time

Psalms 2, 8, 146
Genesis 3.1-15
John 12.27-36a

Tuesday 14 September
Holy Cross Day

Genesis 3.1-15
'... you will be like God, knowing good and evil' (v.5)

The crafty serpent has been listening carefully to God's interaction with the human creatures. Even before they came into being, God declared the intention of sharing divine likeness with them (Genesis 1.27). But somehow, the serpent manages to make that divine gift uncertain, something that the human creatures have to reach for by their own determination, rather than receiving freely.

Eve should have known better than to listen to the serpent. After all, when still part of Adam, she had helped to name the serpent, identifying its characteristic 'craftiness'. But now, she has let the serpent slither out of place and as a result, the whole beautiful web of creation begins to unravel. The human creatures know and fear their difference, where once they had been bone of each other's bone; they hide from God, who used to come and talk to them in the cool of the evening; they blame each other, rather than standing together in penitence.

This is the 'Fall', which mythically depicts how evil becomes an actuality when it should have remained only a theoretical possibility. The fateful tree, which stands in the middle of the garden, will be redeemed by another tree, carrying the body of Christ, given to death to restore the world. On that tree, evil attempts to annihilate good, forever, but finds that it is nothing but a puny, crafty serpent, as it confronts the endless, invincible goodness of God.

> Almighty God,
> who in the passion of your blessed Son
> made an instrument of painful death
> to be for us the means of life and peace:
> grant us so to glory in the cross of Christ
> that we may gladly suffer for his sake;
> who is alive and reigns with you,
> in the unity of the Holy Spirit,
> one God, now and for ever.

COLLECT

Reflection by **Jane Williams**

Ordinary Time

Wednesday 15 September

Psalm **119.57-80**
Ecclesiasticus 2
or Ezekiel 2.3 – 3.11
Mark 13.1-13

Ezekiel 2.3 – 3.11

'I ate it; and in my mouth it was as sweet as honey' (3.3)

In chapter 1, all the imagery is visual, though hard to picture. But now, Ezekiel is about to receive his commission, given to him in speech. Although he could look at the throne room, he cannot look at the One now speaking to him. He is just a 'mortal' – a description often translated as 'son of man', and used regularly throughout the book to contrast the mere messenger with the One who sends.

The message Ezekiel is to carry is not an easy one, and he is given no assurance of its reception. God's people are described in harsh terms: they are rebellious, impudent, stubborn; they will surround Ezekiel like briars and thorns and scorpions. God does not deceive Ezekiel about the isolation and opposition that come with his calling. He is sent to his own people, who should be able to hear and understand him, and yet will not. They and Ezekiel will be like cold, hard statues, standing immovably face to face, for Ezekiel's own protection and as a sign of their condemnation.

Yet, as Ezekiel eats the words of lamentation, mourning and woe that God holds out to him, they become 'as sweet as honey'. From now on, God's message will be food and drink and consolation to Ezekiel. It will become his very substance. To declare, 'Thus says the Lord God' will be his constant reality.

COLLECT

O Lord, we beseech you mercifully to hear the prayers
   of your people who call upon you;
and grant that they may both perceive and know
   what things they ought to do,
and also may have grace and power faithfully to fulfil them;
through Jesus Christ our Lord.

Reflection by **Jane Williams**

Ordinary Time

Psalms 56, **57** (63*)
Ecclesiasticus 3.17-29
or Ezekiel 3.12-end
Mark 13.14-23

Thursday 16 September

Ezekiel 3.12-end

'Mortal, I have made you a sentinel for the house of Israel' (v.17)

Now Ezekiel's hard task begins. The glorious, extravagant, mysterious dwelling of God and the presence of the indescribable living creatures all vanish, leaving Ezekiel dazed, heartbroken and weighed down by his calling, until God speaks again.

Again, God addresses the 'mortal' whom God has deigned to call, and again, the message is hardly a cheering one for Ezekiel. He is to become a 'sentinel' for the people, bearing the heavy responsibility of keeping watch, looking always to the horizons, ready to give the vital warning. He must never be too tired, too afraid, too negligent to warn the people, because if he is, the blame for their fate will be on his shoulders. But he is not to be held to account for their response. It is one of the strong themes in the book of Ezekiel that people can and must choose. God's prophets will offer them the vision of truth, but they must make decisions for themselves.

To illustrate that, Ezekiel is told to enact a prophetic sign. He is to shut himself in his house and neither move nor speak until the Lord speaks through him, so that the people shall be in no doubt about where the message comes from, whether they choose to listen or to refuse to hear. They will not be able to persuade themselves that it is 'only that strange Ezekiel' they are ignoring. It is the Lord.

COLLECT

Lord of creation,
whose glory is around and within us:
open our eyes to your wonders,
that we may serve you with reverence
and know your peace at our lives' end,
through Jesus Christ our Lord.

Reflection by **Jane Williams**

Ordinary Time

Friday 17 September

Psalms **51**, 54
Ecclesiasticus 4.11-28
or Ezekiel 8
Mark.13.24-31

Ezekiel 8

'The Lord does not see us' (v.12)

Ezekiel's fellow exiles are clearly intrigued by the prophet, even if they do not obey him. But as they sit around and stare at him, Ezekiel is far away, lifted by his hair, carried away by something slightly like a hand of a figure who is shaped quite like a human being but fiery and gleaming.

His flight takes him 'home', to Jerusalem and its temple. But there is nothing to gladden a homesick prophet's heart, for everywhere he looks, there are idolatry and 'vile abominations'. The people have always known that God is a jealous God (Exodus 20.5), protecting the people from the fundamental category mistake of worshipping what is not God. And yet here, in that most holy place, the people have persuaded themselves that the Lord is negligible. The descriptions of their practices are deliberately horrible: the images are not just of ordinary animals but of 'creeping things'; men turn their backs on the temple to worship the sun; women weep over the death of a non-existent god. Everywhere there is horror and betrayal.

Do the elders, still sitting by Ezekiel's house in Babylon, see the horror on his face as he is forced to look on the degradation of the temple? Is it entertaining for them to watch the heartbroken prophet in his fearful trance, and then go home to their suppers?

COLLECT

O Lord, we beseech you mercifully to hear the prayers
    of your people who call upon you;
and grant that they may both perceive and know
    what things they ought to do,
and also may have grace and power faithfully to fulfil them;
through Jesus Christ our Lord.

Reflection by **Jane Williams**

Ordinary Time

Psalm **68**
Ecclesiasticus 4.29 – 6.1
or Ezekiel 9
Mark 13.32-end

Saturday 18 September

Ezekiel 9

'... the glory of the God of Israel had gone up' (v.3)

We are on our knees beside the prophet, weeping for the appalling sins of the people, but also for the apparently implacable wrath of God. This is the kind of reading that provokes the heretical belief that the God of the Old Testament and the God of the New cannot be the same.

But we have to remember that Ezekiel is being shown a vision, not a historical occurrence. Ezekiel's body is still in his house by the River Chebar, being examined by the curious elders (8.1), and he is returned there at the end of the vision (11.25). In the valley of the dry bones (Ezekiel 37), Ezekiel's vision enables him to prophesy hope; here in the desecrated temple, from which God's glory has withdrawn, he must cry out, 'Danger!'.

God's people must not assume that God is a doting and short-sighted grandparent who can be ignored at will. The armed destroyers and the sinister clerk with his satchel and pen are unquestioningly, inhumanly obedient; their contempt for their prey is an uncomfortable mirror of the people's contempt for God. The people have persuaded themselves, 'The Lord does not see', and now they are experiencing what it is not to be seen.

Ezekiel is shown these things so that he can speak, beg, warn, exhort. This is his hard calling as a 'sentinel', whose job is to see so that disaster can be averted.

COLLECT

Lord of creation,
whose glory is around and within us:
open our eyes to your wonders,
that we may serve you with reverence
and know your peace at our lives' end,
through Jesus Christ our Lord.

Reflection by **Jane Williams**

Ordinary Time

Monday 20 September

Psalm 71
Ecclesiasticus 6.14-end
or Ezekiel 10.1-19
Mark 14.1-11

Mark 14.1-11

'… an alabaster jar of very costly ointment' (v.3)

One denarius was the usual day's pay for a labourer; 300 was almost a year's wages. That would go a long way among the needy, but the poor will live another day; Jesus' days on earth are numbered.

Who raised the voice of criticism against the woman for her wastefulness? 'Some who were there' is all Mark says, but in Matthew's telling of the story, it was the disciples, and in John's account, Judas Iscariot alone. That sounds convincing in the context of Mark's own narrative.

Judas was the disciples' treasurer, the keeper of the common purse in which Jesus and his followers kept their shared funds. The Gospels speak of him as a thief who pilfered the money entrusted to him. In his avarice and greed, he sees nothing of the beautiful deed that Jesus praised, only a means by which the common purse could be increased and his own pocket lined. His mendacious pretence of concern for the poor adds to his greed the trait of deceit.

Smell the fragrance of the costly perfume. Sense its opulence and its luxury, its extravagance and its excess. Savour its wealth and its richness, its affluence and its indulgence. Then know the abundant love and devotion of the woman who poured it out and pray that the same might overflow from you today.

COLLECT	Almighty God, you have made us for yourself, and our hearts are restless till they find their rest in you: pour your love into our hearts and draw us to yourself, and so bring us at last to your heavenly city where we shall see you face to face; through Jesus Christ our Lord,.

Reflection by **Tim Heaton**

Ordinary Time

Psalms 49, 117
1 Kings 19.15-end
2 Timothy 3.14-end

Tuesday 21 September
Matthew, Apostle and Evangelist

2 Timothy 3.14-end
'... from childhood you have known the sacred writings' (v.15)

If this really is a letter of Paul – let us assume it is – it was probably his last, written from prison in Rome shortly before his execution in AD 64, to Timothy, his most faithful companion and co-worker.

The 'sacred writings' are the Hebrew Scriptures, the only Bible known to Paul and Timothy. After all, none of the Gospels had been written; there was as yet no testament of Christ. As he wrote these words to Timothy, Paul could never have imagined, even for a moment, that they would one day be added to the sacred writings and accepted by future generations of Christians as holy Scripture 'inspired by God' – literally *God-breathed*.

The same goes for Matthew, whom we remember on this his feast day, as both Apostle and Evangelist. Questionable though it may be, the author of the Gospel that bears his name is held by Christian tradition to be the same person as Matthew the tax collector – Levi in the Gospels of Mark and Luke – who was called by Jesus to be his disciple.

Paul-once-Saul, Matthew-once-Levi. Transformed by Christ in name and nature. Uprooted from their previous lives as ruthless Christian persecutor and despised Roman collaborator to be born again from above, born of water and the Spirit. Sons of Abraham who knew only the sacred writings and unknowingly became authors of the Christian canon. Thank God for them today.

> O Almighty God,
> whose blessed Son called Matthew the tax collector
> to be an apostle and evangelist:
> give us grace to forsake the selfish pursuit of gain
> and the possessive love of riches
> that we may follow in the way of your Son Jesus Christ,
> who is alive and reigns with you,
> in the unity of the Holy Spirit,
> one God, now and for ever.

COLLECT

Reflection by **Tim Heaton**

Ordinary Time

Wednesday 22 September

Psalm **77**
Ecclesiasticus 10.6-8, 12-24
or Ezekiel 12.1-16
Mark 14.26-42

Mark 14.26-42

'Keep awake and pray' (v.38)

The place at the foot of the Mount of Olives called Gethsemane – a Hebrew name meaning 'oil press' – is the scene of the spectacular failure of Jesus' inner circle of disciples to understand what is about to happen. Three times Jesus has predicted his Passion. Now, as he prepares for it through vigilance and prayer, the sleeping disciples effectively abandon him to his fate.

Peter, James and John were the three who had come to be regarded as closest to the Lord. They had been taken aside from the rest on other occasions – the raising of Jairus' daughter and the transfiguration – and the explanation here probably stems from their recent actions: Peter has just declared he will never deny Jesus and is ready to die with him, while James and John have recently affirmed their readiness to drink his cup of suffering (Mark 10.39).

Jesus takes them with him so they can watch how he prays. He shows them by example how *they* should prepare spiritually for what is to come, to keep awake and pray not for Jesus but for themselves, to be alert to the danger of failure in the struggle that is about to overwhelm them.

Despite their earlier boasting, they fall asleep – not once, not twice, but three times. Sometimes we just hope for the best to avoid having to prepare for the worst.

COLLECT

Almighty God,
you have made us for yourself,
and our hearts are restless till they find their rest in you:
pour your love into our hearts and draw us to yourself,
and so bring us at last to your heavenly city
where we shall see you face to face;
through Jesus Christ our Lord.

Reflection by **Tim Heaton**

Ordinary Time

Psalm **78.1-39***
Ecclesiasticus 11.7-28
or Ezekiel 12.17-end
Mark 14.43-52

Thursday 23 September

Mark 14.43-52

'Now the betrayer had given them a sign' (v.44)

Gethsemane was an old haunt of Jesus and the Twelve. Mark doesn't tell us this, but John, who calls the place a 'garden', says 'Jesus often met there with his disciples'. Luke also tells us that Jesus often went there.

Whether the place was an olive oil press or a garden is not important. In fact, Christian tradition has fused the two narratives to create a place called the 'Garden of Gethsemane', which exists nowhere in the Gospels. What is important is that its location was the secret that Judas Iscariot betrayed.

This secluded spot, removed from all the hustle and bustle of the city, was not known to the authorities as a place where Jesus could be found. They wanted to arrest him quickly and by stealth, before the festival and out of public sight, to avoid any civil disorder, so the insider information that Judas possessed was well worth their 30 pieces of silver.

The sign of identification is the finest irony: a kiss, a mark of love and friendship, and with that the traitor's work is done. Judas turns his back on the light and sets out on the way of darkness. In a paradox of human wilfulness (greed) and divine purpose ('let the scriptures be fulfilled'), Judas surrenders to the power of evil and leaves behind him the beauty and the joy of knowing Jesus.

COLLECT

> Gracious God,
> you call us to fullness of life:
> deliver us from unbelief
> and banish our anxieties
> with the liberating love of Jesus Christ our Lord.

Reflection by **Tim Heaton**

Ordinary Time

Friday 24 September

Psalm **55**
Ecclesiasticus 14.20 – 15.10
or Ezekiel 13.1-16
Mark 14.53-65

Mark 14.53-65

'Are you the Messiah, the Son of the Blessed One?' (v.61)

The defendant is seated before the Sanhedrin of Jerusalem, the highest Jewish court in the land. Its members include former holders of the high priestly office (the chief priests), the wealthy and influential aristocracy (the elders), and experts in the law of Moses (the scribes). Two court clerks are recording the minutes of the proceedings.

The charge is blasphemy; the sentence prescribed by law upon conviction: death by stoning (Leviticus 24.16). However, a capital sentence cannot be handed down by this court under Roman provincial rule and, should the accused be found guilty, he must be referred to the Roman prefect, Pontius Pilate, who alone holds the power of life and death.

Witnesses come forward to testify. Deuteronomic Law required that evidence of at least two must correspond if the charge is to be upheld, but in this case no two can be found whose testimony agrees. The high priest, Caiaphas, determined to secure a guilty verdict, intervenes: he asks one decisive question, 'Are you the Messiah?' A hush descends over the courtroom. The success or failure of the conspiracy to kill Jesus depends entirely on the response that follows.

Jesus makes no attempt to save himself. He replies clearly, 'I am' – the very name of God (Exodus 3.14). With this confession the fate of the Son of Man is sealed. God, the great I AM, is condemned.

COLLECT

Almighty God,
you have made us for yourself,
and our hearts are restless till they find their rest in you:
pour your love into our hearts and draw us to yourself,
and so bring us at last to your heavenly city
where we shall see you face to face;
through Jesus Christ our Lord.

Reflection by **Tim Heaton**

Ordinary Time

Psalms **76**, 79
Ecclesiasticus 15.11-end
or Ezekiel 14.1-11
Mark 14.66-end

Saturday 25 September

Mark 14.66-end

'... the cock crowed for the second time' (v.72)

The interrogation of Peter in the courtyard below occurs at the same time as the trial of Jesus in the courtroom above. The two narratives are interwoven and the irony inherent in this is clear: at the very moment Jesus confesses to be the Messiah, the prophecy that Peter would deny him is being fulfilled. Integrity and faithlessness are brought into sharp contrast.

Cocks are conscientious timekeepers and the Romans reckoned the time of night by them. The four nocturnal watches were called evening (6–9pm), midnight (9pm–midnight), cockcrow (midnight–3am) and dawn (3–6am). Studies carried out in Jerusalem have shown that cocks crow at three distinct times between midnight and 3am, at roughly hourly intervals, the second occurring at about half-past-one in the morning.

Failure comes in many guises. While Judas' betrayal of Jesus was the more heinous action, Peter's ignominious denial may be the most haunting. His infamous act of self-preservation, portended by his failure to watch and pray in Gethsemane, stands as a solemn warning to all disciples. Bold affirmations of fidelity – 'Even though I must die with you, I will not deny you' (Mark 14.31) – do not guarantee faithfulness.

In our secular age, the temptation to deny our association with Jesus is real and strong. We must prepare for our own hour of testing and be able to hold fast to our confession that Jesus is Lord.

> Gracious God,
> you call us to fullness of life:
> deliver us from unbelief
> and banish our anxieties
> with the liberating love of Jesus Christ our Lord.

COLLECT

Reflection by **Tim Heaton**

Ordinary Time

Monday 27 September

Psalms **80**, 82
Ecclesiasticus 16.17-end
or Ezekiel 14.12-end
Mark 15.1-15

Mark 15.1-15

'Are you the King of the Jews?' (v.2)

Blasphemy, the charge on which Jesus had been found guilty under Jewish law, was not a crime for which Roman law provided punishment. It was therefore necessary for the Sanhedrin to conjure up a new charge before handing Jesus over to Pilate – the so-called 'consultation'.

It is evident from Pilate's question that this trumped-up charge was lèse-majesté, or treason. 'King of the Jews' still meant 'Messiah' so far as the charge of blasphemy was concerned, but to Pilate it meant something more like 'Leader of the Resistance'. Jesus' pretensions to kingship were politically subversive, a crime against the authority of imperial Rome, punishable by death.

Jesus' reply, 'You say so' (the NIV is clearer here: 'Yes, it is as you say') is a candid confession, enough for Pilate to pass sentence. But because the hearing continues, we must deduce – though Mark does not report it – that Jesus qualified his statement in some way, such as recorded in the Fourth Gospel, 'My kingdom is not from this world' (John 18.36). This would explain the continuing questioning.

But Jesus made no further reply. To Pilate's amazement, he refused to defend himself. Instead, he manifested the exalted, sublime silence of the suffering servant of God: 'like a lamb that is led to the slaughter, and like a sheep that before its shearers is silent, so he did not open his mouth' (Isaiah 53.7).

COLLECT

Almighty and everlasting God,
increase in us your gift of faith
that, forsaking what lies behind
and reaching out to that which is before,
we may run the way of your commandments
and win the crown of everlasting joy;
through Jesus Christ our Lord.

Reflection by **Tim Heaton**

Ordinary Time

Psalms 87, **89.1-18**
Ecclesiasticus 17.1-24
or Ezekiel 18.1-20
Mark 15.16-32

Tuesday 28 September

Mark 15.16-32

'It was nine o'clock in the morning when they crucified him' (v.25)

It was always going to end like this, God's plan from the very beginning, 'destined before the foundation of the world' (1 Peter 1.20), God's way of restoring fallen humanity to himself: an innocent man goes willingly to his death in place of a guilty man (Barabbas), one sinless person for all the sinful people who ever lived. And there was only one human being like that, the incarnation of God himself, able to bear the burden of divine judgement on the world's transgressions.

Pilate thought that he was in control, that Jesus' life was in his hands. Barabbas was a pawn in his game, a lifeline thrown to Jesus, who Pilate never thought for a moment was guilty of treason. But it wasn't his game; it was God's game, and the stakes were far higher than Pilate ever knew. He was a piece on the chessboard, just like Judas and Caiaphas, and the only thing the outcome ever depended on was Jesus' obedience to his Father's will. He never wavered.

It was God's game all along and it was always going to end like this – except, of course, this is not the end. It cannot end like this, not with thorns and nails, blood and agony, mockery and derision. The grandmaster of the universe has one last spectacular move to make. The end is still to come.

COLLECT

God, our judge and saviour,
teach us to be open to your truth
and to trust in your love,
that we may live each day
with confidence in the salvation which is given
through Jesus Christ our Lord.

Reflection by **Tim Heaton**

Ordinary Time

Wednesday 29 September
Michael and All Angels

Psalms 34, 150
Tobit 12.6-end
or Daniel 12.1-4
Acts 12.1-11

Acts 12.1-11

'Suddenly an angel of the Lord appeared' (v.7)

Michaelmas interrupts our reading of the Passion. The flow is abruptly suspended as we mark this feast with a tale of angelic derring-do and Peter's dramatic release from prison in Jerusalem. Suddenly, without any forewarning, the deadly plans of Herod Agrippa are foiled.

Angels have a habit of interrupting things, breaking into our temporal world in sudden and quite unexpected ways. A young woman from Nazareth named Mary knew this better than most. Whereas the archangel Gabriel is the archetype of a messenger of God, Peter's rescue from prison conforms to the idea of a personal guardian angel in the popular imagination. This role of angels as ministers to humankind, of active help and support to God's servants in time of need, is perceived also in the earlier release of the apostles from prison (Acts 5.19) and recalls the succour given to Elijah under the broom tree. The archangel Michael is the guardian angel of Israel and, in the New Testament, leader of the heavenly army that defeats Satan when war breaks out in heaven (Revelation 12), earning his place as the protector of all Christians.

Someday, one of God's holy angels might be interrupting your life, unexpectedly breaking into your world and changing things forever. The interruption will be only brief, but life may never be the same again.

COLLECT

Everlasting God,
you have ordained and constituted
    the ministries of angels and mortals in a wonderful order:
grant that as your holy angels always serve you in heaven,
so, at your command,
they may help and defend us on earth;
through Jesus Christ our Lord.

Reflection by **Tim Heaton**

Ordinary Time

Psalms 90, **92**
Ecclesiasticus 19.4-17
or Ezekiel 20.1-20
Mark 15.42-end

Thursday 30 September

Mark 15.42-end

'... he granted the body to Joseph' (v.45)

It is almost impossible to comprehend the death of God. But dead he was, the centurion in charge of the crucifixion squad confirms it. The creator of all life: lifeless. And yet we know this to be important, not only for what is about to happen but because now God knows what suffering and death are like for us.

After crucifixion, the release of the body to a family member for dignified burial was quite normal – except for those, like Jesus, who had been convicted of treason. Their bodies would be left to decay, eaten by predatory animals. Perhaps Mary knew this, which is why she did not herself petition Pilate for the body.

In an extraordinary turn of events, a sympathizer emerges from the ranks of Jesus' enemies. He is a member of the Sanhedrin, the supreme court that had convicted Jesus, and he boldly claims the body for burial. The disciples, even if they hadn't fled, could not have succeeded in this: Pilate would never have agreed to such an unusual and irregular request had it not come from a member of the wealthy aristocracy.

No individual should be judged because of their background or associations. Sympathetic outsiders – even believers – can be found everywhere. They shall receive their reward. Perhaps it is not so hard for a rich person to enter the kingdom of God, after all.

> Almighty and everlasting God,
> increase in us your gift of faith
> that, forsaking what lies behind
> and reaching out to that which is before,
> we may run the way of your commandments
> and win the crown of everlasting joy;
> through Jesus Christ our Lord.

COLLECT

Reflection by **Tim Heaton**

Ordinary Time

Friday 1 October

Psalms **88** (95)
Ecclesiasticus 19.20-end
or Ezekiel 20.21-38
Mark 16.1-8

Mark 16.1-8

'He has been raised; he is not here' (v.6)

Mark's Gospel in its original form ends here at the empty tomb, the verses that follow being a later addition drawn from the post-resurrection appearances of Jesus reported in the other Gospels. The emptiness of the tomb possesses no factual value in itself; it only raises the question: what happened to the body?

The truth is unveiled in the words of divine revelation given by the angel, who appears as God's messenger to announce the fact of the resurrection. This is the crystallization point for faith: do you believe it? Jesus' resurrection is open to understanding only through these words of revelation received in faith.

The observation that it was three women who received the announcement of the angel is significant in view of contemporary attitudes: Jewish law declared women to be ineligible as witnesses. If their presence had been invented, it would, therefore, be a rather troublesome and inconvenient detail, leading us to the conclusion that the presence of the women at the tomb must actually be factual.

The women are instructed to remind the disciples of the promise that Jesus had already made, that he will go ahead of them to Galilee and 'there you will see him'. Unlike Matthew, Mark sees no need to relate the event itself; his ending is sufficient: the centre of our faith is a crucifix behind which stands an empty tomb.

COLLECT

Almighty and everlasting God,
increase in us your gift of faith
that, forsaking what lies behind
and reaching out to that which is before,
we may run the way of your commandments
and win the crown of everlasting joy;
through Jesus Christ our Lord.

Reflection by **Tim Heaton**

Ordinary Time

Psalms 96, **97**, 100
Ecclesiasticus 21.1-17
or Ezekiel 24.15-end
Mark 16.9-end

Saturday 2 October

Mark 16.9-end

'... he appeared first to Mary Magdalene' (v.9)

These verses are missing from the earliest and most reliable manuscripts of Mark's Gospel and were added later by someone else, probably in the first half of the second century. They summarize some of the post-resurrection appearances of Jesus recorded in Matthew, Luke and John, which were all written after Mark.

Jesus' conquest of death was manifested among the living. The New Testament attests to perhaps eleven separate encounters with the risen Jesus, some involving single individuals, one a group of more than five hundred. For some weeks, Jesus continued to appear to his followers in this way, convincing them of his victory over death and transforming a frightened and demoralized group of disciples into a confident and prayerful company of apostles waiting with quiet assurance for the coming of the promised Holy Spirit and the power to continue God's mission that Jesus had begun.

What place do these 'proofs' of the resurrection have for us today? Resurrection faith is grounded in lived experience and personal encounters with the living Lord. They change people. The most convincing proof of the resurrection is the effect the risen Jesus has on the individual believer and the community of faith. The everyday testimony of the faithful that the work of Christ's kingdom continues – the countless deeds of love and kindness done daily in his name – are proof enough that Jesus lives.

COLLECT

God, our judge and saviour,
teach us to be open to your truth
and to trust in your love,
that we may live each day
with confidence in the salvation which is given
through Jesus Christ our Lord.

Reflection by **Tim Heaton**

Ordinary Time

Monday 4 October

Psalms **98**, 99, 101
Ecclesiasticus 22.6-22
or Ezekiel 28.1-19
John 13.1-11

John 13.1-11

'... he loved them to the end' (v.1)

We know from the Gospels that Jesus made fellowship meals a priority. He ate regularly with his disciples and used them as opportunities to teach. Unbelievably for his culture, he even had meals with prostitutes, tax-gatherers and people with leprosy. He shared his bread with sinners. It was one of the reasons why the religious establishment despised him. But the Last Supper was of a different order, and not just because it was Jesus' last meal on earth.

In the Middle East, it was the job of the house-slave to wash the feet of guests as they arrived; this ensured that the dirt and dust of the streets were not trampled all over the house. And very sensible the custom was too. Except here is Jesus, the host, not only washing his disciples' feet, but doing so *after* the meal, not before it. It was a deliberate act to burn a truth into their memory.

St John describes Jesus 'taking off his outer robe' or 'laying down his garments' before washing his disciples' feet. He uses the same word to describe the Good Shepherd laying down his life for his sheep. The two actions are inextricably linked. Jesus loved his disciples to the end. He shows us what God does, and on the cross does what he shows us and invites us to follow him in the way of sacrificial service. Is there someone to whom we might express the love of God in a practical way today?

COLLECT

O God, forasmuch as without you
we are not able to please you;
mercifully grant that your Holy Spirit
may in all things direct and rule our hearts;
through Jesus Christ our Lord.

Reflection by **Robert Atwell**

Ordinary Time

Psalms **106*** (*or* 103)
Ecclesiasticus 22.27 – 23.15
or Ezekiel 33.1-20
John 13.12-20

Tuesday 5 October

John 13.12-20

'I have set you an example' (v.15)

Feet are not that romantic. Nor are they particularly symbolic. Yet for Jesus, the action of washing his disciples' feet on the night of his betrayal is hugely symbolic. He was acting out a prophetic sign of his life and mission.

The disciples remembered the Last Supper they shared with Jesus, not least because of the way he used the bread and wine of the meal to signify his forthcoming death. However, unlike the other Gospel writers, John does not record this. Instead, he invests the foot-washing with a sacramental quality: an outward and visible sign of an inward and spiritual reality. Jesus tells his disciples that he has come to lay down his life, and he invites us to follow him in the same way of self-giving love.

If the Eucharist is at the heart of our life as Christians, so also should foot-washing be. The Eucharist is the place to which we are drawn and the centre from which we are sent out to bring Christ to the world.

The call to the Eucharist is a call to get our feet dirty in our service of others. We cannot love and keep our own feet clean.

Faithful Lord,
whose steadfast love never ceases
and whose mercies never come to an end:
grant us the grace to trust you
and to receive the gifts of your love,
new every morning,
in Jesus Christ our Lord.

COLLECT

Reflection by **Robert Atwell**

Ordinary Time

Wednesday 6 October

Psalms 110, 111, 112
Ecclesiasticus 24.1-22
or Ezekiel 33.21-end
John 13.21-30

John 13.21-30

'And it was night' (v.30)

In John's Gospel, day, night, light and darkness are not merely statements about the time of day: they are spiritual declarations. This was the night that the close-knit band of Jesus' disciples fell apart. This was the night that the community disintegrated.

No one will ever know what pushed Judas to betray Jesus. Perhaps he was obsessed with the thought of getting rid of the Romans from his country and thought that in forcing Jesus' hand at Passover, when Jerusalem was packed full of pilgrims, he might provoke an uprising. Whatever his reasoning, Judas abandons the company of Jesus, abandons the light, and in the process falls into his own shadow. He destroys not only his Lord and Master, but himself. We learn from Matthew 27.3-10 and from the opening chapter of Acts that, overcome by remorse for what he had done, Judas hanged himself.

We should not forget that Jesus had washed Judas' feet along with all the others, which makes his betrayal all the more difficult to fathom. It is not for nothing that, as Judas leaves the upper room, John says, 'And it was night'.

As we reflect on this event, at some level, deep within us, we need to repent of our own betrayals and disloyalties. We pray for grace to forgive those who have undermined and betrayed us because, in the end, only forgiveness can mend broken lives.

COLLECT

O God, forasmuch as without you
we are not able to please you;
mercifully grant that your Holy Spirit
may in all things direct and rule our hearts;
through Jesus Christ our Lord.

Reflection by **Robert Atwell**

Ordinary Time

Psalms 113, **115**
Ecclesiasticus 24.23-end
or Ezekiel 34.1-16
John 13.31-end

Thursday 7 October

John 13.31-end

'I give you a new commandment' (v.34)

Judas leaves the upper room and heads off to rendezvous with the temple police. The trap set for Jesus in the garden of Gethsemane is about to be sprung. Judas' departure becomes the cue for some of the most intimate teaching of Jesus. When someone is nearing death, their words and actions have a peculiar intensity. They begin a process of leave-taking in preparation for that last great journey, which one day we must all make and which we can only make alone.

On the night of his betrayal, however, Jesus is not detached: he is intensely present. It is his disciples who are absent. They cannot fathom what is going on and will shortly abandon him. Bizarrely, Peter asks Jesus where he is going. He professes undying loyalty but will deny knowing him three times.

In these so-called 'Farewell Discourses', Jesus offers his disciples the simplest but hardest command of all: 'Love one another'. He calls it a 'new commandment'. In truth, it is not new: the Old Testament is full of exhortations to love. What makes it new is the measure of love: 'as I have loved you, so you also should love one another'. Jesus' sacrificial love is the measure and, in the words of the poet T. S. Eliot, the cost will be 'not less than everything'.

COLLECT

Faithful Lord,
whose steadfast love never ceases
and whose mercies never come to an end:
grant us the grace to trust you
and to receive the gifts of your love,
new every morning,
in Jesus Christ our Lord.

Reflection by **Robert Atwell**

Ordinary Time

Friday 8 October

Psalm **139**
Ecclesiasticus 27.30 – 28.9
or Ezekiel 34.17-end
John 14.1-14

John 14.1-14

'In my Father's house there are many dwelling-places' (v.2)

Many will be familiar with this reading at funerals, though probably in its traditional form: 'In my Father's house there are many mansions' (KJV). The old language is grand as well as comforting and echoes words of Psalm 31 in the Book of Common Prayer: 'Thou hast set my feet in a large room' (v.9). The picture it paints of heaven is one of freedom and adventure.

Jesus speaks of his 'going away', and the disciples are understandably anxious. Where is he going? Can they come too?

In the face of the unknown and in response to the disciples' questioning, Jesus invites us to trust God. He speaks of his 'Father's house'. The only other time in the fourth Gospel that Jesus uses this expression occurs when he cleared out the moneychangers, referring to the temple (John 2.16). In the life of the people of Israel, the temple was holy ground, the sacred meeting place of heaven and earth. Here, Jesus uses the phrase to speak of a new 'house', one not constrained by time or geography, but spacious and open to all, part of God's renewal of creation.

Jesus is recasting death as a homecoming in which God our Father is there to greet us and of which he is 'the way, and the truth, and the life'. We have nothing to fear and everything to hope for.

COLLECT

O God, forasmuch as without you
we are not able to please you;
mercifully grant that your Holy Spirit
may in all things direct and rule our hearts;
through Jesus Christ our Lord

Reflection by **Robert Atwell**

Ordinary Time

Psalms 120, **121**, 122
Ecclesiasticus 28.14-end
or Ezekiel 36.16-36
John 14.15-end

Saturday 9 October

John 14.15-end

'I will not leave you orphaned.' (v.18)

The death of a parent is one of the great watershed moments of life for which there is no adequate psychological preparation. The experience can be particularly traumatic for a child. Jesus uses the word *orphanos* here when speaking to his disciples, and it captures the sense of foreboding and impending loss.

In the ancient Greek world, *orphanos* was also used of disciples and students bereaved at the loss of an honoured teacher. Speaking of the death of Socrates, Plato says that his disciples 'thought that they would have to spend the rest of their days forlorn as children bereft of a father'. There may be this double resonance in Jesus' words.

In saying that they would not be left orphaned, Jesus is offering his disciples (and us) deep reassurance. 'I am coming to you,' he insists. Jesus alludes to his resurrection and risen presence, which will transform loss into joy: 'because I live, you also will live'. Christian spirituality is 'aliveness', and it is rooted in the risen life of Jesus Christ. It is characterized by a sense of homecoming that is shaped by Jesus' own words: 'those who love me will keep my word, and my Father will love them, and we will come to them and make our home with them.' God will be with us. We have nothing to fear.

> Faithful Lord,
> whose steadfast love never ceases
> and whose mercies never come to an end:
> grant us the grace to trust you
> and to receive the gifts of your love,
> new every morning,
> in Jesus Christ our Lord.

COLLECT

Reflection by **Robert Atwell**

Ordinary Time

Monday 11 October

Psalms 123, 124, 125, **126**
Ecclesiasticus 31.1-11
or Ezekiel 37.1-14
John 15.1-11

John 15.1-11

'Abide in me' (v.4)

In the Hebrew Scriptures, the vine is the supreme image of the people of God (see Isaiah 5.1-4 and Psalm 80.8), and here Jesus relates the image to himself: 'I am the true vine, and my Father is the vine-grower.' Just as Jesus is the *true* bread and the *true* light, so he is also the *true* vine – the real Israel. Not only that, he says that we are the vine's branches.

The task of the vine-grower includes pruning both barren and living branches to encourage the vine to be more fruitful. You prune for growth. In midwinter, a vine is cut back to the main stock to create a strong structure and the branches tied in to protect them from wind damage. From time to time, we need to stand back and do a bit of judicious pruning of ourselves. Are there things we need to stop doing because we have become over-extended at home, at work or at church? When we do too much, we will be vulnerable when winter winds blow.

Branches can only survive as an intimate part of the vine. Which is why Jesus tells us to 'abide in me as I abide in you'. The verb variously translated as 'abide', 'dwell' or 'live' is one of the great words of this Gospel. We need to be rooted in Christ to allow his life-giving sap to flow through us. Only so will we bear fruit for God.

COLLECT

God, the giver of life,
whose Holy Spirit wells up within your Church:
by the Spirit's gifts equip us to live the gospel of Christ
and make us eager to do your will,
that we may share with the whole creation
the joys of eternal life;
through Jesus Christ our Lord.

Reflection by **Robert Atwell**

Ordinary Time

Psalms **132**, 133
Ecclesiasticus 34.9-end
or Ezekiel 37.15-end
John 15.12-17

Tuesday 12 October

John 15.12-17

'You did not choose me but I chose you' (v.16)

Rabbis did not usually look for disciples. Instead, young devotees did the rounds of the synagogues, listening to the local rabbis, looking for someone who appealed to them and then attaching themselves to their entourage. When we read the Gospels, we witness a reversal of roles. It is not the disciples who choose Jesus: it is Jesus who chooses his disciples. And what a rum lot they were. Just like you and me.

The good news is that not only does Jesus call us to follow him, but he also invites us into friendship. According to Exodus, Moses was 'a friend of God' (Exodus 33.11). Jesus invites us into nothing less than friendship with God because 'whoever has seen me has seen the Father' (John 14.9). Sometimes we can be so busy working in God's vineyard that we lose sight of the joy of that invitation. We revert to becoming servants, not friends.

Teresa d'Ávila, the Spanish Carmelite and spiritual writer, trundling across the Sierra Nevada on the back of an ox cart, famously remarked when she fell from it into the mud: 'If this is how you treat your friends, God, it's no wonder you've got so few of them.' But the fact is, she enjoyed an extraordinary intimacy with God that was evident to all who knew her. Are we friends of Jesus or just acquaintances?

COLLECT

God, our light and our salvation:
illuminate our lives,
that we may see your goodness in the land of the living,
and looking on your beauty
may be changed into the likeness of Jesus Christ our Lord.

Reflection by **Robert Atwell**

Ordinary Time

Wednesday 13 October

Psalm 119.153-end
Ecclesiasticus 35
or Ezekiel 39.21-end
John 15.18-end

John 15.18-end

'I have chosen you out of the world' (v.19)

We may not be living under the constant threat of persecution, as many Christians are in other parts of the world, but we often encounter suspicion and animosity. Hatred is a strong word, but it does capture the opprobrium that Christians sometimes attract.

The American lawyer Oliver Wendell Holmes famously jibed: 'Some people are so heavenly minded that they are of no earthly good.' The accusation is that Christians are a waste of space because we are not in touch with reality. When Jesus said that he was calling his disciples 'out of the world', he did not mean that we have divine permission to abdicate responsibility for the world and its problems. We are summoned by God to be *in* the world, but not *of* the world. As Paul wrote to the Christians in Rome: 'Do not be conformed to this world, but be transformed by the renewing of your minds' (Romans 12.2).

Writing in the sixth century, Gregory the Great comments on this call to personal transformation: 'Hold the things of this world in such a way that you are not held by them. Earthly goods must be possessed; do not let them possess you. Otherwise, you will be possessed by your own possessions.' Today, let us pray for the renewing of our minds and imaginations.

COLLECT

God, the giver of life,
whose Holy Spirit wells up within your Church:
by the Spirit's gifts equip us to live the gospel of Christ
and make us eager to do your will,
that we may share with the whole creation
the joys of eternal life;
through Jesus Christ our Lord.

Reflection by **Robert Atwell**

Psalms **143**, 146
Ecclesiasticus 37.7-24
or Ezekiel 43.1-12
John 16.1-15

Thursday 14 October

John 16.1-15

'When the Spirit of truth comes' (v.13)

A wise old monk, commenting on these words of Jesus, said they were the scariest words in the Bible. 'We all tell lies,' he said, 'but the worst lies are the ones we tell ourselves.'

In George Orwell's prophetic novel *Nineteen Eighty-Four*, the 'Ministry of Truth' controls the corporate memory of society: it continuously edits history to ensure that there is no memory of a time when Big Brother was not right. With the reach of digital platforms, fake news has become a burgeoning industry. Assaults on truth and the abuse of free speech are now major threats to democratic institutions and our way of life.

In the light of this, we should not be surprised that cynicism is widespread. It takes root in soil poisoned by lies and cover-ups, particularly when those in positions of public trust are discovered to have been economical with the truth. The prospect that the Holy Spirit will lead us into all truth is good news, full of hope because lies distort, damage and degrade both individuals and society.

Let us pray that the Holy Spirit's work of renewal may begin in each of us today by helping us be truthful and open in all our dealings.

COLLECT

God, our light and our salvation:
illuminate our lives,
that we may see your goodness in the land of the living,
and looking on your beauty
may be changed into the likeness of Jesus Christ our Lord.

Reflection by **Robert Atwell**

Ordinary Time

Friday 15 October

Psalms 142, **144**
Ecclesiasticus 38.1-14
or Ezekiel 44.4-16
John 16.16-22

John 16.16-22

'No one will take your joy from you' (v.22)

In an interview she gave shortly before her death, Joyce Grenfell, famous for her humorous monologues, said that she wasn't a bit interested in happiness, but was deeply interested 'in the roots of joy'. What are the roots of joy in our life? It is a good question to ponder.

Joy is one of the distinctive words in the fourth Gospel. For John, the root of joy is abiding in Christ. In the Gospel, Jesus doesn't promise happiness. On the contrary, he says that we will 'have pain' and 'persecution' (v.33). However, what Jesus does promise is joy: 'I have said these things to you so that my joy may be in you, and that your joy may be complete' (John 15.11). Happiness may come; happiness may go; but joy has a tough, enduring quality. The thing about joy is that you can be joyful even in dark times.

Gardeners know all about protecting the roots of plants and feeding them lest they wither through their inability to take up water and nutrients. When we abide in Christ, we put down roots into the love of God and discover the Christ-sap flowing through our veins, bringing us alive. And when that happens, no one will be able to rob us of the joy.

COLLECT

God, the giver of life,
whose Holy Spirit wells up within your Church:
by the Spirit's gifts equip us to live the gospel of Christ
and make us eager to do your will,
that we may share with the whole creation
the joys of eternal life;
through Jesus Christ our Lord.

Reflection by **Robert Atwell**

Psalm 147
Ecclesiasticus 38.24-end
or Ezekiel 47.1-12
John 16.23-end

Saturday 16 October

John 16.23-end

'I have conquered the world!' (v.33)

It is difficult to correlate Jesus' arrest and execution as a common criminal with the language of victory and conquest. What did he mean? Clearly, something qualitatively different from being the general at the head of a triumphant army.

The reputed words of Napoleon Bonaparte are fascinating to contemplate: 'Alexander the Great, Julius Caesar and I conquered the world by force, but Jesus Christ conquered the world by love, and still today millions follow his teaching.' These three historical figures are reckoned as the most successful military leaders the world has ever seen, but no one today follows them. With Jesus Christ, it is different.

Jesus lived his life in response to the call of love. When he was executed, many people thought that his life and ministry were a failure. Yet his powerful message of love in the face of hatred and forgiveness in the face of violence outlived all his enemies; it still inspires millions of people today. St Paul knew just how much the preaching of a crucified Saviour was a scandal to Jews and sheer stupidity to Greeks (1 Corinthians 1.23), but it is why we honour his victory and have the courage to proclaim him Lord.

God, our light and our salvation:
illuminate our lives,
that we may see your goodness in the land of the living,
and looking on your beauty
may be changed into the likeness of Jesus Christ our Lord.

COLLECT

Reflection by **Robert Atwell**

Ordinary Time

Monday 18 October
Luke the Evangelist

Psalms 145, 146
Isaiah 55
Luke 1.1-4

Luke 1.1-4

'... so that you may know the truth' (v.4)

Luke writes for Theophilus to know the truth about the things in which they have been instructed. Theophilus, we guess, is a baptized disciple on the Way, belonging to a community of believers. What is missing which prompts Luke to write? The answer may be in the content and style of Luke's Gospel. The narrative about Zechariah leads to the beautiful accounts of Elizabeth, Mary, and their meeting. We are able to be present as human encounters give way to glorious poetry. The words of the Magnificat, with all their hope and challenge, are set in a very specific context of a conversation between two women. Luke offers us intimate details about the birth of Jesus and an insight into his teenage years. Luke's Gospel is especially attentive to women and to social outcasts.

Luke's writing enhances our understanding of context and our insight into Jesus' encounters with ordinary people. Luke also includes parables not found elsewhere, such as the Prodigal Son and the Good Samaritan, with their emphasis on grace, generosity and inclusion.

Christian teaching is incomplete without contemplation on the human encounters Luke offers us. We can spend time with the narratives, poetry and parables in Luke. In imagination, we can be with Elizabeth, Mary and the young Jesus. With Mary, we might treasure these things in our hearts and sing with her of grace and justice.

COLLECT

Almighty God,
you called Luke the physician,
whose praise is in the gospel,
to be an evangelist and physician of the soul:
by the grace of the Spirit
and through the wholesome medicine of the gospel,
give your Church the same love and power to heal;
through Jesus Christ our Lord.

Reflection by **Julia Mourant**

Ordinary Time

Psalms **5**, 6 (8)
Ecclesiasticus 39.13-end
or Ecclesiastes 2
John 17.6-19

Tuesday 19 October

John 17.6-19

'I have sent them into the world' (v.18)

This long prayer discourse of Jesus reminds me of the plaited bread loaves I once used to make. Stretching the soft dough, gently attending to each section, keeping the strands distinct, but shaping into one loaf. Repeated words and phrases weave around each other, each with a distinct meaning but appearing and reappearing. Analysis of each phrase may not help any more than analyzing each line of a poem or every bar of a piece of music will really take us to its heart. Perhaps we have to listen to it, again and again, so that its deep music takes root in our souls and we know what Jesus is saying, not by a kind of translation or unpicking but more by attending to cadence, resonance and echo.

Jesus prays for protection, deeply aware of the misunderstanding and even hate his followers may face. Vulnerability in need of protection is not the same as weakness. There is no suggestion here of weakness, but Jesus knows the scale of the task that lies ahead. Their protection will lie in belonging to God in a life sanctified by the word. The words and themes in this prayer are part of a whole. When you cut open a plaited loaf of bread, there are no separate threads inside; these are only visible on the outside. Inside, it is just bread. Taste and see.

COLLECT

Grant, we beseech you, merciful Lord,
to your faithful people pardon and peace,
that they may be cleansed from all their sins
and serve you with a quiet mind;
through Jesus Christ our Lord.

Reflection by **Julia Mourant**

Ordinary Time

Wednesday 20 October

Psalm 119.1-32
Ecclesiasticus 42.15-end
or Ecclesiastes 3.1-15
John 17.20-end

John 17.20-end

'The glory that you have given me ...' (v.22)

The recurring theme of 'glory' emerges again here. Glory is a multifaceted concept that refers to the weight of God's presence and life. Glory draws our gaze, our wonder as we behold the divine radiance. We are drawn in, unable to take our eyes away and yet overwhelmed by brilliance. This does not have to be a 'super spiritual' experience – sometimes we find ourselves immersed in glory and radiance in unexpected places and people.

Jesus gives his glory to his followers so that the world may know that they belong to him. This gift of glory is given first so that 'they may be one'. The Church has had many debates about how to become one, and there have been questions about whether it is even desirable. What we are offered here is a reminder that the only starting point for unity is to gaze on God. God's glory is made visible and tangible in Jesus and in those followers who have received his gift and live in his light.

Sometimes it is hard to see; we focus first on the difficulties and the cracks. These will not easily disappear, but perhaps we can find ways to behold the glory of God together in silence and wonder. A genuine experience of glory leaves all other agendas in deep shade.

Where have you encountered glory?

COLLECT

Grant, we beseech you, merciful Lord,
to your faithful people pardon and peace,
that they may be cleansed from all their sins
and serve you with a quiet mind;
through Jesus Christ our Lord.

Reflection by **Julia Mourant**

Ordinary Time

Psalms 14, **15**, 16
Ecclesiasticus 43.1-12
or Ecclesiastes 3.16 – end of 4
John 18.1-11

Thursday 21 October

John 18.1-11

'Jesus said to them "I am he"' (v.6)

Jesus steps forward into the light with the words 'I am he'. Picture the scene. Perhaps the disciples had a lantern between them, but this was no cosy evening gathering. This garden in a valley had provided a place of shade, shelter, refuge and companionship for Jesus and the disciples. Now it is a place of darkness, shadows and threat. The soldiers come with torches, weapons – and treachery. The light plays tricks; no face is clearly discernible. So, the words 'I am he' are a deliberate self-identification and self-offering. Some step back and fall down, such is the presence of glory here.

The words 'I am he' with their echoes of other times when Jesus has said 'I am', echoing the divine name, are a manifestation of ultimate authority and light. Jesus is unafraid to say who is he is. Peter panics – he does not look to Jesus for a lead but simply reacts. He fails to see that Jesus is intentional, committed and does not need defending. Jesus has not sought the protection of humankind, nor is he fleeing from its violence. It is he who has kept the flock safe; this is his vocation. It is not theirs to protect him.

Earlier, Jesus says he has lost none except the one destined to be lost (John 17.12). Now he says he has not lost a single one. Perhaps, in the eyes of Jesus, even now Judas is not lost.

> Almighty God,
> in whose service lies perfect freedom:
> teach us to obey you
> with loving hearts and steadfast wills;
> through Jesus Christ our Lord.

COLLECT

Reflection by **Julia Mourant**

Ordinary Time

Friday 22 October

Psalms 17, **19**
Ecclesiasticus 43.13-end
or Ecclesiastes 5
John 18.12-27

John 18.12-27

'Did I not see you in the garden?' (v.26)

Jesus is bound. It seems disproportionate to restrain a man who has given himself up, but the authorities act from fear and a need to control. They use physical force to compensate for their lack of moral or spiritual authority. This will not be hard for us to recognize.

Peter is feeling his own fears, washing over him in place of the passionate loyalty he has previously expressed. No one would judge Peter; Peter is all of us. 'I don't know the man' stands in stark contrast to the words of Jesus, 'I am he'. Jesus steps into the light to be identified, while Peter seeks to slip into the shadows of the firelight and become anonymous. The bravado of the sword has evaporated. Perhaps Peter found it hard to believe that Jesus is now an arrested prisoner, held by the authorities he has eluded for so long. Peter does not want to leave, but he is torn and conflicted. Judas betrays Jesus openly. Peter's denial is more an act of omission, dissemblance, silence. Lingering in the shadows is not much of a strategy when we are asked where our loyalties lie. It takes courage to identify openly with those who are persecuted, suffering or marginalized. Jesus stands alone.

Where can we see Jesus in the other now? How do we find courage to step out of the flickering firelight?

COLLECT

Grant, we beseech you, merciful Lord,
to your faithful people pardon and peace,
that they may be cleansed from all their sins
and serve you with a quiet mind;
through Jesus Christ our Lord.

Reflection by **Julia Mourant**

Ordinary Time

Psalms 20, 21, **23**
Ecclesiasticus 44.1-15
or Ecclesiastes 6
John 18.28-end

Saturday 23 October

John 18.28-end

'... my kingdom is not from here' (v.36)

We are offered further reminders of the human capacity for denial of responsibility. The authorities want Pilate to be the one who condemns Jesus. They will not even name the charge but manipulate Pilate, saying that it should not be difficult since Jesus is clearly a criminal. Their avoidance of culpability is not a mere legal technicality but reflects moral and spiritual bankruptcy. Their chief concern is to avoid being defiled. John makes the point that this is ritual defilement. Perhaps we are meant to note that their souls are already defiled by their actions. It is not which architectural or power thresholds are crossed that matter, but the lines we cross in our hearts.

Pilate, too, seeks to avoid responsibility. He had some limited power to take a risk and do the right thing. Yet it probably did not seem worth the risk when he had one eye on the political figures who could remove him in an instant. The possibility of sidestepping responsibility will always be present, for the humble disciple such as Peter as well as for religious figures and political leaders. Peter's denial, the authorities' dishonesty and Pilate's cowardice look different, but they all reflect our inability to step into the light with Jesus. Jesus lives, and will soon die, on an entirely different plane. Jesus knows who he is, his vocation from God, and all that he says and does will reflect that integrity.

> Almighty God,
> in whose service lies perfect freedom:
> teach us to obey you
> with loving hearts and steadfast wills;
> through Jesus Christ our Lord.

COLLECT

Reflection by **Julia Mourant**

Ordinary Time

Monday 25 October

Psalms 27, **30**
Ecclesiasticus 44.19 – 45.5
or Ecclesiastes 7.1-14
John 19.1-16

John 19.1-16

'I find no case against him' (v.4)

Pilate is afraid; he has political standing but no real security. Jesus appears unwilling to help himself, much less give Pilate a way out. Briefly, Pilate resists the pressure, but the moment passes, and in fear and weakness, he surrenders Jesus. In some deeply buried place, Pilate knows there is no case, but to attend to that possibility could be dangerous. It is better not to think about it, to tell himself he has no option, even though he colludes with people who are merely using him.

'I had no choice' is not always the truth. Jesus goes to the cross because of human fear. His teaching was not understood, or if it was, the message was too costly to embrace. Hardened religious or political positions can be a smokescreen for deeper fears. Human perspectives, agendas and motivations are worked out. Humankind was always going to reject Jesus. It is a rejection of God, but in the name of both expediency and religion.

The passion of Jesus is a seminal event in Christian understanding, yet not an isolated one. Where truth and beauty, compassion and justice meet institutional insecurity and toxic religiosity, there will be crucifixion. We take Jesus to the cross again and again; it is what we do as ordinary people. There is, however, hope. We may temporarily hide in the shadows of the courtyard, yet if we run to the garden, we can rediscover our vocation from the risen Christ.

COLLECT

Blessed Lord,
who caused all holy Scriptures to be written for our learning:
help us so to hear them,
to read, mark, learn and inwardly digest them
that, through patience, and the comfort of your holy word,
we may embrace and for ever hold fast
    the hope of everlasting life,
which you have given us in our Saviour Jesus Christ.

Reflection by **Julia Mourant**

Ordinary Time

Psalms 32, **36**
Ecclesiasticus 45.6-17
or Ecclesiastes 7.15-end
John 19.17-30

Tuesday 26 October

John 19.17-30

'Here is your mother' (v.27)

There is a heart-wrenching tone to this unfolding narrative. As is often the way when recounting a death, every detail is told, like precious jigsaw pieces that must not be lost. The agony is not glossed over; those present must have been marked for life by these traumatic events. The focus narrows to a small group of women. Their discipleship is courageous, yet without bravado or violent protest. These women do not hide behind denials of their relationship, nor do they run. Perhaps they said little, but they are visible and present. 'We are here' is their gift; an active presence, a shared witness. They will have nothing to regret, later, when they measure out the spices with their tears and their tenderness.

Jesus draws his mother and the beloved disciple together. Perhaps this is not simply a protective gesture, the last care of Jesus for his mother. Mary is as much a gift to the beloved disciple as he is to her. The beloved disciple welcomes into his home the witness who has seen it all. She has lived from the shocking angelic announcement to the life of a child in an ordinary family. Confused and hurt at times, she has seen the teacher, heard the prophet and healer find his voice. Now, she has stood and silently borne his death. The beloved disciple may be her protector, but surely, she is his teacher.

COLLECT

Merciful God,
teach us to be faithful in change and uncertainty,
that trusting in your word
and obeying your will
we may enter the unfailing joy of Jesus Christ our Lord.

Reflection by **Julia Mourant**

Ordinary Time

Wednesday 27 October

Psalm **34**
Ecclesiasticus 46.1-10
or Ecclesiastes 8
John 19.31-end

John 19.31-end

'They took the body of Jesus' (v.40)

The law, which has been manipulated in order to put Jesus to death, now dictates, conveniently, that the embarrassment and challenge of his body is removed. However, Joseph of Arimathea will not allow an unceremonious clearing up and sanitizing of the scene. He emerges from the shadows, with Nicodemus, who once again (John 3.2) will only come at night. Perhaps it seems less dangerous now that Jesus is dead. Joseph and Nicodemus offer gifts in death that they could not offer in life. Some cannot declare openly their discipleship. Joseph and Nicodemus offer what they can, when they can. Perhaps in their tender service to Jesus in death, there was a sense of a vocation that could not be fulfilled openly while Jesus lived. Joseph had spoken out in the Sanhedrin (Luke 23.50). Could he have distanced himself further? There is a moment to follow a call and those who let it pass can be left wondering if they might have been more vocal, more visible, more willing to take a risk.

It is never too late to respond to Jesus, and if at one time in our lives we went as far as we could in our response, that need not be the end of the story. The invitation of God has no expiration, no 'best before' date. Jesus calls Joseph and Nicodemus again, even in his death, and they go to him with the gifts they have.

COLLECT

Blessed Lord,
who caused all holy Scriptures to be written for our learning:
help us so to hear them,
to read, mark, learn and inwardly digest them
that, through patience, and the comfort of your holy word,
we may embrace and for ever hold fast
    the hope of everlasting life,
which you have given us in our Saviour Jesus Christ.

Reflection by **Julia Mourant**

Ordinary Time

Psalms 116, 117
Wisdom 5.1-16
or Isaiah 45.18-end
Luke 6.12-16

Thursday 28 October
Simon and Jude, Apostles

Luke 6.12-16

'... when day came, he called his disciples' (v.13)

The Twelve are called from an existing group of disciples, a discernment that began in a night of prayer. Jesus drew this group from real human beings; he never expected perfection or even reliability. The little we know about Simon and Jude is from Christian tradition rather than Scripture. It seems they had missionary ventures, possibly together, and both were martyred. Jude has become the patron saint of hopeless cases and lost causes; some miracles are attributed to him. It is a rather beautiful thing that the Church has such a saint.

Some pray to the saints; others are more comfortable with an imaginary conversation or the lighting of a candle. Perhaps Jude's vocation now, however you understand that in the context of the communion of saints, is to hear our longings and laments. I imagine Jude sitting quietly in some half-forgotten corner of the Residence of the Saints, door open, ready to hear it all. Miracles might be in short supply (sometimes we are surprised by one), but what we most need is to be heard, not for someone to tell us it will all be ok. Sometimes we don't want to be cheered up or pointed to Scriptures we already know. The lostness is real; we may find a way forward in due course, in our own time.

What would you say to the patron saint of lost causes?

> Almighty God,
> who built your Church upon the foundation
> of the apostles and prophets,
> with Jesus Christ himself as the chief cornerstone:
> so join us together in unity of spirit by their doctrine,
> that we may be made a holy temple acceptable to you;
> through Jesus Christ our Lord.

COLLECT

Reflection by **Julia Mourant**

Ordinary Time

Friday 29 October

Psalm 31
Ecclesiasticus 51.1-12
or Ecclesiastes 11.1-8
John 20.11-18

John 20.11-18

'Jesus said to her "Mary!"' (v.16)

After the turmoil of the last few days, all that is left to Mary is to tend the body of Jesus. How important the physicality of a body is for those who mourn. Death means the complete loss of an embodied connection. Mary's tears are specifically because there is no body. She is devastated. This agony is grief upon grief, loss upon loss. She needs to see, to touch, to tend, to process and in due course to say goodbye to this body. What unfolds is one of the most tender and poignant encounters in all Scripture.

As with other accounts of the resurrection, grief and despair shift to bemusement in which it is impossible to make sense of what is happening. Then there is a pivotal point, a moment of invitation to stay with the wondering. Mary does not scream, run away in fright or tell this man to go away. She stays still and listens, and hears her name spoken. That voice changes everything.

Her instinct is to grasp this body, breathing again. 'Don't hold on to me,' he says. At times of confusion, it can be important to stay with the wrestling, stand still and listen. Then, perhaps we will hear our name spoken again in a voice we know so well. It is enough – just a name. Mary has seen the Lord; now she can walk away from his physical presence in the garden and tell the disciples.

COLLECT

Blessed Lord,
who caused all holy Scriptures to be written for our learning:
help us so to hear them,
to read, mark, learn and inwardly digest them
that, through patience, and the comfort of your holy word,
we may embrace and for ever hold fast
    the hope of everlasting life,
which you have given us in our Saviour Jesus Christ.

Reflection by **Julia Mourant**

Ordinary Time

Psalms 41, **42**, 43
Ecclesiasticus 51.13-end
or Ecclesiastes 11.9 – end of 12
John 20.19-end

Saturday 30 October

John 20.19-end

'Receive the Holy Spirit' (v.22)

Jesus comes not so much to offer evidence of his resurrected life as to breathe the Holy Spirit on the disciples and commission them as agents of forgiveness. Forgiveness is the currency of the kingdom. Where there is forgiveness, there will be more grace, more compassion. Where there is hardness of heart, desire for self-justification or even revenge, it self-replicates. We cannot claim to stand between God and the one seeking forgiveness. Our unforgiveness must never prevent someone from finding peace with God. The words of Jesus both warn and invite. If you do not forgive, then that person may never find forgiveness at all. When we model forgiveness, it becomes the lifeblood of a community.

Thomas has missed out, but a week later, he must make up his own mind. He sees the wounds in the body, but more importantly, looks into the face of Jesus, hears the familiar voice. Thomas responds with faith, but also humility, realizing perhaps that he has missed the point. Those who need physical evidence will always look for more, the 'final proof' that will always evade us. But to see and be seen, to hear Jesus speak, this is relationship. It will always be an encounter that compels us to follow Jesus, not 'proof'.

Again and again in John, it is the voice of Jesus that evokes faith, heals and calls. What evokes faith: 'evidence', or the grace of forgiveness?

> Merciful God,
> teach us to be faithful in change and uncertainty,
> that trusting in your word
> and obeying your will
> we may enter the unfailing joy of Jesus Christ our Lord.

COLLECT

Reflection by **Julia Mourant**

Ordinary Time: All Saints to Advent

Monday 1 November
All Saints' Day

Psalms 15, 84, 149
Isaiah 35.1-9
Luke 9.18-27

Luke 9.18-27

'Peter answered, "The Messiah of God"' (v.20)

Peter's astonishing insight into Jesus' identity is a leap of faith, and Jesus immediately qualifies it with an account of the suffering that he will endure and of the glory that will follow it. This is what Messiahship will look like: his identity is bound up with his suffering, death and rising. That is who he is.

This is what the followers of Jesus can also expect. Peter, who would deny Jesus three times, did indeed finally pick up his own cross, in literal terms. So did the majority of Jesus' friends and early followers.

When we truly focus on who Jesus is, we begin to discover who we are too. We learn what kind of 'yes' we have said to him when he called us to come and follow him. We learn too whether our faith will bring shame on us.

On this All Saints' Day, when we recall and honour the lives and deaths of the saints, what is clear is that they were people who had found that one thing – or rather, the one person – they most desired to say 'yes' to. When we know what we most need to say 'yes' to, it becomes clearer that we can say 'no' to all sorts of other things – we become free to deny what we thought was ourselves, and discover our true identity in the kingdom of God.

COLLECT

Almighty God,
you have knit together your elect
in one communion and fellowship
　　in the mystical body of your Son Christ our Lord:
grant us grace so to follow your blessed saints
in all virtuous and godly living
that we may come to those inexpressible joys
that you have prepared for those who truly love you;
through Jesus Christ our Lord.

Reflection by **Ally Barrett**

Ordinary Time: All Saints to Advent

Psalms **5**, 147.1-12 *or* **48**, 52
Isaiah 1.21-end
Matthew 2.1-15

Tuesday 2 November

Matthew 2.1-15

'In the time of King Herod ...' (v.1)

In the ancient world, it was accepted that the movement of heavenly bodies was inextricably bound up with earthly events. The arrival of the magi – visitors from the gentile world – is essential to Matthew's perspective, that the true King of the Jews (unlike the unworthy Herod) would not only lead God's people into freedom, but bring in a reign of justice and peace for the whole world. Such a momentous event on earth finds its reflection in the behaviour of the cosmos itself.

The gifts of gold, incense and myrrh are fit for a king, or even for a God. They point to the reality that Jesus' birth ushers in something new and world changing. No wonder Herod is afraid and, as we will see tomorrow, turns to violence in an attempt to shore up his own status and authority in the face of this new threat.

The gift of myrrh points to both death and healing, the incense to Jesus' priestly ministry (both of which are reflected in All Souls' Day commemorations). The gold signifies kingship – though the crown Jesus will wear is made from thorns, and his earthly throne is a cross. The light that drew the magi will be turned to darkness, and it is in that darkness that another gentile voice – an officer of the occupying powers – will proclaim that Jesus truly is the Son of God (Matthew 27.54).

> Almighty and eternal God,
> you have kindled the flame of love in the hearts of the saints:
> grant to us the same faith and power of love,
> that, as we rejoice in their triumphs,
> we may be sustained by their example and fellowship;
> through Jesus Christ our Lord.

COLLECT

Reflection by **Ally Barrett**

Ordinary Time: All Saints to Advent

Wednesday 3 November

Psalms **9**, 147.13-end
or **119.57-80**
Isaiah 2.1-11
Matthew 2.16-end

Matthew 2.16-end

'Rachel weeping for her children; she refused to be consoled' (v.18)

All Souls' Day was yesterday, and today we read of death.

The murder of the children of Bethlehem is an act of such unspeakable violence that we might doubt that anyone could bring themselves to enact it, were it not echoed in the news on a daily basis – in conflict zones, and in so many other contexts where violence should have no place. We rightly rail against a world that regularly enables such abominations against the most vulnerable and innocent. The world is such that an annual commemoration of the faithful departed is not a line in the sand after which we can cry, 'no more'; each day brings fresh grief, until that day when God wipes away all our tears (Revelation 21.4).

Meanwhile, the lone survivor of the massacre is Jesus himself. Having lived as refugees, the Holy Family returns from Egypt, and Jesus continues to fulfil all that Mary and Joseph had been promised and warned about him, and which has already been proved terrifyingly true. Mary's little son survived the wrath of Herod the Great, but his life of love will also be a purposeful journey towards a self-sacrificial death on the cross, with Herod Antipas as a key antagonist. So Mary, too, will weep for her child; as countless mothers continue to weep today, she weeps with them.

COLLECT

Almighty and eternal God,
you have kindled the flame of love in the hearts of the saints:
grant to us the same faith and power of love,
that, as we rejoice in their triumphs,
we may be sustained by their example and fellowship;
through Jesus Christ our Lord.

Reflection by **Ally Barrett**

Ordinary Time: All Saints to Advent

Psalms 11, **15**, 148 *or* 56, **57** (63*)
Isaiah 2.12-end
Matthew 3

Thursday 4 November

Matthew 3

'This is my son, the Beloved' (v.17)

John the Baptist emerges from the wilderness, wild, untamed but not chaotic – his message has a devastating clarity and focus. In the moment that prophecy turns to revelation and fulfilment, his voice rings out, calling people to repent not as punishment but as preparation. We are to turn towards God's promise, and all that it brings, levelling the rough places of our hearts so that the Lord may come.

When Jesus steps into the waters of the Jordan, the scene shifts from prophetic words to actions. The one without sin joins the crowd of sinners, choosing solidarity over separation, and opening up heaven itself in blessing and affirmation. Jesus, standing in the water alongside us, allows us all to hear the words of God the Father that claim us, along with Christ, as beloved children.

For Jesus, and for all of us, God names us as his own before we can be sent out, and God's grace is the foundation of all that we go on to do. The Father is pleased with the Son not because of what he has done (for his ministry is only just beginning) but because he is the Son, and he is beloved. In the strength of that, Jesus is ready to face whatever the next 40 days – and indeed the next three years – have in store.

COLLECT

God of glory,
touch our lips with the fire of your Spirit,
that we with all creation
may rejoice to sing your praise;
through Jesus Christ our Lord.

Reflection by **Ally Barrett**

Ordinary Time: All Saints to Advent

Friday 5 November

Psalms **16**, 149 *or* **51**, 54
Isaiah 3.1-15
Matthew 4.1-11

Matthew 4.1-11

'Away with you, Satan!' (v.10)

The temptations that the devil devises are well chosen, playing into the lure of physical comfort, protection and cheap power. Perhaps unwittingly, the devil provides an opportunity for something of a trial run of some of the temptations Jesus will face during his ministry and especially as he approaches his passion and death. It is one thing to know an action can't be good when the devil suggests it, and quite another to resist the same temptation when it comes to you from a friend: remember Peter rejecting Jesus' coming suffering, and the ensuing rebuke, 'Get behind me, Satan' (Matthew 16.22-23).

The devil had hoped to derail Jesus' mission before it even began, but instead, Jesus takes the opportunity to articulate out loud what he already knows. Bread miracles are not for his own comfort, but for hungry crowds; he himself will be broken and shared as both living Word and living bread; his kingship is not like that of earthly kings, and his vocation will bring suffering and death from which he will choose not to save himself.

Everything that the devil offers Jesus runs contrary to who Jesus is, what he came to do, and how he would accomplish it. In the wilderness, Jesus names the path that he will follow, and in everything he does from that moment on, we see him again and again embracing what this means.

COLLECT

Almighty and eternal God,
you have kindled the flame of love in the hearts of the saints:
grant to us the same faith and power of love,
that, as we rejoice in their triumphs,
we may be sustained by their example and fellowship;
through Jesus Christ our Lord.

Reflection by **Ally Barrett**

Psalms **18.31-end**, 150 *or* **68**
Isaiah 4.2 – 5.7
Matthew 4.12-22

Saturday 6 November

Matthew 4.12-22

'... light has dawned' (v.16)

It's a liminal place, located on a shoreline – a border – with a diverse population, and Jesus is there intentionally, drawing on the prophet Isaiah to reveal himself as the light that shines in darkness – a key scriptural theme (Isaiah 9.1–2). In the first chapter of John's Gospel, Jesus is the personified, embodied light echoed as one of the great 'I am' sayings (John 9.5). In Matthew chapter 5, the image is flipped round as a challenge to his followers, that they should live as lights of the world (5.14).

This is who Jesus is as he continues John's call to repent. In Hebrew, the word 'repent' means to turn, perhaps like a seedling germinating in darkness turns towards the light. We are to turn towards Jesus, for in him the kingdom has come near, and it is in his kingdom that we will know both light and life.

It is this light that helps the fishermen mending their nets to see the world – and themselves – so differently that, without hesitation and without full understanding, they get up and follow him and become part of the way that this light is shared. The shore of the lake becomes a place where dawn breaks, and they will spend the next three years learning, following, doubting and struggling, as they grow into this vocation. So it is for all who hear that call to follow.

COLLECT

God of glory,
touch our lips with the fire of your Spirit,
that we with all creation
may rejoice to sing your praise;
through Jesus Christ our Lord.

Reflection by **Ally Barrett**

Ordinary Time: All Saints to Advent

Monday 8 November

Psalms 19, **20** *or* **71**
Isaiah 5.8-24
Matthew 4.23 – 5.12

Matthew 4.23 – 5.12

'Blessed are you' (5.11)

Jesus walks through Galilee, teaching, proclaiming good news and healing – ministering to body, mind and spirit. His fame spreads because his compassion spreads: the kingdom he announces is not an idea but a whole new way of seeing the world, into which he invites everyone he meets.

On the mountain, he begins to describe the kind of life that flourishes in the kingdom. The Beatitudes are not moral instructions so much as glimpses into the heart of God. Each 'blessed' subverts expectation, as power, wealth and control give way to poverty of spirit, mercy and hunger for righteousness. Jesus paints a picture of a new community where vulnerability is not a defect but a place where blessing takes root. Those who grieve are not abandoned, but held. The meek are noticed and given an inheritance. The peacemakers, even in their struggle, reveal the likeness of God.

This is not a reward system but a statement of fact: God is already near to those who seem most disenfranchised. So the mountain becomes a place where the kingdom of heaven is revealed on earth, and a teacher heals weary souls by naming blessedness in unexpected places. The seeds of the kingdom are planted in the soil of our vulnerability and lack; blessing is ours not because it is something we can possess, but because it transforms us into God's holy people for God's needy world.

COLLECT

Almighty Father,
whose will is to restore all things
in your beloved Son, the King of all:
govern the hearts and minds of those in authority,
and bring the families of the nations,
divided and torn apart by the ravages of sin,
to be subject to his just and gentle rule;
who is alive and reigns with you,
in the unity of the Holy Spirit,
one God, now and for ever.

Reflection by **Ally Barrett**

Ordinary Time: All Saints to Advent

Psalms **21**, 24 *or* **73**
Isaiah 5.25-end
Matthew 5.13-20

Tuesday 9 November

Matthew 5.13-20

'You are the light of the world' (v.14)

Jesus always asks for more, perhaps because he sees in us such incredible potential, longing for us to become who we were created to be. His evident frustration is born of love, and delight in all that we are and can be, as well as out of sorrow at the very many ways in which we fail, or fail to try.

We are to be the salt of the earth, called to flavour the world around us with the kingdom of God. We are to be the light of the world, called to shine brightly and to do so in places where the whole household is illuminated. The salt and the light are both divine gifts, set within us, and divine callings, as people of faith within the world. This vocation is for the good of the whole of creation, as it has always been for God's beloved people. So there can be no half measures.

Jesus' teaching is both revolutionary and in continuity with all that has gone before. The law is therefore to be fulfilled, its purpose bound up with how 'all is accomplished'. For Jesus, the law is more wonderful and generative than we seem to be able to imagine, and its fulfilment is nothing less than the full realization of God's kingdom on earth. In him, we see the givenness of the law expressed in its fullness as a gift that brings abundant life.

COLLECT

God, our refuge and strength,
bring near the day when wars shall cease
and poverty and pain shall end,
that earth may know the peace of heaven
through Jesus Christ our Lord.

Reflection by **Ally Barrett**

Ordinary Time: All Saints to Advent

Wednesday 19 November

Psalms **23**, 25 *or* **77**
Isaiah 6
Matthew 5.21-37

Matthew 5.21-37

'Let your word be "Yes, Yes" or "No, No"' (v.37)

It's hard to control our thoughts, and research shows that it's easier to act our way into new patterns of thinking than it is to think ourselves into new behaviours. Cognitive behavioural therapy also works on the basis of a powerful relationship between what we think, what we feel, and how we act. No wonder Jesus is so adamant about the importance of our thinking patterns about each other. We cannot hope always to act well if we indulge in destructive thinking; at the same time, intentionally practising wholesome behaviours trains our brains into healthier patterns of thought.

Jesus advocates drastic action to break unhealthy thinking. Though we might not advocate removing body parts, we can certainly undertake other intentional actions to retrain our minds and hearts. Knowing our weaknesses, we can take steps to increase the cognitive and practical distance between ourselves and the temptations we may face, and to focus particular qualities of attention on people and situations to which such attention is rightly given.

The same applies to repentance and reconciliation: intentionally making the first move towards reparation when we are at fault not only reduces the risk of losing in court, but opens up possibilities of real reconciliation and healing.

When we reduce the dissonance between what we think and how we act, our 'yes' and our 'no' will be rooted in our integrity, and will be all that is needed.

COLLECT

Almighty Father,
whose will is to restore all things
in your beloved Son, the King of all:
govern the hearts and minds of those in authority,
and bring the families of the nations,
divided and torn apart by the ravages of sin,
to be subject to his just and gentle rule;
who is alive and reigns with you,
in the unity of the Holy Spirit,
one God, now and for ever.

Reflection by **Ally Barrett**

Ordinary Time: All Saints to Advent

Psalms **26**, 27 *or* **78.1-39***
Isaiah 7.1-17
Matthew 5.38-end

Thursday 11 November

Matthew 5.38-end

'Be perfect, therefore, as your heavenly Father is perfect' (v.48)

The expansiveness of the love of God appears again and again in Scripture, and every time, it is presented as a surprise that the love of God is broader and deeper and higher than the scope of human society.

Perfection is, both individually and collectively, beyond us in this life, and we will always find ways to fall short of the vision of generosity set out by Jesus here. But we are nevertheless called explicitly by God not just to raise the bar of our aspiration (to generosity, love and forgiveness) but to remove it completely: everyone is our neighbour; people who hate us might also be cold and need our spare coat.

Jesus sets out a pattern for self-sacrificial living – and dying. In short, he is offering us in words, here, what he then embodies in his passion: he is struck on the cheek; they cast lots for his garment; he walks the long road to Golgotha; and as he dies, he prays for his executioners to be forgiven.

Jesus' radical, challenging teaching is not just about us; it is more deeply about what God has done for us. It is humanity that sent Jesus (who chose his own vulnerability) to his death, and it is human conflict that still makes casualties of the most vulnerable.

COLLECT

God, our refuge and strength,
bring near the day when wars shall cease
and poverty and pain shall end,
that earth may know the peace of heaven
through Jesus Christ our Lord.

Reflection by **Ally Barrett**

Ordinary Time: All Saints to Advent

Friday 12 November

Psalms 28, **32** *or* **55**
Isaiah 8.1-15
Matthew 6.1-18

Matthew 6.1-18

'… your Father knows what you need' (v.8)

Jesus has no need of ostentatious piety because he embodies wholeness of relationship with God. Nor does he need to offer acts of performative generosity because his love and compassion for people is enacted in everything he does. Jesus' whole life and being witnesses to God's love, and brings the world's brokenness before the throne of heaven.

Jesus was also good at praying; not because his prayers were eloquent and wordy, but because they cut to the heart of what it means to be a human being among other human beings, and before God, and in a wayward and troubled world. He understands temptation and the proximity of evil (he met the Devil face to face just two chapters ago), and he knows hunger and a longing for bread from that same wilderness experience. He knows, too, the nearness of the kingdom, for he himself is making it real in a world that is in so many ways still at odds with the will of God. And he knows both the majesty and intimate love of the Father.

Jesus prays and lives as a human being and as the Son of God, and in a way that shows us all how we might also both pray and live as people who can call God 'Abba, Father', trusting that we are heard and seen, known and loved.

COLLECT | Almighty Father,
whose will is to restore all things
in your beloved Son, the King of all:
govern the hearts and minds of those in authority,
and bring the families of the nations,
divided and torn apart by the ravages of sin,
to be subject to his just and gentle rule;
who is alive and reigns with you,
in the unity of the Holy Spirit,
one God, now and for ever.

Reflection by **Ally Barrett**

Ordinary Time: All Saints to Advent

Psalm **33** or **76**, 79
Isaiah 8.16 – 9.7
Matthew 6.19-end

Saturday 13 November

Matthew 6.19-end

'... where your treasure is, there your heart will be also' (v.21)

What happens when we consider the lilies of the field and look at the birds of the air? An intentional pause in which we fix our attention on the ordinary beauty of God's creation is as countercultural as it is beneficial for our mental and spiritual wellbeing. The eye, as the lamp of the body (as with all our senses), enables us to pay attention to the world in a way that shapes the character of our own existence and participation in the world.

When we consider the lilies and the birds, we may start to notice that their particular way of being does not seem like *toil*, perhaps because it is in keeping with their true identity and vocation. They are not at odds with who they really are; their very existence in all its beauty is a continual act of praise and service to their creator.

This kind of attention paying to God's creation is, paradoxically, one of the ways in which we learn to sit lightly to the material treasures that might keep us from the kingdom. The ephemeral beauty of all things living – which cannot be possessed, only delighted in – reminds us that all our striving and focusing on having and storing is a distraction from the deeper reality that we, like the lilies and the birds, are God's treasure.

> God, our refuge and strength,
> bring near the day when wars shall cease
> and poverty and pain shall end,
> that earth may know the peace of heaven
> through Jesus Christ our Lord.

COLLECT

Reflection by **Ally Barrett**

Ordinary Time: All Saints to Advent

Monday 15 November

Psalms 46, **47** *or* **80**, 82
Isaiah 9.8 – 10.4
Matthew 7.1-12

Matthew 7.1-12

'... knock, and the door will be opened' (v.7)

How can you have a fulfilling life as a follower of Jesus?

Live with a sense of proportion. You are so far short of God's perfection that from his perspective, the difference between you and the neighbour whose attitudes you despise is negligible. If your reaction to someone's behaviour is disapproval, use it as a prompt to examine your own need for forgiveness.

Live with a sense of reverence. There are some aspects to your salvation that are too good to mock or treat lightly. In what you prioritize; in what you say; in the jokes you tell; in the language you use: remember that there are some things that are pearls.

Live with a sense of prayerfulness. Go on asking, searching, knocking. Even when you feel you have been given a raw deal by life, hold on to the truth that you have a good God who is on your side.

Live with a sense of goodwill. If you don't know what to do for someone, start by imagining what you would like them to do for you in similar circumstances. Take the initiative with imagination and positivity.

And while you're at it, live with a sense of humour. If you've read all those teachings about eyes, logs, pigs and snakes, imagining Jesus saying them with a face like a curmudgeon, you may have missed the point.

COLLECT

Heavenly Father,
whose blessed Son was revealed
    to destroy the works of the devil
and to make us the children of God and heirs of eternal life:
grant that we, having this hope,
may purify ourselves even as he is pure;
that when he shall appear in power and great glory
we may be made like him in his eternal and glorious kingdom;
where he is alive and reigns with you,
in the unity of the Holy Spirit,
one God, now and for ever.

Reflection by **Peter Graystone**

Psalms 48, **52** *or* 87, **89.1-18**
Isaiah 10.5-19
Matthew 7.13-end

Tuesday 16 November

Matthew 7.13-end

'You will know them by their fruits' (v.16)

The end of the Sermon on the Mount brings us to a point of decision. We are confronted with absolutes between which we must choose: life or death, truth or fake, Jesus' welcome or Jesus' dismissal, survival or collapse.

Jesus makes an all-or-nothing demand. His followers must be recognized not by their knowledge of him, but by their obedience to him. A similar account of Jesus' teaching in Luke 6.47 spells out three things that Jesus asks. 'Come to me' – open yourself to a captivating personal friendship with Jesus. 'Hear my words' – spend time discovering what he did and said. 'Put them into practice' – live out what he taught, and that goes way beyond pleasantly saying, 'Lord, Lord,' because it impacts the tough areas of which Jesus has spoken in these chapters: money, sex, marriage, community, justice, work.

Making your Christian life as easy as you can for yourself is a wide gate. It's alluring, but it's not enough. Wrapping yourself in your national flag and yelling that yours is a Christian country is a bad tree. It attracts attention, but it's not enough. Only the hard work of obedience is enough. But its consequences are utterly worthwhile. When the storm comes (whether that is illness, unemployment, attack, divorce, loneliness or the presence of death), the relationship you have forged with Jesus will make you strong enough to endure. You will be on a rock.

> Heavenly Lord,
> you long for the world's salvation:
> stir us from apathy,
> restrain us from excess
> and revive in us new hope
> that all creation will one day be healed
> in Jesus Christ our Lord.

COLLECT

Reflection by **Peter Graystone**

Ordinary Time: All Saints to Advent

Wednesday 17 November

Psalms **56**, 57 *or* **119.105-128**
Isaiah 10.20-32
Matthew 8.1-13

Matthew 8.1-13

'I do choose' (v.3)

It's surely no accident that these two stories appear side by side in Matthew's Gospel. The man with leprosy was lowly and rejected. The centurion from the Roman army was a person of stature and influence. Coming to Jesus in need made them equal. But the way Jesus responded to that need was completely different in each case. For someone untouchable, there was the taboo-breaking comfort of a human touch. For someone living in a world of military chains of command, there was a demonstration of absolute authority.

I am at neither of those extremes. I'm not a high-flier nor an outcast. I'm a recently retired man, bumbling through my new circumstances and trying to do something worthwhile. Jesus chose to do a beautiful thing in the life of someone unexpected – a person whose illness made others walk away. And a beautiful thing in the life of someone equally unexpected – a Gentile whose army was brutally occupying his own homeland. I am both moved and challenged that Jesus found the right words and the right actions for people in such contrasting circumstances. It gives me courage to say to him, 'Lord, if you choose, we could spend my remaining years working together on something life-changing in my corner of the world.' So that is what I have prayed after reading this Bible passage. How thrilling it will be if I hear him say, 'I do choose.'

COLLECT

Heavenly Father,
whose blessed Son was revealed
    to destroy the works of the devil
and to make us the children of God and heirs of eternal life:
grant that we, having this hope,
may purify ourselves even as he is pure;
that when he shall appear in power and great glory
we may be made like him in his eternal and glorious kingdom;
where he is alive and reigns with you,
in the unity of the Holy Spirit,
one God, now and for ever.

Reflection by **Peter Graystone**

Ordinary Time: All Saints to Advent

Psalms 61, **62** *or* 90, **92**
Isaiah 10.33 – 11.9
Matthew 8.14-22

Thursday 18 November

Matthew 8.14-22

'I will follow you wherever you go' (v.19)

During his lifetime, people said all sorts of things about Jesus, and Matthew recorded the good, the bad and the ugly. Some had great insight (such as the centurion who recognized Jesus' authority, about whom we read yesterday); some said things that were just stupid (such as the Pharisee who thought Jesus was invoking Satan to perform miracles in Matthew 12.24). At the end of today's reading, Jesus deals with an outburst by someone with naive enthusiasm, to whom he wearily explains that following him will not be comfortable. Then Jesus responds to someone whose devotion has conditions attached, shocking him with what the personal cost of commitment might be.

Among all those who met Jesus and attempted an appropriate response, who got it right? Maybe an older woman who was sick and whose name we don't even know. She encountered Jesus in a state of helplessness. She received the restoration he wanted her to have. And she responded in a practical way by serving him. It is recognizable as a pattern for an ordinary Christian life, lived with down-to-earth realism. The commitment Jesus asks for might involve heroism and anguish. But it doesn't always. Instead, it can mean quietly devoted action over the course of a lifetime. People notice a life lived like that and are attracted to Jesus, just as large numbers were in Capernaum all those years ago.

COLLECT

Heavenly Lord,
you long for the world's salvation:
stir us from apathy,
restrain us from excess
and revive in us new hope
that all creation will one day be healed
in Jesus Christ our Lord.

Reflection by **Peter Graystone**

Ordinary Time: All Saints to Advent

Friday 19 November

Psalms **63**, 65 *or* **88** (95)
Isaiah 11.10 – end of 12
Matthew 8.23-end

Matthew 8.23-end

'What sort of man is this …?' (v.27)

In these stories, Jesus stilled two storms and then created one. The first storm was actual. The part that makes us gasp is that he had such control over the world he created, but actually what Jesus wanted to do was address the disciples' fear and increase their faith. They still didn't fully comprehend what kind of man they had alongside them. The second storm was a mental illness. The eye-catching part of this healing gets so much attention that we sometimes overlook the fact that two men who felt ravaged by evil were calmed and had their lives dramatically improved.

The storm that Jesus caused came about because he entered Gadara, a Gentile area heavily populated by Roman soldiers. How utterly offensive it was to the Jews to know those pigs were there. Vermin! But the Romans loved their bacon, so pigs were intensively farmed in that area. With a mighty display of power, Jesus swept the vermin off the land and into the sea. It was an unforgettable picture of how God viewed the empire that had occupied the homeland of the Jews and now controlled it with brutality. Tyranny would be swept away.

No wonder the town's inhabitants begged Jesus to leave. They were intrigued, but scared of the uproar that might follow if he stayed. Jesus had chosen a dangerous route and made his future unsafe. Was that going to deter him? Pigs might fly!

COLLECT

Heavenly Father,
whose blessed Son was revealed
　to destroy the works of the devil
and to make us the children of God and heirs of eternal life:
grant that we, having this hope,
may purify ourselves even as he is pure;
that when he shall appear in power and great glory
we may be made like him in his eternal and glorious kingdom;
where he is alive and reigns with you,
in the unity of the Holy Spirit,
one God, now and for ever.

Reflection by **Peter Graystone**

Ordinary Time: All Saints to Advent

Psalm **78.1-39** *or* 96, **97**, 100
Isaiah 13.1-13
Matthew 9.1-17

Saturday 20 November

Matthew 9.1-17

'Take heart, son; your sins are forgiven' (v.2)

Claiming to forgive sins is really easy – it's an invisible process that nobody has to prove. Claiming to heal disabilities is really difficult – everyone can see the result with their own eyes. However, to the scribes, a claim to be able to forgive sins was outrageous, because it was an assertion that only God could make. So Jesus was deliberately propelling himself into controversy. But in front of their eyes, he did the really difficult thing. He left the scribes with no choice but to contemplate that, if he could do the impossible, his extraordinary claims about his relationship with God might also be true.

Jesus never claimed straightforwardly to be God. I suppose if he had, he would have been stabbed in a backstreet and that would have been that. The world would have gone unsaved. But if you have your own obdurate views about how God should be described, you wouldn't recognize him when he came to you anyway. Or (a case in point) when she came to you.

When God did walk on this planet, he sought the company of the despised, not the respectable; he came proclaiming mercy, not demanding better religious rituals; he spread joy, rather than demanding abstinence; and he didn't just patch up an old religion, he inaugurated something magnificently new. If that appeals to you, Matthew the tax collector will let you know precisely what to do.

> Heavenly Lord,
> you long for the world's salvation:
> stir us from apathy,
> restrain us from excess
> and revive in us new hope
> that all creation will one day be healed
> in Jesus Christ our Lord.

COLLECT

Reflection by **Peter Graystone**

Ordinary Time: All Saints to Advent

Monday 22 November

Psalms 92, **96** *or* **98**, 99, 101
Isaiah 14.3-20
Matthew 9.18-34

Matthew 9.18-34

'Never has anything like this been seen' (v.33)

Unaware of the science that now seems commonplace, Jewish leaders of Jesus' day did not understand what made a woman bleed. So at that point in her monthly cycle, a woman was declared 'unclean' and isolated from everyone until seven days had passed. After a ritual wash, she was then allowed back into the community by the leader of the synagogue.

But what if your bleeding never stopped? What if you had been cast out of worship, of friendship, of the ability to earn, of acceptability for twelve years? Imagine the desperation. People at the time commonly believed that there were mystical powers in the clothes of rabbis, especially the tassels of their garments. So it's no accident that the woman touched Jesus' clothes. She thought they might be magic. You may think it was totally the wrong attitude, but Jesus overlooked that entirely and focused on her need.

We don't know the name of the woman. However, we do know the name of the synagogue leader who kept her outcast. His name was Jairus. It would be easy to see him as the villain. He believed he was doing God's will. His story is wrapped around the woman's, and it's clear that he had issues of his own. He was engulfed in a family tragedy. The Bible doesn't choose who to blame. It simply challenges us that no one, absolutely no one, should be kept from Jesus' compassion.

COLLECT

Eternal Father,
whose Son Jesus Christ ascended to the throne of heaven
    that he might rule over all things as Lord and King:
keep the Church in the unity of the Spirit
and in the bond of peace,
and bring the whole created order to worship at his feet;
who is alive and reigns with you,
in the unity of the Holy Spirit,
one God, now and for ever.

Reflection by **Peter Graystone**

Ordinary Time: All Saints to Advent

Psalms **97**, 98, 100 or **106*** (or 103)
Isaiah 17
Matthew 9.35 – 10.15

Tuesday 23 November

Matthew 9.35 – 10.15

'… proclaiming the good news of the kingdom' (9.35)

We don't have many sheep in Croydon where I live. My main encounters with them are in knitted or butchered format. But Jesus' simile is nevertheless vivid. I imagine sheep without a shepherd confusedly following one of their number who appears to be giving a lead, but is equally unaware of which way is best to go. In contrast, a good shepherd, if he or she follows the example of Jesus, offers direction ('teaching'), inspiration ('good news'), wellbeing ('curing'), and care ('compassion') to the sheep. And, of course, to the humans.

Jesus recognized those qualities in twelve of his circle and sent them to do as he had done. But with twelve times the impact! His mission was multiplying. His expectations of them were that they should be leaders who offered both words and actions, so that people thrilled by the hope they held out were not disappointed by the reality that they experienced. And leaders who had no interest in using their position for personal gain, so that there could be no accusation of owning possessions unless their own hard work had earned them. And leaders who were intent on peace, working with all who shared that aim and walking away from any who would foster division.

Oh, how the whole world needs leaders like that – both secular and Christian! If the whole world is too big to contemplate, I'll attempt to make a start with Croydon.

> God the Father,
> help us to hear the call of Christ the King
> and to follow in his service,
> whose kingdom has no end;
> for he reigns with you and the Holy Spirit,
> one God, one glory.

COLLECT

Reflection by **Peter Graystone**

Ordinary Time: All Saints to Advent

Wednesday 24 November

Psalms 110, 111, **112**
or 110, **111**, 112
Isaiah 19
Matthew 10.16-33

Matthew 10.16-33

'... the hairs of your head are all counted' (v.30)

Just reading this passage scares the wits out of me. Please God, may I never experience it in actuality. And may I never forget to pray for those for whom it is the reality of a life walked in Jesus' footsteps. What qualities are needed to be resilient in life-threatening circumstances? And (if I may ask this without trivializing the enormous cost of persecution) are they the same qualities that those of us whose worship is comfortable need when confronting our petty hurdles?

First, model your attitude on Jesus. He is the teacher and you are his disciple. So if you have made a decision that you want to be like him, bear in mind that not everybody loved him. But that didn't stop him loving them. Second, be honest about your Christian faith. Secret Christians don't cut it. If you are prepared to tell a churchgoer that you're a person who prays, don't avoid the subject with your neighbour. Third, be bold. Every time you introduce God into conversation, Jesus is whispering to his Father, 'Look at him, look at her – what a superhero!' (I may perhaps be letting my imagination run away with me, but you get the point!)

One thing alone makes these qualities possible. We have a God who knows every single atom, every microscopic synapse of our being. He understands them, values them, loves them. So nothing need hold you back. Courage!

COLLECT

Eternal Father,
whose Son Jesus Christ ascended to the throne of heaven
    that he might rule over all things as Lord and King:
keep the Church in the unity of the Spirit
and in the bond of peace,
and bring the whole created order to worship at his feet;
who is alive and reigns with you,
in the unity of the Holy Spirit,
one God, now and for ever.

Reflection by **Peter Graystone**

Ordinary Time: All Saints to Advent

Psalms **125**, 126, 127, 128
or 113, **115**
Isaiah 21.1-12
Matthew 10.34 – 11.1

Thursday 25 November

Matthew 10.34 – 11.1

'Whoever welcomes you welcomes me' (10.40)

'You shall have no other gods before me' is the first of the Ten Commandments. It would have been deep-rooted in the thinking and actions of Jesus' first disciples. Although recognition of religious texts is diminishing in this century, many today are still familiar with it even if they don't know where it comes from. In a statement that would be outrageous were it not true, Jesus put himself in God's place and demanded total allegiance.

As usual, he taught using dramatically memorable extremes. However, this time he wasn't doing it to make his listeners laugh, but to make them gasp. A person who took up his cross to follow Jesus was someone following a condemned criminal on his way to execution. He wouldn't be going back home to a loving family. Jesus was asking, 'How committed are you to this world-changing mission? Committed enough to die with me?'

The devotion Jesus asks of us is daunting, but the rewards are extraordinary. Jesus describes us as if we were ambassadors for God, with all the dignity and respect that accompanies the role. It's not even the case that we need to accomplish great feats to receive his acclaim. Something small on behalf of a vulnerable or needy person is sufficient – maybe just a glass of water. As the missionary and martyr Jim Elliot put it: 'He is no fool who loses what he cannot keep to gain what he cannot lose.'

COLLECT

God the Father,
help us to hear the call of Christ the King
and to follow in his service,
whose kingdom has no end;
for he reigns with you and the Holy Spirit,
one God, one glory.

Reflection by **Peter Graystone**

Ordinary Time: All Saints to Advent

Friday 26 November

Psalm **139** *or* **139**
Isaiah 22.1-14
Matthew 11.2-19

Matthew 11.2-19

'… are we to wait for another?' (v.3)

There was a widespread expectation among first-century Jews that before their Messiah came, there would be a revival of the golden age of prophecy, and Elijah would reappear. Anticipation was feverish. Into that setting strode a firebrand. He got himself up in fancy dress to look like Elijah – coarse clothes and wild appearance. He roared and denounced like Elijah. His name was John. Jesus recognized exactly what was going on and acclaimed his ministry.

I wonder whether John had assumed that the Messiah would share his lifestyle – abstemious, flinty, severe. So much of what he heard about Jesus fitted the expectations of the Messiah, but the party-going and the company he kept were completely opposite to John's way. From prison, where he had been locked up for speaking truth to power, he sent messengers to Jesus to ask, 'Are you the one?' As so often, Jesus did not answer the question, but said, 'Look at the evidence and make up your mind.'

Tragically, John died before the resurrection of Jesus and the events of Pentecost. They would have given him the certainty he craved. But Matthew the Gospel writer mentions him again and again as a key player in God's plan to bring salvation to humankind through Jesus the Messiah. It is as if his whole Gospel is there precisely to answer John's question. So go on – read the evidence and make up your mind.

COLLECT

Eternal Father,
whose Son Jesus Christ ascended to the throne of heaven
    that he might rule over all things as Lord and King:
keep the Church in the unity of the Spirit
and in the bond of peace,
and bring the whole created order to worship at his feet;
who is alive and reigns with you,
in the unity of the Holy Spirit,
one God, now and for ever.

Reflection by **Peter Graystone**

Ordinary Time: All Saints to Advent

Psalm **145** *or* 120, **121**, 122
Isaiah 24
Matthew 11.20-end

Saturday 27 November

Matthew 11.20-end

'I will give you rest' (v.28)

Every Jewish rabbi of the first century taught a particular way of fulfilling the requirements of God, and his followers lived by that pattern. The metaphor rabbis used for their way of living was the yoke by which oxen were steered. Jesus was clearly concerned that Jews who followed other rabbis were being asked to bear too burdensome a yoke. So he offered an easier one. He was saying, 'I'm a different kind of rabbi. Choose the way of serving God that I model and follow that. Because you'll be less stressed.' What a marvellous offer! Who could possibly turn down the invitation to be less stressed?

Lots of people apparently. The locations upon which Jesus had lavished his greatest care had turned their back on him. In Capernaum, a paralysed man lowered through a roof had walked. In Bethsaida, 5,000 hungry people had been served more food than they could eat. Not enough? No. In Capernaum, he was accused of blasphemy. In Bethsaida, they proposed a military coup. People loved the spectacle but were unresponsive to Jesus' spiritual message.

Those who had been given the greatest chance to respond to God's love had spurned it and that angered Jesus. Perhaps their brains were too big to appreciate the simplicity of what Jesus said. That's why, in his infinite kindness, Jesus tried again with words so simple and tender that any toddler can appreciate them: 'Are you tired? Come here.'

> COLLECT
>
> God the Father,
> help us to hear the call of Christ the King
> and to follow in his service,
> whose kingdom has no end;
> for he reigns with you and the Holy Spirit,
> one God, one glory.

Reflection by **Peter Graystone**

Seasonal Prayers of Thanksgiving

Advent

Blessed are you, Sovereign God of all,
to you be praise and glory for ever.
In your tender compassion
the dawn from on high is breaking upon us
to dispel the lingering shadows of night.
As we look for your coming among us this day,
open our eyes to behold your presence
and strengthen our hands to do your will,
that the world may rejoice and give you praise.
Blessed be God, Father, Son and Holy Spirit.
Blessed be God for ever.

Christmas Season

Blessed are you, Sovereign God,
creator of heaven and earth,
to you be praise and glory for ever.
As your living Word, eternal in heaven,
assumed the frailty of our mortal flesh,
may the light of your love be born in us
to fill our hearts with joy as we sing:
Blessed be God, Father, Son and Holy Spirit.
Blessed be God for ever.

Epiphany

Blessed are you, Sovereign God,
king of the nations,
to you be praise and glory for ever.
From the rising of the sun to its setting
your name is proclaimed in all the world.
As the Sun of Righteousness dawns in our hearts
anoint our lips with the seal of your Spirit
that we may witness to your gospel
and sing your praise in all the earth.
Blessed be God, Father, Son and Holy Spirit.
Blessed be God for ever.

Lent

Blessed are you, Lord God of our salvation,
to you be glory and praise for ever.
In the darkness of our sin you have shone in our hearts
to give the light of the knowledge of the glory of God
in the face of Jesus Christ.
Open our eyes to acknowledge your presence,
that freed from the misery of sin and shame
we may grow into your likeness from glory to glory.
Blessed be God, Father, Son and Holy Spirit.
Blessed be God for ever.

Passiontide

Blessed are you, Lord God of our salvation,
to you be praise and glory for ever.
As a man of sorrows and acquainted with grief
your only Son was lifted up
that he might draw the whole world to himself.
May we walk this day in the way of the cross
and always be ready to share its weight,
declaring your love for all the world.
Blessed be God, Father, Son and Holy Spirit.
Blessed be God for ever.

Easter Season

Blessed are you, Sovereign Lord,
the God and Father of our Lord Jesus Christ,
to you be glory and praise for ever.
From the deep waters of death
you brought your people to new birth
by raising your Son to life in triumph.
Through him dark death has been destroyed
and radiant life is everywhere restored.
As you call us out of darkness into his marvellous light
may our lives reflect his glory
and our lips repeat the endless song.
Blessed be God, Father, Son and Holy Spirit.
Blessed be God for ever.

Ascension Day

Blessed are you, Lord of heaven and earth,
to you be glory and praise for ever.
From the darkness of death you have raised your Christ
to the right hand of your majesty on high.
The pioneer of our faith, his passion accomplished,
has opened for us the way to heaven
and sends on us the promised Spirit.
May we be ready to follow the Way
and so be brought to the glory of his presence
where songs of triumph for ever sound:
Blessed be God, Father, Son and Holy Spirit.
Blessed be God for ever.

From the day after Ascension Day
until the Day of Pentecost

Blessed are you, creator God,
to you be praise and glory for ever.
As your Spirit moved over the face of the waters
bringing light and life to your creation,
pour out your Spirit on us today
that we may walk as children of light
and by your grace reveal your presence.
Blessed be God, Father, Son and Holy Spirit.
Blessed be God for ever.

From All Saints until the day before
the First Sunday of Advent

Blessed are you, Sovereign God,
ruler and judge of all,
to you be praise and glory for ever.
In the darkness of this age that is passing away
may the light of your presence which the saints enjoy
surround our steps as we journey on.
May we reflect your glory this day
and so be made ready to see your face
in the heavenly city where night shall be no more.
Blessed be God, Father, Son and Holy Spirit.
Blessed be God for ever.

The Lord's Prayer and The Grace

Our Father in heaven,
hallowed be your name,
your kingdom come,
your will be done,
on earth as in heaven.
Give us today our daily bread.
Forgive us our sins
as we forgive those who sin against us.
Lead us not into temptation
but deliver us from evil.
For the kingdom, the power,
and the glory are yours
now and for ever.
Amen.

(or)

Our Father, who art in heaven,
hallowed be thy name;
thy kingdom come;
thy will be done;
on earth as it is in heaven.
Give us this day our daily bread.
And forgive us our trespasses,
as we forgive those who trespass against us.
And lead us not into temptation;
but deliver us from evil.
For thine is the kingdom,
the power and the glory,
for ever and ever.
Amen.

The grace of our Lord Jesus Christ,
and the love of God,
and the fellowship of the Holy Spirit,
be with us all evermore.
Amen.

An Order for Night Prayer (Compline)

Preparation

The Lord almighty grant us a quiet night and a perfect end.
Amen.

Our help is in the name of the Lord
who made heaven and earth.

A period of silence for reflection on the past day may follow.

The following or other suitable words of penitence may be used

**Most merciful God,
we confess to you,
before the whole company of heaven and one another,
that we have sinned in thought, word and deed
and in what we have failed to do.
Forgive us our sins,
heal us by your Spirit
and raise us to new life in Christ. Amen.**

O God, make speed to save us.
O Lord, make haste to help us.

**Glory to the Father and to the Son
and to the Holy Spirit;
as it was in the beginning is now
and shall be for ever. Amen.
Alleluia.**

The following or another suitable hymn may be sung

Before the ending of the day,
Creator of the world, we pray
That you, with steadfast love, would keep
Your watch around us while we sleep.

From evil dreams defend our sight,
From fears and terrors of the night;
Tread underfoot our deadly foe
That we no sinful thought may know.

O Father, that we ask be done
Through Jesus Christ, your only Son;
And Holy Spirit, by whose breath
Our souls are raised to life from death.

The Word of God

Psalmody

One or more of Psalms 4, 91 or 134 may be used.

Psalm 134

1 Come, bless the Lord, all you servants of the Lord, ♦
 you that by night stand in the house of the Lord.

2 Lift up your hands towards the sanctuary ♦
 and bless the Lord.

3 The Lord who made heaven and earth ♦
 give you blessing out of Zion.

**Glory to the Father and to the Son
and to the Holy Spirit;
as it was in the beginning is now
and shall be for ever. Amen.**

Scripture Reading

One of the following short lessons or another suitable passage is read

You, O Lord, are in the midst of us and we are called by your name; leave us not, O Lord our God.

Jeremiah 14.9

(or)

Be sober, be vigilant, because your adversary the devil is prowling round like a roaring lion, seeking for someone to devour. Resist him, strong in the faith.

1 Peter 5.8,9

(or)

The servants of the Lamb shall see the face of God, whose name will be on their foreheads. There will be no more night: they will not need the light of a lamp or the light of the sun, for God will be their light, and they will reign for ever and ever.

Revelation 22.4,5

The following responsory may be said

Into your hands, O Lord, I commend my spirit.
Into your hands, O Lord, I commend my spirit.
For you have redeemed me, Lord God of truth.
I commend my spirit.
Glory to the Father and to the Son
and to the Holy Spirit.
Into your hands, O Lord, I commend my spirit.

Or, in Easter

Into your hands, O Lord, I commend my spirit.
　Alleluia, alleluia.
Into your hands, O Lord, I commend my spirit.
　Alleluia, alleluia.
For you have redeemed me, Lord God of truth.
Alleluia, alleluia.
Glory to the Father and to the Son
and to the Holy Spirit.
Into your hands, O Lord, I commend my spirit.
　Alleluia, alleluia.

Keep me as the apple of your eye.
Hide me under the shadow of your wings.

Gospel Canticle

Nunc Dimittis (The Song of Simeon)

**Save us, O Lord, while waking,
and guard us while sleeping,
that awake we may watch with Christ
and asleep may rest in peace.**

1　Now, Lord, you let your servant go in peace:
　　your word has been fulfilled.

2　My own eyes have seen the salvation
　　which you have prepared in the sight of every people;

3　A light to reveal you to the nations
　　and the glory of your people Israel.

Luke 2.29-32

**Glory to the Father and to the Son
and to the Holy Spirit;
as it was in the beginning is now
and shall be for ever. Amen.**

**Save us, O Lord, while waking,
and guard us while sleeping,
that awake we may watch with Christ
and asleep may rest in peace.**

Prayers

Intercessions and thanksgivings may be offered here.

The Collect

Visit this place, O Lord, we pray,
and drive far from it the snares of the enemy;
may your holy angels dwell with us and guard us in peace,
and may your blessing be always upon us;
through Jesus Christ our Lord.
Amen.

The Lord's Prayer (see p. 325) may be said.

The Conclusion

In peace we will lie down and sleep;
for you alone, Lord, make us dwell in safety.

Abide with us, Lord Jesus,
for the night is at hand and the day is now past.

As the night watch looks for the morning,
so do we look for you, O Christ.

[Come with the dawning of the day
and make yourself known in the breaking of the bread.]

The Lord bless us and watch over us;
the Lord make his face shine upon us and be gracious to us;
the Lord look kindly on us and give us peace.
Amen.

Index of Readings

Genesis 3.1-15 **257**
Genesis 28.10-17 **239**

Exodus 35.30–36.1 **146**

Numbers 11.16-17, 24-29 **147**
Numbers 27.15-end **148**

Deuteronomy 8.2-16 **163**

Joshua 1.1-9 **134**

1 Samuel 2.1-10 **166**
1 Samuel 2.27-35 **152**
1 Samuel 10.1-10 **149**

1 Kings 19.1-18 **150**

Isaiah 11.1-10 **104**
Isaiah 43–56, 57, 59–65 **11–31, 35–45**

Jeremiah 1–25 **70–105**

Ezekiel 1–3, 8–9 **256–61**
Ezekiel 11.14-20 **151**
Ezekiel 47.1-12 **10**

Daniel 9.3-6, 17-19 **72**

Micah 1–7 **226–33**
Micah 3.1-8 **153**

Habakkuk 1–3 **234–7**

Haggai 1–2 **238, 240**

Zechariah 1–14 **241–55**

Matthew 1.18-25 **32**
Matthew 2–11 **299–321**
Matthew 18.1-10 **34**
Matthew 28.16-end **114**

Mark 1–4 **214–25**
Mark 14–16 **262–73**
Mark 16.1-8 **112**

Luke 1.1-4 **286**
Luke 3.1-17 **187**
Luke 6.12-16 **295**
Luke 7.11-17 **115**
Luke 8.1-3 **211**
Luke 8.41-end **116**
Luke 9.18-27 **298**
Luke 22–23, 24 **106–9, 113**

John 2.18-22 **111**
John 11.1-16 **195**
John 11.17-44 **117**
John 13–20 **274–97**
John 20–21 **119–23**

Acts 6 **33**
Acts 11.1-18 **191**
Acts 12.25–13.13 **136**

Romans 1–16 **154–89**
Romans 5.12-end **118**
Romans 12.1-5 **65**

1 Corinthians 1–16 **46–69**

2 Corinthians 1–13 **190–205**

Ephesians 1–6 **124–35**

Philippians 3.1-14 **58**

2 Timothy 3.14-end **263**

Hebrews 7. [11-25] 26-end **145**
Hebrews 10.1-10 **110**

James 1.1-12 **141**
James 1–5 **206–13**

1 Peter 1–5 **137–45**

1 John 3.1-3 **224**

REFLECTIONS FOR DAILY PRAYER
App

Make Bible study and reflection a part of your routine wherever you go with the Reflections for Daily Prayer App for Apple and Android devices.

Download the app for free from the App Store (Apple devices) or Google Play (Android devices) and receive a week's worth of reflections free. Then purchase a monthly, three-monthly or annual subscription to receive up-to-date content.

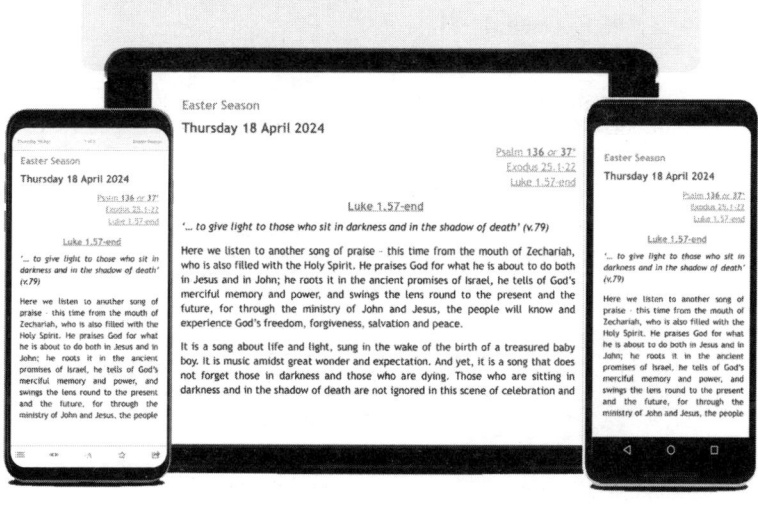

REFLECTIONS FOR SUNDAYS (YEAR B)

Reflections for Sundays offers over 250 reflections on the Principal Readings for every Sunday and major Holy Day in Year B, from the same experienced team of writers that have made *Reflections for Daily Prayer* so successful. For each Sunday and major Holy Day, they provide:

- full lectionary details for the Principal Service
- a reflection on each Old Testament reading (both Continuous and Related)
- a reflection on the Epistle
- a reflection on the Gospel.

This book also contains a substantial introduction to the Gospels of Mark and John, written by Paula Gooder.

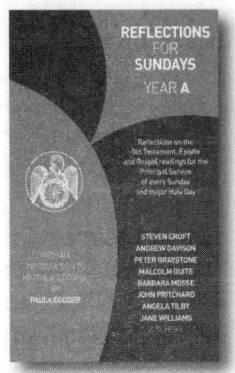

288 pages
ISBN 978 1 78140 030 2

REFLECTIONS ON THE PSALMS

192 pages
ISBN 978 0 7151 4490 9

Reflections on the Psalms provides original and insightful meditations on each of the Bible's 150 Psalms.

Each reflection is accompanied by its corresponding Psalm refrain and prayer from the *Common Worship Psalter*, making this a valuable resource for personal or devotional use.

Specially written introductions by Paula Gooder and Steven Croft explore the Psalms and the Bible and the Psalms in the life of the Church.

COMMON WORSHIP: DAILY PRAYER

The official daily office of the Church of England, **Common Worship: Daily Prayer** is a rich collection of devotional material that will enable those wanting to enrich their quiet times to develop a regular pattern of prayer. It includes:

- Prayer During the Day
- Forms of Penitence
- Morning and Evening Prayer
- Night Prayer (Compline)
- Collects and Refrains
- Canticles
- Complete Psalter

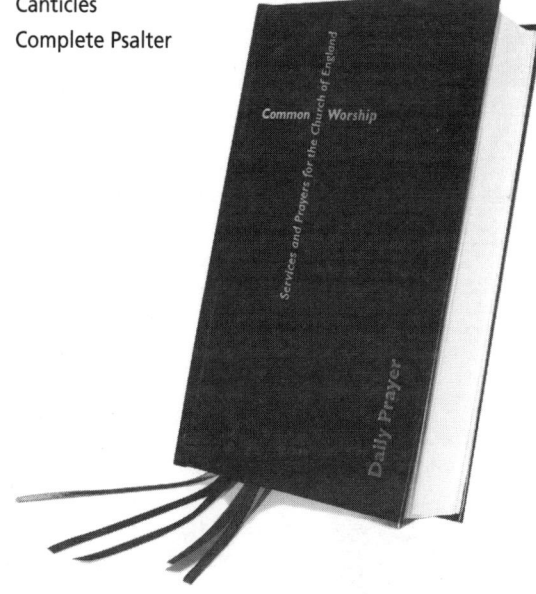

896 pages • with 6 ribbons • 202 x 125mm
Hardback   978 0 7151 2199 3
Bonded leather 978 0 7151 2277 8